A COMPENDIUM OF THE DOCTRINES OF THE GOSPEL

A COMPENDIUM OF THE DOCTRINES OF THE GOSPEL

**VARIOUS,
FRANKLIN DEWEY RICHARDS,
JAMES AMASA LITTLE**

ISBN: 978-93-5614-112-4

Published: 1884

LECTOR HOUSE LLP
E-MAIL: lectorpublishing@gmail.com

A COMPENDIUM OF THE DOCTRINES OF THE GOSPEL.

BY

FRANKLIN D. RICHARDS,

One of the Twelve Apostles of the Church of Jesus Christ
of Latter-day Saints,

AND

ELDER JAMES A. LITTLE,

COMPILERS AND PUBLISHERS.

SECOND STEREOTYPE EDITION.

1884

PREFACE.

We consider the Bible, Book of Mormon, Book of Doctrine and Covenants, Pearl of Great Price and sayings of Joseph, the Seer, our guides in faith and doctrine. The first four have been adopted as such by a vote of the Saints in General Conference. Reference to other writings are only for illustration of the subject.

We have sought to furnish the best available material for the use of the Elders. It is for them to seek for the wisdom of the Holy Spirit to enable them to use it with discretion.

On most of the subjects treated, only a portion of the passages that refer to them have been cited, but we have endeavored to use the best. We designed to make the Compendium sufficiently elaborate to give it a wide range of usefulness, and, at the same time, not make it so large as to be burdensome to the Elders who travel and preach the Gospel. Practically, we have aimed to get up a book that would contain a great amount of information for its bulk.

The arguments on each subject are so plain and direct, that, we trust, they may be made available by the most inexperienced Elders. At the same time, the references and citations are considered sufficient for the more advanced student to acquire a thorough knowledge of the subjects treated on.

The references in small type are not designed to be verbatim, but only to embody, as near as may be, the leading idea of the passage referred lo. They should be studied before being used. The passages included within the usual quotation marks, thus, " ", are designed to be correctly quoted, and may be used without referring to the original.

We are indebted to Elder George Reynolds for the carefully prepared Chronology of the Book of Mormon. It is evidently the result of much study and thought, and as such is entitled to credence.

While we have aimed at accuracy, we should be pleased to have our friends inform us of any material error they may discover.

We expect our labors will elicit some criticism, but we trust the thoughtful and experienced will allow much for the complicated character of the work.

THE COMPILERS.

CONTENTS

CONTENTS

A COMPENDIUM OF THE DOCTRINES OF THE GOSPEL.

ARTICLES OF FAITH.

1. We believe in God, the Eternal Father, and in His Son, Jesus Christ, and in the Holy Ghost.

2. We believe that men will be punished for their own sins, and not for Adam's transgression.

3. We believe that, through the atonement of Christ, all mankind may be saved, by obedience to the laws and ordinances of the Gospel.

4. We believe that these ordinances are: First, Faith in the Lord Jesus Christ; second, Repentance; third, Baptism by immersion for the remission of sins; fourth, Laying on of hands for the Gift of the Holy Ghost.

5. We believe that a man must be called of God, by "prophecy, and by the laying on of hands," by those who are in authority, to preach the Gospel and administer in the ordinances thereof.

6. We believe in the same organization that existed in the primitive church, viz: apostles, prophets, pastors, teachers, evangelists, etc.

7. We believe in the gift of tongues, prophecy, revelation, visions, healing, interpretation of tongues, etc.

8. We believe the Bible to be the word of God, as far as it is translated correctly; we also believe the Book of Mormon to be the word of God.

9. We believe all that God has revealed, all that he does now reveal, and we believe that he will yet reveal many great and important things pertaining to the Kingdom of God.

10. We believe in the literal gathering of Israel and in the restoration of the ten tribes. That Zion will be built upon this continent. That Christ will reign personally upon the earth, and that the earth will be renewed and receive its paradisic glory.

11. We claim the privilege of worshiping Almighty God according to the dictates of our conscience, and allow all men the same privilege, let them worship how, where, or what they may.

12. We believe in being subject to kings, presidents, rulers and magistrates, in obeying, honoring and sustaining the law.

13. We believe in being honest, true, chaste, benevolent, virtuous, and in doing good to all men; indeed, we may say that we follow the admonition of Paul, "We believe all things, we hope all things;" we have endured many things, and hope to be able to endure all things. If there is anything virtuous, lovely, or of good report, or praiseworthy, we seek after these things. —Joseph Smith.

THE FALL OF ADAM.

"Honor thy Father and thy Mother." This was one of the ten special commandments given to Israel, during a grand display of God's power and glory on Mount Sinai.

In the past centuries of darkness it appears to have lost its significance with the Christian world. They do not appear to realize that honor is due to the first parents of the human race. They have been long taught that Adam and Eve were great transgressors, and have mourned over the fact that they partook of the forbidden fruit and brought death into the world.

There is no possibility that the fall of man was an accident or chance, any more than was his creation. If an accident, then why was Christ prepared from before the foundation of the world as a propitiation for sin, and to open up the way for man to immortality?

Christ's mediation was a sequence of the fall. "Him hath God exalted with his right hand to be a Prince and a Savior, for to give repentance to Israel, and forgiveness of sins;" Acts 5. 31. Without the fall there would have been no broken law, and therefore nothing to repent of; and there could be no forgiveness of sin without the atonement of Christ.

The Book of Mormon makes this subject very plain: "And now, behold, if Adam had not transgressed, he would not have fallen; but he would have remained in the garden of Eden. And all things which were created, must have remained in the same state which they were, after they were created; and they must have remained for ever, and had no end. And they would have had no children; wherefore they would have remained in a state of innocence, having no joy, for they knew no misery; doing no good, for they knew no sin;" 2 Nephi 2. 22, 23.

It is evident, not only from this passage, but from all that is recorded on this subject, that, if Adam and Eve had not attained to a knowledge of evil, by partaking of the forbidden fruit, the human race could not have existed under present conditions. It is also evident, that without a knowledge of both good and evil, man would be incapable of exercising a free agency, and therefore not capable of independent, self-reliant action—a necessary condition for development and progress.

We, the children of Adam, have no right to bring accusations against the Patriarch of the race. But father, we should rejoice with them, that through their fall and the atonement of Jesus Christ, the way of eternal life has been opened up to us. It was after an angel had administered to Adam, and made known to him the atonement through the Only Begotten Son of the Father, that he and Eve gave expression to their joy, in view of the glorious future of the race.

"And in that day Adam blessed God and was filled, and began to prophesy concerning all the families of the earth, saying, Blessed be the name of God, for because of my transgression my eyes are opened, and in this life I shall have joy, and again in the flesh I shall see God. And Eve, his wife, heard all these things and was glad, saying, Were it not for our transgression we never should have had seed, and never should have known good and evil, and the joy of our redemption, and the eternal life which God giveth unto all the obedient;" Pearl of Great Price, page 10.

The principle of obedience could only be developed in man through the fall, and only through that can they realize the joys of redemption and eternal life. The woman fell first, and led Adam out of Eden and the presence of the Lord. "Adam was not deceived, but the woman being deceived was in transgression;" 1 *Tim.* 2. 14.

When the Lord asked Adam if he had eaten of the fruit of the tree, of which he had commanded him that he should not eat, he replied, "The woman whom thou gavest *to be* with me, she gave me of the tree, and I did eat;" *Gen.* iii, 12. Adam had been previously commanded to multiply and replenish the earth, and he could not do so unless he remained with Eve. She, being deceived, forced upon him the necessity of partaking of the forbidden fruit with her, or of remaining in a condition where it would have been impossible to fulfil the first great commandment of the Father.

Bible.

Gen. 3. gives a general account of the fall of man.

15 enmity between the seed of the woman and that of the serpent.

16 woman to bring forth children in sorrow, and be subject to her husband.

19 man to labor for his bread, and to return to the ground.

22 man became as the Gods, knowing good and evil.

Rom. 5. 12 by one man sin came into the world and death by sin.

Book of Mormon.

Alma 12. 22, 23 by the fall all mankind became lost.

Chap. 42 explains the plan for the exaltation of man through the fall of Adam, and the atonement of Jesus Christ.

Mormon 9. 12 by Adam came the fall of man, because of the fall came Jesus Christ and the redemption.

Doctrine & Covenants.

Sec. 29. 36 Adam being tempted of the devil, for the devil was before Adam.

40 Adam partook of the forbidden fruit, and became subject to the devil.

41 through the fall Adam became spiritually dead.

Pearl of Great Price.

Pages 7, 8. a general account of the fall of man.

See our Article on Atonement, and also an examination and elucidation of the mediation and atonement of our Lord and Savior, Jesus Christ: by Prest. John Taylor.

Article, by O. Pratt, Mil. Star. Vol. 28. pages 577, 593 and 609.

Article by C. W. Penrose, Mil. Star, Vol. 29, page 645. Sermon by O. Pratt, Journal of Discourses Vol. I, page 328.

FREE AGENCY OF MAN.

The doctrine of free agency is plainly elucidated in the written revelations from God. The plan for man's redemption was predicated on his fall.

No law could have been given to our first parents, and no penalty affixed for the breaking of a law, unless they had been free to act without constraint. The liberty to choose was given by the Creator to the progenitors of the race, and that liberty has been fully recognized in all his dealings with their posterity.

As the Patriarch of the race entailed on it an experimental knowledge of good and evil, through sufferings and death, so, through the sufferings and death of the Only Begotten Son, they are redeemed from the effects of his transgression, independent of any act of theirs.

Man was created in the image of God, with the possibility of becoming like him. But he cannot attain to that position without a knowledge of good and evil. Through the act of the Father he has attained to that knowledge; through the act of the Son he is delivered from the effects of original transgression.

Thus, with the privilege of exercising his free agency, he is placed on an equality with the parents of the race, and has the choice of good or evil for himself, with the results of that choice. If he chooses evil, a second death will be the result. If the good, it will prove to be the way to all the powers, glories and exaltations that the Gods enjoy, in whose image man is created.

The Book of Mormon is very plain on this subject: "Wherefore, men are free according to the flesh; and all things are given them which are expedient unto man. And they are free to choose liberty and eternal life, through the great mediation of all men, or to choose captivity and death, according to the captivity and power of the devil;" 2 *Nephi* 2. 27.

Bible.

Gen. 2. 17 in the day thou eatest thereof thou shalt surely die.

3, 6 Eve eat of the fruit of the tree and gave to her husband and he did eat. 12, 17.

4. 7 if thou doest well thou shalt be accepted.

Book of Mormon.

1 *Nephi* 6. 4 that I may persuade men to come to God.

2 *Nephi* 2. 16 Lord gave unto man that he should act for him-

self.

10. 23 ye are free to act for yourselves.

Mos. 2, 33 if he listeth to obey him, the same drinketh damnation.

Alma 3. 26 reap eternal happiness or misery, according to the spirit they obey.

12. 31 in a state to act according to their will.

13. 3 being left to choose good or evil.

29. 4, 5 he allotteth to man according to their wills.

30. 9 a man's privilege to believe in God or not.

41. 3, 4 evil or good is restored to men, as they have chosen.

Hel. 14. 30 ye are permitted to act for yourselves.

Doctrine & Covenants.

Sec. 10. 66 may come and partake of the waters of life freely.

29. 35 Adam to be an agent to himself. 36.

39 men must needs be tempted, or they could not be agents to themselves. *Sec.* 58. 27, 28.

98. 8 I, the Lord, make you free.

Pearl of Great Price.

Page 7. thou mayest choose for thyself. Satan sought to destroy the agency of man.

16. given to men to know good and evil; they are agents to themselves.

17. many have believed and become sons of God; many have not believed and perished.

See a sermon by B, Young, J. of D., Vol. I., page I.

Sermon by B. Young, J. of D., Vol. 3, page 80.

Sermon by O. Pratt, J. of D. Vol. I, page 328.

Sermon by D. H. Wells, J. of D. Vol. 9, page 259.

THE ATONEMENT.

The word atonement signifies deliverance, through the offering of a ransom, from the penalty of a broken law. The sense is expressed in *Job* 33. 24: "Deliver him from going down to the pit: I have found a ransom."

As effected by Jesus Christ, it signifies the deliverance, through his death and resurrection, of the earth and everything pertaining to it, from the power which death has obtained over them through the transgression of Adam.

The following passage is very comprehensive on the atonement of Christ: "And the end shall come, and the heaven and the earth shall be consumed and pass away, and there shall be a new heaven and a new earth, for all old things shall pass away, and all things shall become new, even the heaven and the earth, and all the fulness thereof, both men and beasts, the fowls of the air, and the fishes of the sea; and not one hair, neither mote, shall be lost, for it is the workmanship of mine hand;" *Doc. & Cov.* 29. 23-25. In the revelations of St. John we read, "And he that sat upon the throne said, Behold, I make all things new;" 21. 5.

The righteous could not inherit all things in their immortal, exalted condition, if all things were not resurrected to immortality as well as themselves.

The Apostle Paul quite comprehensively sums up the results of Christ's death and resurrection: "But now is Christ risen from the dead, and become the first fruits of them that slept. For since by man *came* death, by man *came* also the resurrection of the dead. For as in Adam all die, even so in Christ shall all be made alive;" I *Cor.* 15. 21, 22. That is, death having come on all men through the disobedience of Adam, so must all be raised to immortality and eternal life through the death and resurrection of Christ.

Paul also asserted that "the last enemy *that* shall be destroyed *is* death;" *Verse* 26. John the Revelator declares that he saw death and hell cast into the lake of fire; *Rev.* 20. 14.

The atonement, as wrought out by Jesus Christ, further signifies that he has opened up the way for man's redemption from his own sins, through faith in Christ's sufferings, death and resurrection. The Apostle Paul well expresses this, "For all have sinned, and come short of the glory of God; being justified freely by his grace through the redemption that is in Christ Jesus: whom God hath set forth *to be* a propitiation through faith in his blood, to declare his righteousness for the remission of sins that are past, through the forbearance of God; to declare, *I say*, at this time his righteousness: that he might be just, and the Justifier of him which believeth in Jesus;" *Rom.* 3. 23-26.

These passages evidence that redemption from death, through the sufferings of Christ, is for all men, both the righteous and the wicked; for this earth, and for all things created upon it. The whole tenor of the Scriptures assure us, that while they may be sure of resurrection from death, regardless of their personal acts, yet they will be rewarded for their works, whether they be good or evil, and that redemption from personal sins can only be obtained through obedience to the requirements of the Gospel, and a life of good works.

The transgression of Adam being infinite in its consequences, those consequences cannot be averted, except through an infinite atonement. The Prophet Nephi makes this very plain: "Wherefore it must needs be an infinite atonement; save it should be an infinite atonement, this corruption could not put on incorruption. Wherefore, the first judgment which came upon man, must needs have remained to an endless duration. And if so, this flesh must have laid down to rot and to crumble to its mother earth, to rise no more. O the wisdom of God! his mercy and grace! For behold, if the flesh should rise no more, our spirits must become subject to that angel who fell from before the presence of the eternal God, and became the devil, to rise no more.

O how great the goodness of our God, who prepareth a way for our escape from the grasp of this awful monster; yea, that monster, death and hell, which I call the death of the body, and also the death of the spirit;" 2. *Nephi* 7, 8, 10. "There is one thing, however, which the atonement does for us, immediately upon our entrance into this mortal life; it sets us free from the first spiritual death."

"As in Adam all died spiritually, even so in Christ all, in their infancy, are made alive spiritually. Christ, by the atonement, became the life and the light of men; he is the true light by which all are lighted who come into the world. Without this light all would have suffered in the eternal night of darkness, from which there would have been no return. But little children, by the atonement, are made alive, and are all subjects of salvation, being redeemed by the blood of Christ from the fall, being pure, and spotless, and innocent, and thus are made heirs of the kingdom of heaven. This redemption from the spiritual death upon all mankind in their infant state, is brought about without any conditions on the part of the creature; it is wrought out by the free grace of Christ alone, without works;" *O. Pratt.*

"I say unto you, that little children are redeemed from the foundation of the world through mine Only Begotten: wherefore, they cannot sin, for power is not given unto Satan to tempt little children, until they begin to become accountable before me;" *Doc. & Cov.* 29. 46, 47.

"Wherefore, it came to pass that the devil tempted Adam, and he partook the forbidden fruit and transgressed the commandment, wherein he became subject to the will of the devil, because he yielded unto temptation. Wherefore I the Lord God caused that he should be cast out from the Garden of Eden, from my presence, because of his transgression, wherein he became spiritually dead, which is the first death, even that same death, which is the last death, which is spiritual, which shall be pronounced upon the wicked when I shall say—Depart, ye cursed. But, behold, I say unto you, that I the Lord God gave unto Adam and unto his seed that they should not die as to the temporal death, until I the Lord God should send forth angels to declare unto them repentance and redemption, through faith on the name of mine Only Begotten Son. And thus did I, the Lord God, appoint unto man the days of his probation that by his natural death he might be raised in immortality unto eternal life, even as many as would believe; and they that believe not unto eternal damnation, for they cannot be redeemed from their spiritual fall, because they repent not; for they will love darkness rather than light, and their deeds are evil, and they receive their wages of whom they list to obey;" *Doc. & Cov.* 29. 40-45.

Bible.

Isa. 45. 22 look unto me and be ye saved.

53. 10 when thou shalt make his soul an offering for sin.

63. 9 he, redeemed them and carried them all the days of old.

Matt. 1. 21 Jesus shall save his people from their sins.

18. 11 the Son of Man hath come to save that which was lost.

John 1. 29 the Lamb of God which taketh away the sin of the world.

3. 14, 15 even so must the Son of Man be lifted up. 16.

4. 42 this is Christ the Savior of the world.

12. 32 if I be lifted up I will draw all men to me.

Acts 5. 31 him hath God exalted to be a Prince and Savior.

Chap. 13. 23.

Rom. 3. 24 being justified through the redemption that is in Christ Jesus.

25 whom God hath sent forth to be a propitiation. 26

5. 6 in due time Christ died for the ungodly. 8-11.

15 if through the offence of one many be dead, the gift of grace by one man, Christ Jesus, hath abounded to many. 18.

6. 23 the gift of God is eternal life through Jesus Christ.

8. 32 spared not his own Son but delivered him up for us all.

11. 26 there shall come out of Zion a deliverer.

1 *Cor.* 1. 30 Christ Jesus who is made to us sanctification and redemption.

5. 7 for even Christ our Passover is sacrificed for us.

2 *Cor.* 5. 18 who hath reconciled us to himself, by Jesus Christ.

Gal. 3. 13 Christ hath redeemed us from the curse of the law.

4. 4, 5 God sent his Son to redeem them that were under the law. 7.

Eph. 1. 7 in whom we have redemption through his blood. *Col.* 1. 14.

5. 2 as Christ also hath loved us, and given himself for us.

1 *Tim.* 1. 15 faithful saying, that Christ came into the world to save sinners.

2. 5 one God, one Mediator between God and man, the man Christ Jesus.

4. 10 we trust in the living God who is the Savior of all men.

Titus 2. 14 who gave himself for us, that he might redeem us.

Heb. 5. 9 being made perfect, he became the author of eternal salvation.

7. 25 able to save them that come to God by him.

9. 26, 28 so Christ was once offered to bear the sins of the world.

1 *Peter* 1. 19 with the blood of Christ, as of a lamb without blemish.

3. 18 Christ hath once suffered for our sins, the just for the unjust.

1 *John* 1. 7 the blood of Christ cleanseth from all sin.

2. 2 he is the propitiation for the sins of the world.

4. 9 God sent his son into the world that we might live through him. 14.

Rev. 5. 9 and hath redeemed us by his blood, out of every nation.

Book of Mormon.

1 *Nephi* 11. 27 I looked and beheld the Redeemer of the world 33.

12. 11 made white in the blood of the Lamb.

15. 14 the very points of his doctrine, that they may come to him and be saved.

2 *Nephi* 1. 10 if the day come, they reject the Messiah. 15.

2. 3 thou art redeemed, for thou hast beheld, that, in the fulness of time he cometh to bring salvation to men.

9. 21, 22 he suffereth the pains of all men.

25, 26 the atonement satisfies the demands of justice, on those without law.

10. 25 may God raise you from everlasting death by the power

of the atonement.

26. 24 layeth down his own life, that he may draw all men to him.

31. 21 no other name given whereby men can be saved.

Jacob 4. 15-17 Jews will reject the only foundation on which they can build.

Omni 1. 26 come to Christ and partake of the power of his redemption.

Mos. 4. 6-9 the atonement which has been prepared from the foundation of the world for all who have been, or will be.

27. 25 becoming his sons and daughters. 30.

Alma 7. 12 take upon him death that he may loose the bands of death.

11. 39, 40 the eternal Father shall come into the world to redeem his people.

34. 11-16 the law of Moses fulfilled in the infinite atonement of Christ.

39. 18 as necessary that the plan of salvation should be made known to this people, as to their children?

Hel. 5. 9-12 will not redeem his people in their sins, but from their sins.

3 *Nephi* 12. 17 in Christ is the law of Moses fulfilled. 21, 22.

Ether 3. 14 was prepared from the foundation of the world to redeem my people.

12. 33 to the laying down of thy life, that thou mightest take it again.

Moroni 8 he that says little children need baptism setteth at naught the atonement of Christ.

Doctrine & Covenants.

Sec. 18. 11 Lord suffered the pain of all men that they might come to him.

23. 25 Jesus Christ, the only name given under heaven whereby men can be saved.

19. 16 I, God, have suffered these things for all, that they might not suffer.

20. 26, 27 not only those who believed after he came in the meridian of time.

29. 42 Lord gave to Adam and his seed that they should not

die until the plan of redemption was declared to them.

46 little children are redeemed from the foundation of the world. *Sec.* 74. 6, 7. *Sec.* 93. 38.

76. 41-44 Jesus was crucified that all might be saved, except the sons of Perdition.

Pearl of Great Price.

Page 1. My Only Begotten is and shall be the Savior.

3. For this is my work and my glory, to bring to pass the immortality and eternal life of man.

9. Wherefore, thou shalt do all that thou doest in the name of the Son, and thou shalt repent and call upon God in the name of the Son evermore.

16. Jesus Christ the only name given whereby salvation shall come.

17. Plan of salvation to all men through the blood of mine Only Begotten.

See An examination and elucidation of the mediation and atonement of Jesus Christ; by Prest. J. Taylor.

Articles on the fall and atonement, by O. Pratt, Mil. Star, Vol. 28, pages 577, 593 and 609.

Sermon by O. Pratt, J. of D., Vol. 1, page 280.

Sermon by O. Pratt, J. of D., Vol. 2, Page 328.

Sermon by O. Pratt, J. of D., Vol. 2, page 368.

Sermon by B. Young, J. of D. Vol. 3, page 80.

Article by W. Woodruff, Mil. Star, Vol. 6, page 113.

Article by C. W. Penrose, Contributor, Vol. 2, page 362.

FAITH.

"Faith is the first principle of revealed religion and the foundation of all righteousness." "Now faith is the substance (assurance) of things hoped for, the evidence of things not seen;" *Heb*. 11. 1, *Doc. and Cov., Lecture on Faith*, 1. 1-8. That to use the word assurance, instead of substance, would be the proper rendering of the above passage, is evident from the 22d verse of the previous chapter: "Let us draw near with a true heart in full assurance of faith."

Faith begets trust and confidence. "In whom we have boldness and access with *confidence* by the faith of him;" (Jesus Christ.) *Eph*. 3. 12. Faith is the gift of God. "Saved through faith; and that not of yourselves: *it is* the gift of God;" 2. 8. "To another faith by the same Spirit;" 1 *Cor*. 12. 9. "But to think soberly, according as God hath dealt to every man the measure of faith;" *Rom*. 12. 3. *Moroni* 10. 11.

Through repentance, baptism and the laying on of hands man may receive the Holy Ghost. It will open his spiritual vision and he will begin to comprehend himself, the object of his creation, and his affinity to his Heavenly Father. Then through the further observance of all the ordinances of the Gospel, will the righteousness of God be revealed to him, from faith to faith, until by keeping the commandments and seeking after knowledge through the inspirations of the Holy Ghost, in time, he will reach that assurance of faith which is unto eternal life.

The *Lectures on Faith*, by Joseph Smith, Jun., in *Doc. and Cov.*, may justly be considered the most elaborate treatise on the subject in the sacred writings. They are written in such simplicity, that they can be easily understood by all who will honestly study them, to obtain a knowledge of the nature of faith. Their fulness, their comprehensiveness, is one of the many evidences of the Divine inspiration of the Prophet Joseph.

The first lecture shows that faith is an assurance that men have of the existence of things that they have not seen, and that it is an element of power. "It is the principle by which Jehovah works, and through which he exercises power over all temporal as well as eternal things."

The second lecture informs us how faith, in the beginning was based on a knowledge of God and his attributes, and that faith in God has existed in man in proportion to that knowledge.

The third lecture teaches us that to exercise faith in God, man must have an idea that he exists, and also of his character and attributes. He must, as well, feel an assurance that he is living in accordance with the will of God. Consequently, those who fail to obtain this knowledge by living in the spirit and power of the

Gospel, cannot exercise a true and understanding faith in God, no matter what their pretentions.

Lecture fourth treats of the connection between correct ideas of God's attributes, of his Knowledge, Faith or Power, Justice, Judgment, Mercy and Truth; and the exercise of faith unto salvation, in a rational being.

The fifth lecture shows the necessity of faith in God the Father, and in his Son Jesus Christ.

Lecture sixth evidences the necessity of men knowing that their course of life is in accordance with the will of God, in order to exercise faith in him unto salvation. "It was this that enabled the ancient Saints to endure all their afflictions and persecutions, and to take joyfully the spoiling of their goods, knowing (not believing merely) that they had a more enduring substance. *Heb.* 10. 34.

The seventh lecture treats of the effects of faith. That working by faith is working by mental exertion instead of physical force; illustrating the fact by numerous examples. It also elucidates the principle that the mental powers are far superior to the physical forces of nature, and that through them the power of faith is manifested.

FAITH IN GOD THE FATHER, THE SON, AND THE HOLY GHOST.

Bible.

Gen. 15. 6 Abraham believed in God and he counted it to him for righteousness. *Rom.* 4. 3; *Gal.* 3. 6.

Exod. 4. 5 that they may believe that the God of their fathers hath appeared unto thee.

Num. 20. 12 ye believed me not; ye shall not bring this congregation into the land.

Psalm 119. 66 teach me judgment and knowledge, for I have believed thy commandments.

Prov. 16. 20 whoso trusteth in the Lord, happy is he.

Jonah 3. 5 so the people of Nineveh believed God.

John 1. 12 to as many as believed on him he gave power to become the sons of God.

3. 15 that whosoever believeth in him should not perish.

4. 42 know that this is the Christ, the Savior of the world.

5. 24 he that believeth on him that sent me hath everlasting life.

8. 24 if ye believe not I am he, ye shall die in your sins. 31.

11. 25 he that believeth in me, though he were dead, yet shall he live. 26, 27, 40-48.

13. 19 when it comes to pass ye may believe I am he. *Chap*. 14. 29.

14. 1 ye believe in God believe also in me. *Chap*. 10. 11.

16. 9 of sin because they believe not on me. 27, 30, 31.

17. 8 they have believed thou didst send me.

20. 29 blessed are they who have not seen, and yet have believed. 31.

Acts 8. 29 the Spirit said to Philip, go near and join thyself to him.

37 eunuch answered, I believe Jesus Christ is the Son of God.

10. 43 all the prophets witness that whosoever believe in him shall receive remission of sins.

13. 39 by him all that believe are justified from all things, &c.

14. 23 they commended them to the Lord on whom they believed.

16. 31 believe on Jesus Christ, and thou shalt be saved.

19. 4 should believe on him who should come after him.

20. 21 testifying to Jews and Greeks faith towards Jesus Christ.

27. 25 Paul said, I believe God; that it shall be as was told me.

Rom. 1. 16 Gospel of Christ the power of God unto salvation.

17 therein is the righteousness of God revealed from faith to faith. The just shall live by faith.

3. 26 the justifier of him who believeth in Jesus. *Chap*. 4, 5.

4. 24 if we believe in him that raised Jesus from the dead.

6. 8 if we be dead with Christ, we believe we shall live with him.

8. 26, 27 the Spirit itself maketh intercession for us, according to the will of God.

9. 33 a rock of offence, they that believe on him shall not be ashamed. *Chap*. 10. 4, 11.

10. 9 believe God has raised Christ from the dead, thou shalt be saved.

14 how shall they believe in him of whom they have not heard?

2 *Cor*. 1. 9 not trust in ourselves, but in God who raiseth the dead.

Gal. 2. 20 I live by the faith of the Son of God, who gave himself for me.

Col. 1. 4 faith in Christ and love for all the Saints.

1 *Tim.* 1. 16 for a pattern for those who should hereafter believe on him.

3. 16 God manifest in the flesh, justified in the Spirit, believed on in the world, received up into glory.

4. 10 who is the Savior of all men, especially of those who believe.

Titus 3. 8 they who believe in God might maintain good works.

Heb. 3. 18 they that believe not should not enter into his rest.

James 2. 19 thou believest there is one God; devils believe and tremble.

1 *Peter* 1. 21 by him believe in God that raised him from the dead, &c.

1 *John* 4. 16 we have believed the love God hath for us.

5. 10 he that believeth on the Son of God hath the witness in himself.

Book of Mormon.

1 *Nephi* 10. 6, 17 which power he received by faith on the Son of God.

2 *Nephi* 11. 6, 7 my soul delighteth in proving to my people, that, save Christ should come, all men must perish.

25. 25 because of our faith we are made alive in Christ. 26.

26. 8 forward to Christ with steadfastness, they are they who shall not perish.

31. 19 ye have not come thus far except by unshaken faith in Christ.

32. 5 receive the Holy Ghost, it will show you what ye shall do.

33. 4 my words persuade them to believe in Jesus. 7, 10.

Jacob 3. 1 pray to God with great faith.

7. 3 Sherem, knowing that I, Jacob, had faith in Christ, who should come.

Enos 1. 8 he said to me, because of thy faith in Christ.

Jarom 1. 11 persuading them to believe in the Messiah to come.

Mos. 4. 2 for we believe in Christ who shall come.

8. 18 God has provided means that man through faith might work mighty miracles.

Alma 5. 15 do you exercise faith in the redemption of him who created you? 48.

13. 10-31 an exhortation to repentance and faith in Christ. *Chap.* 22. 14.

25. 15 they looked forward to the coming of Christ.

27. 27 the Lamanites were firm in the faith of Christ.

44. 3 is done to us because of our religion and faith in Christ.

46. 41 those who died in the faith of Christ are happy in him.

48. 13 Moroni was a man who was firm in the faith of Christ.

Hel. 3. 35 they grew firmer and firmer in the faith of Christ.

5. 9 no way a man can be saved, only through Christ who shall come. 47.

3 *Nephi* 11. 32 the Holy Ghost bears record of the Father and Son. 34, 35, 36.

12. 19 that ye shall believe in me and repent of your sins.

17. 8 I see that your faith is sufficient that I should heal you. 20.

19. 9 they desired that the Holy Ghost be given unto them.

28 thou hast purified these whom I have chosen because of their faith. 29, 35.

27. 19 none can enter the kingdom unless they wash their garments in the blood of Christ, by faith. 20.

Chap. 28. The three Nephite disciples of Jesus had the faith that enabled them to receive a change in their bodies, that they might remain on the earth until his coming.

4 *Nephi* 1. 48 being constrained by the Holy Ghost, Ammaron hid up the records.

Mormon 7. 7 Father, Son and Holy Ghost are one God. 10.

Ether 5. 4 the Father, Son and Holy Ghost beareth record. *Chap.* 12. 41.

12. 10 by faith they of old were called after the holy order of God.

Moroni 6. 4 were wrought upon and cleansed by the power of the Holy Ghost. *Chap.* 7. 32.

8. 7-9 the word of the Lord came by the power of the Holy Ghost. 26.

10. 4-7 the truth will be manifested by the power of the Holy Ghost.

Doctrine & Covenants.

Sec. 18. 18 ask the Father in faith and you shall receive the Holy Ghost. 19.

41. 3 by prayer of faith ye shall receive my law.

44. 2 if they exercise faith in me I will pour my Spirit on them.

45. 8 to those that believe on my name, gave I power to obtain eternal life.

136. 42 Be diligent in keeping all my commandments lest your faith fail you.

Pearl of Great Price.

Page 2. Moses declared to Satan that he would worship only the God of glory. God blessed Moses for his faith in him.

9. Adam and Eve called on the name of the Lord and offered sacrifice.

Thou shalt call upon God in the name of the Son for evermore.

13. Adam hearkened to the voice of God and glorified his name.

17. many believed and became the sons of God, many believed not and perished.

21. Enoch asked the Lord that he would have mercy on Noah and his seed, inasmuch as he was God and he knew him.

24. Noah walked with God, and all his three sons, also.

29. through faith in the Lord, Abraham left Ur to go into the land of Canaan.

NECESSITY OF FAITH IN THE HOLY PRIESTHOOD.

In every dispensation in which God has made known his will to man, it has been done through a living, inspired Priesthood. Passages from the sacred writings might be multiplied, indefinitely, on this subject. But this is not necessary, inasmuch as all the sacred records attest the necessity of an inspired Priesthood, and obedience to it on the part of the people, if they would understand the will of the Lord concerning them.

Fifteen centuries of the history of Israel, from the Exodus to the destruction of Jerusalem by the Romans, is a record of adversity through disobedience to seers and prophets, and of prosperity, the result of listening to their teachings.

Mankind, with a wide range of religious tenets, are instinctively imbued with a sentiment of reverence and obedience to those who minister in the ordinances of religion. After the apostacy of the early apostolic church, it had a strong hold on the minds of the people during the supremacy of the Romish church.

We may consider that this doctrine began to lose its hold on the masses of the people, professing Christianity, after the Reformation and the splitting up of the Christian world into a great multiplicity of sects. With the introduction of the Gospel and the Holy Priesthood, through Joseph Smith, Jun., the necessity of faith in a living Priesthood is daily being made more apparent to the Latter-day Saints.

Bible.

Exod. 4. 1 Moses answered, they will not believe. 8, 9, 30, 31.

14. 31 Israel believed the Lord and his servant Moses.

19. 9 that the people hear when I speak to thee, and believe thee for ever.

32. 19-34 the golden calf, and the intercession of Moses for the people.

Num. 12. 2 hath the Lord, indeed, spoken only by Moses?

Deut. 9. 19, 20 the Lord hearkened to me; I prayed for Aaron also.

Josh. 1. 5 as I was with Moses, so I will be with thee.

2 *Chron.* 20. 20 believe his prophets, so shall ye prosper.

Amos 3. 7 but he revealeth his secrets to his servants the prophets.

Jonah, Chap. 3. the Ninevites saved by the preaching of Jonah.

Matt. 10. 14, 15 more tolerable for Sodom and Gomorrah, than for those who will not hear your words.

40 he that receiveth you receiveth me.

Luke 1. 19 sent to speak to thee, and shew thee these glad tidings. 45.

10. 16 he that heareth you heareth me. 29.

24. 25 O fools, and slow of heart to believe all that the prophets have spoken.

John 5. 46 had ye believed Moses, ye would have believed me.

13. 20 he that receiveth whomsoever I send, receiveth me.

17. 20 but for them, also, which shall believe on me through their word.

1 *Thess.* 2. 13 when ye received from us, ye received it as the word of God.

Heb. 2. 2 for if the word spoken by angels was steadfast?

Book of Mormon.

Jacob 1. 19 taking the responsibility of answering the sins of the people, if we did not teach them the word of the Lord with all diligence.

2. 2 responsibility of magnifying my office, to rid my garments of your sins.

Mos. 2. 28 to assemble together, that I might rid my garments of your blood.

3 *Nephi* 12. 1, 2 blessed are ye if ye give heed to the words of these twelve, whom I have chosen.

13. 25 ye are they whom I have chosen to minister to this people.

15. 12 ye are my disciples, and a light to this people.

Doctrine & Covenants.

Sec. 1. 4 voice of warning to all people, by the mouth of my disciples.

8, 9 to them is given power to seal, both on earth and in heaven.

14 they who will not hear prophets and apostles shall be cut off. 17, 30.

2. 1 I will reveal to you the Priesthood, by the hand of Elijah.

3. 9 thou art Joseph, and wast chosen to do the work of the Lord. *Sec.* 5. 2, 10, 11-18.

10. 33 Satan thinks to overpower your testimony.

19. 13 keep my commandments which you have received by J. Smith, Jun.

24. 4 if they receive them not, I will curse instead of blessing them.

28. 2 no one to receive revelations for the church but J. Smith, Jun. 3.

7 J. Smith, Jun., has the keys of the revelations which are sealed, until I shall appoint another in his stead.

29. 4 ye are chosen out of the world to declare my Gospel. 7, 10, 12.

42. 61 J. Smith. Jun., to receive revelation, and know the mysteries. 69.

43. 3-5 none but Joseph Smith, Jun., appointed to receive revelation. 12.

52. 9 saying none other things than those which the prophets and apostles have written.

58. 45 behold they shall push the people together from the ends of the earth.

64. 5 the keys of the mysteries shall not be taken from J. Smith, Jun.

65. 2 the keys of the kingdom are committed to man on the earth.

68. 4 whatsoever they shall speak when moved upon by the Holy Ghost shall be scripture and the power of God unto salvation.

75. 20 and they receive you not, shake off the dust of your feet.

81. 2 to J. Smith, Jun., I have given the keys belonging to the Presidency.

84. 64 every soul that believes on your words shall receive the Holy Ghost. 74.

89 whoso receiveth you receiveth me. 90-95. *Sec.* 99. 2-4.

90. 3, 4 the keys of the kingdom never to be taken from J. Smith, Jun. Through him the oracles to be given to the church. 6, 14-16.

103. 25 whomsoever ye curse I will curse.

35 J. Smith, Jun., to organize the kingdom, and establish the children of Zion.

110. 16 the keys of this dispensation are committed into your hands.

112. 15 the keys which I have given unto him, and also to you-ward, shall not be taken from him till I come. 16-21, 30-32.

121. 36 the rights of the Priesthood are inseparably connected with the powers of heaven.

124. 58 my servant, Joseph, in thee shall the kingdoms of the earth be blessed.

128 the Twelve hold the keys of the kingdom upon the four corners of the earth.

133. 26 the prophets of the north countries shall hear his voice, and shall no longer stay themselves.

136. 37 ye shall behold it if ye are faithful in keeping all my words, from the days of Adam to Joseph Smith, Jun., whom I called on by my angels.

Miscellaneous Passages.

Hab. 2. 4 the just shall live by faith. *Rom.* 1. 17. *Gal.* 3. 11. *Heb.* 10. 38.

Matt. 6. 30 shall he not much more clothe you, O ye of little faith? *Luke* 12. 28.

8. 10 not found so great faith, no, not in Israel. *Luke* 7. 9.

17. 20 if ye have faith as a grain of mustard seed.

21. 21 if ye have faith, not only do this, but say to this moun-tain.

Mark 4. 40 how is it that ye have no faith?

Luke 18. 8 when the Son of man cometh shall he find faith on the earth?

Acts 15. 9 purifying their hearts by faith.

26. 18 inheritance among those who are sanctified by faith.

Rom. 3. 3 shall unbelief make the faith of God without effect? 27.

4. 5 his faith is counted to him for righteousness. 9-16.

10. 17 so then faith comes by hearing, and hearing by the word of God.

14. 22 hast thou faith? have it to thyself before God. 23.

1 *Cor.* 2. 5 that your faith should not stand in the wisdom of

men.

16. 13 watch ye, stand fast in the faith, be strong.

2 *Cor*. 4. 13 we having the same spirit of faith.

5. 7 for we walk by faith, not by sight.

Gal. 3. 2 received ye the spirit by works of the law, or by faith? 5-25.

5. 5 we wait for the hope of righteousness by faith. 6, 22.

Eph. 6. 16 above all taking the shield of faith. 23.

Phil. 3. 9 the faith of Christ the righteousness which is of God by faith.

1 *Thess*. 1. 3 remembering without ceasing your work of faith.

5. 8 putting on the breastplate of faith and love.

2 *Thess*. 1. 4 we glory for your patience and faith in your persecutions. 11.

1 *Tim*. 1. 5 of a good conscience and faith unfeigned. 14, 19. *Chap*. 3. 9.

2 *Tim*. 3. 8 men of corrupt minds reprobate concerning the faith. 10.

4. 7 I have finished my course, I have kept the faith.

Titus 1. 13 rebuke sharply that they may be sound in the faith.

Heb. 4. 2 the word did not profit, not being mixed with faith.

6. 1 not laying again the foundation of repentance and faith.

Chap. 11. by faith the worlds were created, the violence of fire quenched, the armies of the aliens put to flight, kingdoms subdued, &c.

12. 2 looking unto Jesus, the author and finisher of our faith.

James 1. 6 let him ask in faith, nothing wavering.

2. 5 hath not God chosen the poor of this world, rich in faith.

5. 15 the prayer of faith shall save the sick.

1 *Peter* 1. 5 kept by the power of God through faith unto salvation. 7, 9, 21.

5. 9 whom resist steadfast in the faith.

2 *Peter* 1. 5 add to your faith virtue, to virtue knowledge.

1 *John* 5. 4 this is the victory that overcometh the world, even our faith.

Jude 3. Earnestly contend for the faith once delivered to the Saints.

Rev. 13. 10 here is the patience and faith of the Saints. *Chap.* 14. 12.

Book of Mormon.

1 *Nephi* 7. 12 the Lord can do all things for men through their faith.

16. 28 the pointers on the ball worked according to their faith. 29.

2 *Nephi* 1. 10 having power given them to do all things by faith.

27. 23 God works not among the children of men save it be according to their faith.

Jacob 1. 5 manifest to us by faith, what should happen to our people.

Enos 1. 12-18 through faith Enos obtained a promise that the records should be preserved to come forth to the Lamanites.

Mos. 4. 6 that salvation might come to him who continues in faith to the end. 21, 30.

Alma 7. 6 look forward for the remission of sins, with an everlasting faith.

12. 30 plan of salvation made known according to men's faith. 33, 34, 37.

13. 2, 3, 4 men called to the Holy Priesthood according to their faith.

18. 35 the Spirit gives knowledge and power according to faith.

32. 18 I ask, Is this faith? if a man knoweth a thing, he has no cause to believe. 21, 26, 27.

28-43 faith illustrated by a parable of a seed.

57. 21-27 through faith the young Ammonites were preserved in battle.

Hel. 5. 20-52 deliverance of Nephi and Lehi from prison through their great faith.

6. 1 the Lamanites exceeded the Nephites in righteousness on account of their great faith.

Mormon 3. 12 it was without faith because of the hardness of their hearts.

8. 24 he knoweth their faith, for in his name could they remove mountains.

Ether 3. This chapter gives an account of great manifestations to the brother of Jared, on account of his great faith.

12. 4-33 many examples given of the power of faith.

Moroni 7. 21-44 instructions on faith.

8. 3 will keep you through the endurance of faith on his name.

10. 4 if ye ask, having faith, he will manifest the truth to you. 7, 11.

Doctrine & Covenants.

Sec. 1. 21 that faith might also increase in the earth.

4. 5 faith, hope, charity, love, &c., qualify him for the work *Sec.* 6. 19, and 12. 8.

8. 10 without faith you can do nothing; ask in faith. 11.

26. 2 all things to be done by common consent, by much prayer and faith.

27. 17 taking the shield of faith, wherewith to quench the fiery darts of the wicked.

41. 3 by prayer of faith ye shall receive my law.

52. 20 the days have come when according to men's faith it shall be done unto them.

103. 36 all victory is brought to pass through your diligence and prayers of faith.

FAITH IN CONTINUAL REVELATION.

Bible.

Num. 11. 29 Moses said, would that all the Lord's people were prophets.

Prov. 29. 18 where there is no vision the people perish.

Mark 16. 17 and these signs shall follow them that believe.

John 14. 12 he that believeth on me shall do the works that I do, and greater.

16. 13 Spirit of truth will teach you all things.

Acts 2. 39 the promise is to as many as the Lord our God shall call.

Rom. 1. 17 for therein is the righteousness of God revealed, from faith to faith.

3. 22 the righteousness of God is unto all, and upon all that believe.

Eph. 3. 19 that ye might be filled with all the fulness of God.

James 1. 5 if any lack wisdom let him ask of God.

1 *John* 2. 27 the anointing which you have received teacheth you all things.

Book of Mormon.

1 *Nephi* 10. 17-19 the gifts and mysteries of God to be unfolded to all men and in all times, to those who diligently seek them.

12. 18 the Messiah of whom the Holy Ghost beareth record from the beginning until this time, henceforth and forever.

22. 2 by the Spirit are all things made known to the prophets.

2 *Nephi* 4. 35 God will give liberally to him that asketh.

26. 13 Christ manifesteth himself by the power of the Holy Ghost, to all who believe on him.

27. 23 that I am the same yesterday, to day and forever. *Chap.* 29. 9.

28. 29 wo be to him that shall say, we have received the word of

God and need no more. 30.

29. 6 thou fool that shall say, we have a Bible and need no more. 7-12.

Alma 39. 19 is it not as easy for the Lord to declare these things to us as unto our children, or as after the time of his coming?

3 *Nephi* 27. 29 for he that asketh receiveth; and to him that knocketh it shall be opened.

Mormon 9. 7-11 God, a God of miracles, revelations and prophecy, the same yesterday, to-day and for ever. 15-19. *Moroni* 10. 19.

Moroni 7. 29 have miracles ceased, or have angels ceased to minister to men because Christ has ascended to heaven? 37, 38.

Doctrine & Covenants.

Sec. 1. 11 the voice of the Lord is unto the ends of the earth. 20.

11. 25 wo to him that denieth the Spirit of revelation and prophecy.

20. 11 that God inspires men to do his work in this generation, as well as in generations of old. 12-17.

26-28 not only those who are but who have been and who shall be, who believe in the gifts and callings of God, shall be saved.

35 diminishing nothing from the revelations of John, or from the revelations of God which shall come hereafter, by the power of the Holy Ghost.

35. 8 will show miracles and wonders unto all who believe on my name.

42. 61 if thou shalt ask thou shalt receive revelation upon revelation. 67, 68.

50. 35 by giving heed to what you have received, and shall hereafter receive.

59. 4 with commandments not a few, and with revelations in their time.

70. 3 revelations which I have given them, and which I shall hereafter give.

See sermon by H. C. Kimball, J. of D., Vol. 2, page 220.

See sermon by H. C. Kimball, J. of D., Vol. 3, page 197.

O. Spencer's Letters to Rev. W. Crowell, No. 3.

A Pamphlet, by O. Pratt, on Faith.

Article by F. D. Richards, Mil. Star, Vol. 29, page 681.

REPENTANCE.

The Nephite prophet, Alma, gives a very comprehensive idea of the importance of repentance. "Yea, I would that ye would come forth and harden not your hearts any longer; for behold, now is the time, and the day of your salvation; and therefore, if ye will repent and harden not your hearts, immediately shall the great plan of redemption be brought about unto you. For behold, this life is the time for men to prepare to meet God; yea, behold the day of this life is the day for men to perform their labors. And now as I said unto you before, as ye have had so many witnesses, therefore, I beseech of you that ye do not procrastinate the day of your repentance until the end; for after this day of life, which is given us to prepare for eternity, behold, if we do not improve our time while in this life, then cometh the night of darkness, wherein there can be no labor performed. Ye cannot say, when ye are brought to that awful crisis, that I will repent, that I will return to my God. Nay, ye cannot say this; for that same spirit which doth possess your bodies at the time ye go out of this life, that same spirit will have power to possess your body in that eternal world. For behold, if ye have procrastinated the day of your repentance, even until death, behold, ye have become subject to the spirit of the devil, and he doth seal you his; therefore, the Spirit of the Lord hath withdrawn from you, and hath no place in you, and the devil hath all power over you; and this is the final state of the wicked." *Alma* 34. 31-35.

"For Godly sorrow worketh repentance to salvation not to be repented of: but the sorrow of the world worketh death;" 2 *Cor.* 7. 10. Of the sorrow that worketh death was that of Judas; *Matt.* 27. 3-5 In some passages of the Scriptures repentance signifies a change of purpose in man, as in the case of the son who refused to work in his father's vineyard, but afterwards repented and went; 21. 28, 29.

Again, it expresses the sympathy of the Lord for the sufferings of his people: "For the Lord hearkened because of their groanings by reason of them that oppressed them;" *Judges* 2. 18. It sometimes expresses sympathy in man for the sufferings of others: "And the people repented them for Benjamin, because that the Lord had made a breach in the tribes of Israel;" 21. 15.

In the history of the deliverance of Israel from Egypt, we are informed that Pharaoh's heart was hardened, so that he would not let the people go. We are evidently to understand by this, that on account of the great wickedness of the Egyptians, the Lord did not soften their hearts by the gentle influences of his Spirit, but permitted them to pursue their own chosen way and suffer the consequences.

We read in the Revelations of St. John: "And the rest of the men which were not killed by these plagues yet repented not of the works of their hands;" 9. 20.

"And blasphemed the God of heaven because of their pains and their sores, and repented not of their deeds;" 16. 11. These, like the Egyptians, had passed the day of repentance, and were left to reap the reward of their wickedness.

On account of their former wickedness, it was all the converted Lamanites could do to repent; *Alma* 24. 11.

Repentance is a gift of God: "Then hath God also to the Gentiles granted repentance unto life;" *Acts* 11. 18. "If God peradventure will give them repentance to the acknowledging of the truth;" 2 *Tim.* 2. 25. "Not knowing that the goodness of God leadeth them to repentance;" *Rom.* 2. 4. That is, the Lord grants to men of his Holy Spirit to soften their hearts and enlighten their understandings, that they may see and receive the truth, if they will; but his Spirit will not always strive with man. Confession of sin, and restitution to the injured party, was early made a standing law in Israel; *Num.* 5. 6, 7.

Confession is one of the outward evidences of a godly sorrow for sin: "For with the heart man believeth unto righteousness; and with the mouth confession is made unto salvation;" *Rom.* 10. 10. "Confess your faults one to another, and pray for one another, that ye may be healed;" *James* 5. 16.

On account of the magnitude of sins committed, repentance is not always followed by forgiveness and restoration. For instance, when Peter was preaching to the Jews, who had slain Jesus and taken his blood on themselves and their children, he did not say, repent and be baptized for the remission of sins; but "Repent ye therefore, and be converted, that your sins may be blotted out, when the times of refreshing shall come from the presence of the Lord; and (when) he shall send Jesus Christ, which before was preached unto you: whom the heaven must receive until the times of the restitution of all things;" *Acts* 3. 19-21. That is, repent now, and believe in Jesus Christ, that you may be forgiven when he whom you have slain shall come again in the days of the restitution of all things; and prescribe to you the terms on which you may be saved.

Bible.

1 *Kings* 8. 47 if they repent in the land of their captivity.

Job 42. 6 I abhor myself and repent in dust and ashes.

Psalm 106. 45 repented according to the multitude of his mercies.

110. 4 the Lord hath sworn and will not repent. *Heb.* 7. 21.

Ezk. 14. 6 repent and turn from your idols. *Chap.* 18. 30,

24. 14 neither will I spare, neither will I repent.

Matt. 3. 2 repent ye, for the kingdom of heaven is at hand. *Chap.* 4. 17.

8 bring forth fruit meet for repentance. *Luke* 3. 8.

9. 13 not to call the righteous but sinners to repentance. *Luke* 5. 32.

11. 20 because they repented not. 21. *Luke* 10. 13.

12. 41 the men of Nineveh shall rise in judgment with this generation. *Luke* 11. 32.

Mark 1. 15 repent ye and believe the Gospel.

6. 12 they went and preached that men should repent.

Luke 13. 3 except ye repent ye shall all likewise perish. 5.

15. 7 over one sinner that repenteth, than over ninety-nine that need no repentance.

16. 30 if one went unto them from the dead they will repent.

17. 3 if thy brother trespass against thee, and repent, forgive him. 4.

Acts 17. 30 times of ignorance God winked at but now commands men to repent.

26. 20 to the Gentiles that they should do works meet for repentance.

Rom. 2. 4 not knowing that the goodness of God leadeth thee to repentance.

2 *Cor.* 7. 9 but that ye sorrowed to repentance.

10 Godly sorrow worketh repentance to salvation, not to be repented of.

Heb. 6. 1 not laying again the foundation of repentance from dead works. 6.

12. 17 he found no place of repentance though he sought it.

2 *Peter* 3. 9 that any should perish, but all should come to repentance.

Rev. 3. 8 remember how thou hast received; hold fast and repent.

19 those I love I chasten; be zealous, therefore, and repent.

Book of Mormon.

1 *Nephi* 10. 18 the way is prepared for all men if they will repent.

22. 28 shall dwell safely in the Holy One of Israel, if they will repent.

2 *Nephi* 2. 21 he gave commandment that all men should repent.

9. 24 if they will not repent and be baptized they must be damned.

30. 2 the Gentiles that will repent are the covenant people of the Lord.

Jacob 3. 3 except ye repent the land is cursed for your sakes.

Mos. 4. 10 believe that you must repent of your sins, and forsake them. 18.

12. 8 unless they repent I will utterly destroy them. 12.

18. 7 Alma preached repentance at the waters of Mormon.

20 he commanded they should preach nothing but repentance and faith.

26. 22 shall be baptized unto repentance.

27. 24 Alma said I have repented of my sins and been redeemed.

29. 19 were it not for the interposition of the Creator because of their repentance.

Alma 5. 31-33 repentance necessary to salvation. 49-56.

7. 9 the Spirit saith repent, prepare the way of the Lord.

9. 12 except ye repent ye can in no wise inherit the kingdom of God.

12. 15 power to save all that bring forth fruit meet for repentance.

24 this life a probationary state for repentance.

22. 6 will repent ye shall be saved.

26. 22 to him that repenteth is given to know the mysteries of God.

27. 23 because of their sore repentance on account of their many murders.

29. 1, 2 that I were an angel to cry repentance to all people.

34. 31-35 to delay repentance until death is to become subject to the devil.

42. 4 there was a probationary time granted to man for repentance. 5, 13.

16 repentance could not come unto men except there was a punishment.

Hel. 5. 11 he hath power to redeem them from their sins because of repentance.

7. 17 O repent ye! why will ye die?

19-24, 28 the Nephites warned of great destruction, unless they would repent.

8. 7 the things he saith will come to pass unless we repent. 26

10. 11 Nephites to be smitten unless they would repent. 17.

11. 8-17 the Lord turned away the famine from the Nephites because of repentance.

12. 22-24 that men might be saved, hath repentance been declared.

13. 2 Samuel preached repentance to the people of Zarahemla. 6.

14. 17, 18 the resurrection of Christ brings to pass the conditions of repentance.

3 *Nephi* 9. 2 wo to the inhabitants of the earth unless they repent. 13, 22.

10. 6 how oft will I gather you if ye will repent. *Matt.* 23. 37.

16. 13 if the Gentiles will repent they shall be numbered with my people.

18. 16 as I pray, ye shall pray among those who repent and are baptized. 30-32.

23. 5 he who repents and is baptized shall be saved.

26. 17 whoso repents and is baptized shall be filled.

Mormon 2. 8 although destruction hung over the Nephites they would not repent. 10-13.

3. 22 I would that I could persuade all ye ends of the earth to repent.

5. 22 how can ye stand before the power of God except ye repent? 24.

7. 3 ye must come to repentance or ye cannot be saved. 5, 7, 8

Ether 2. 11 may repent and not continue in your iniquities, until the fulness come.

5. 5 if so be they repent and come unto the Father.

7. 23 there came prophets warning the people to repent. 25, 26

8. 23 that things may be shown to you that ye may repent.

11. 1 many prophecies of the destruction of the people, unless they should repent. 6, 8, 12, 20.

12. 3 Ether exhorted the people to believe in God unto repentance.

Moroni 6. 7 if they repented not their names were blotted out. 8.

8. 24 repentance is unto those who are under the curse of a

broken law. 25.

Doctrine & Covenants.

Sec. 1. 32, 33 from him that repents not shall be taken the light he has received. *Sec.* 5. 21.

3. 10 God commanded Joseph Smith, Jun., to repent.

5. 19 a desolating scourge shall go forth if they repent not.

19. 4 every one must repent or suffer, for I, God, am endless. 3, 15.

20. 29 all men must repent and endure in faith, or they cannot be saved.

29. 17 1 will take vengeance on the wicked for they will not repent.

44 they cannot be redeemed because they repented not. 49.

33. 10 repent, for the kingdom of heaven is at hand.

39. 18 inasmuch as they repent, I will stay mine hand in judgment.

42. 77 if not married, they shall repent and ye shall receive them.

43. 20 call on the nations to repent. Prepare, for the great day of the Lord. 21, 22.

54. 3 if your brethren desire to escape their enemies let them repent.

63. 15 repent speedily, lest judgment come on them as a snare.

68. 24 if he repent he shall be forgiven, according to the covenants.

75. 29 the idler shall not have place in the church, except he repent.

84. 57 to remain under condemnation, until they repent. 76.

90. 34 your brethren in Zion begin to repent and the angels rejoice. 35.

98. 21 will chasten them if they do not repent and observe all things.

109. 21 when thy people transgress, they may speedily repent and return unto thee. 29.

50 that wicked mob may repent, if repentance can be found. 53.

124. 50 visit on the heads of those who hindered my work, if they repent not. 52, 116.

133. 16 he commandeth all men, everywhere, to repent.

136. 35 their sorrow shall be great unless they repent speedily.

Pearl of Great Price.

Page 9. said to Adam, thou shalt repent and call upon God.

13. Adam called on his sons to repent.

14. the sons of Adam called on all men to repent.

16. God hath made known to our fathers that all men must repent. Teach it to your children that all men must repent.

18. the Lord said to Enoch, say to this people repent, lest I smite them with a curse. He called on all but the people of Cainaan to repent.

23. if men do not repent I will send in the floods upon them For it repenteth Noah that I have created them.

History of Joseph Smith, Sept. 1, 1835.

A Pamphlet by O. Pratt, on Repentance.

BAPTISM.

NECESSITY OF BAPTISM.

That Gospel baptism is necessary to salvation, is abundantly evidenced in the sacred writings. Christ, the highest authority known to man, asserted this most emphatically when he said to Nicodemus, "Verily, verily, I say unto thee, Except a man be born of water and of the Spirit, he cannot enter into the kingdom of God;" *John* 3. 5.

So important did the Savior consider baptism, that when he went to John to be baptized, and John forbade him, he replied to him, "Suffer *it to be so* now: for thus it becometh us to fulfil all righteousness;" *Matt.* 3. 13-15. In this he taught John the doctrine that a fulness of righteousness or salvation, could not be received without it.

The prophet Nephi, who lived nearly 600 years before the birth of our Savior, clearly understood the necessity of baptism. Said he, "And now, if the Lamb of God, he being holy, should have need to be baptized by water, to fulfil all righteousness, O then, how much more need have we, being unholy, to be baptized, yea, even by water;" 2 *Nephi* 31. 5.

The prophet Mormon, who lived nearly 1,000 years after Nephi, also taught the necessity of following the example of our Savior in being baptized, first, by water; *Mormon* 7. 10.

In the opening up of the latter-day dispensation, the Lord said to his prophet Joseph, "Whosoever believeth on my words them will I visit with the manifestation of my Spirit, and they shall be born of me, even of water and of the Spirit;" *Doc. & Cov.* 5. 16.

The Lord, in a revelation to Joseph Smith, Jun., and Sidney Rigdon, speaking of those who should be worthy to come forth in the resurrection of the just, says, "They are they who received the testimony of Jesus, and believed on his name and were baptized after the manner of his burial, being buried in the water in his name;" 76. 51.

Bible.

Matt. 28. 19 go ye therefore and teach all nations, baptizing them.

Mark 16. 16 he that believeth and is baptized shall be saved.

John 1. 33 he that sent me to baptize with water.

Acts 2. 41 then they that gladly received his word were baptized.

1 *Cor.* 12. 13 for by one spirit are we all baptized into one body.

Gal. 3. 27 as many as have been baptized into Christ, have put on Christ.

Eph. 4. 5 one Lord, one faith, one baptism.

1 *Peter* 3. 21 the like figure whereunto even baptism doth now save us.

Book of Mormon.

2 *Nephi* 31. 11 the Father said, repent, and be baptized.

17 the gate by which ye shall enter is repentance and baptism.

Alma 5. 62 be baptized unto repentance.

9. 27 cometh to redeem those who will be baptized unto repentance.

3 *Nephi* 18. 5 one shall be ordained to break bread, and give to those who are baptized in my name.

28. 18 uniting to the church those who believe on their preaching, baptizing them.

Mormon 9. 29 see that ye are not baptized unworthily.

Moroni 6. 1-4 explains who are fit subjects for baptism.

8. 4-22 the reasons given why little children are not fit subjects for baptism.

Doctrine & Covenants.

Sec. 68. 8 preach the Gospel to every creature, baptizing in the name of the Father, Son, and Holy Ghost.

112. 29 he that believeth and is baptized shall be saved; he that believeth not and is not baptized shall be damned.

128. 12 baptism by immersion necessary to answer to the likeness of the dead, that one principle might accord with the other. Also in likeness of the resurrection of the dead, in coming forth out of their graves. This passage explains and beautifully accords with *Rom.* 6. 4, and *Col.* 2. 12.

Pearl of Great Price.

Page 16. the Holy Spirit promised to Adam, if he would repent and be baptized. Explanation of the necessity of being born of water and of the Spirit.

17. gives an account of the baptism of Adam.

*   *   *   *   *

MODE OF BAPTISM.

Not only is the necessity of baptism taught us by the highest possible authority, but, as well, the manner in which that ordinance is to be administered.

Adam, the Father of the race, set an example for all his children to follow. "And it came to pass, when the Lord had spoken with Adam, our father, that Adam cried unto the Lord, and he was caught away by the Spirit of the Lord, and was carried down into the water, and was laid under the water, and was brought forth out of the water. And thus he was baptized; and the Spirit of God descended upon him, and thus he was born of the Spirit, and became quickened in the inner man;" *P. of G. P.*, p. 17.

Christ went where John was baptizing in the river Jordan, to be baptized of him, and "when he was baptized, went up straightway out of the water;" *Matt.* 3. 16. That he was immersed, or buried in the water, is evident from the sayings of the Apostle Paul, "Therefore we are buried with him by baptism into death: that like as Christ was raised up from the dead by the glory of the Father, even so we also should walk in newness of life. For if we have been planted together in the likeness of his death, we shall be also *in the likeness of his resurrection;*" Rom. 6. 4, 5. *"Buried with him in baptism, wherein also ye are risen with* him *through the faith of the operation of God;"* Col. 2. 12.

The meaning of these passages is evident. If we would come forth in the resurrection in the likeness of Christ, we must, like him, be buried in the water, and come forth out of the water, in the likeness of his burial and resurrection.

The Nephites knew no other mode of Gospel baptism than immersion. Said Jesus to his Nephite disciples, "And then shall ye immerse them in the water, and come forth again out of the water;" 3 *Nephi* 11. 26.

When our Savior sent forth his Jewish disciples to preach the Gospel, he authorized them to baptize in the name of the Father, the Son, and the Holy Ghost; *Matt.* 28. 19. He instructed his Nephite disciples to use the following words, "Having authority given me of Jesus Christ, I baptize you in the name of the Father, and of the Son, and of the Holy Ghost. Amen;" 3 *Nephi* 11. 25.

Quite explicit instructions on this subject are given to the Latter-day Saints in the *Doc. & Cov.*: "The person who is called of God, and has authority from Jesus Christ to baptize, shall go down into the water with the person who has presented him or herself for baptism, and shall say, calling him or her by name—Having been commissioned of Jesus Christ, I baptize you in the name of the Father, and of the Son, and of the Holy Ghost. Amen. Then shall he immerse him or her in the water, and come forth again out of the water;" 20. 73, 74.

Under date of May, 1829, we find the following account of the baptism of J. Smith, Jun., and O. Cowdery, being the first baptisms in the Church of Jesus Christ of Latter-day Saints: "Accordingly we went and were baptized, I baptized him first, and afterwards he baptized me, after which I laid my hands upon his head and ordained him to the Aaronic Priesthood, afterwards he laid his hands on me and ordained me to the same Priesthood—for so were we commanded. * * * It was on the fifteenth day of May, 1829, that we were ordained under the hand of the Messenger, and baptized. Immediately on our coming up out of the water, after we had been baptized, we experienced great and glorious blessings."

Bible.

Matt. 3. 6 all baptized of him in Jordan, confessing their sins.

3. 13 then cometh Jesus from Galilee to Jordan unto John.

John 3. 23 John was baptizing in Enon near Salem, because there was much water there.

Acts 8. 38, 39 Philip went down into the water with the eunuch.

22. 16 arise and be baptized and wash away thy sins.

1 *Cor.* 10. 2 all baptized unto Moses in the cloud and in the sea.

Titus 3. 5 by the washing of regeneration and renewing of the Holy Ghost.

Book of Mormon.

Mos. 18. 12-17 a description of the manner in which Alma baptized the Lamanites in the waters of Mormon.

26. 15 blessed are they who were baptized in the waters of Mormon.

Alma 4. 4 many were baptized by Alma in the river Sidon.

3 *Nephi* 11. 23-28 conditions for and form of baptism.

19. 11-13 Nephi, and his brethren, went down into the water, and came up out of the water.

Pearl of Great Price.

Page 17. Adam was laid under the water, and brought forth out of the water.

18. Enoch was commanded to baptize in the name of the Father, Son, and Holy Ghost.

*   *   *   *   *

OBJECT OF BAPTISM.

The primary aim and end of baptism is the remission of sins. This subject is fully explained by the Lord to our Father Adam. "Therefore I give unto you a commandment, to teach these things freely unto your children, saying, That by reason of transgression cometh the fall, which fall bringeth death, and inasmuch as ye were born into the world by water, and blood, and the spirit, which I have made, and so became of dust a living soul, even so ye must be born again into the kingdom of heaven, of water, and of the spirit, and be cleansed by blood, even the blood of mine Only Begotten; that ye might be sanctified from all sin, and enjoy the words of eternal life in this world, and eternal life in the world to come, even immortal glory: For by the water ye keep the commandment; by the spirit ye are justified, and by the blood ye are sanctified; therefore it is given to abide in you; the record of heaven; the Comforter; the peaceable things of immortal glory;" *P. of G. P.*, p. 16.

The above quotation is full of meaning, but it is evident, at once, that the object of baptism is to open the way through which, alone, men may attain to all the blessings of salvation and eternal life. It was especially the mission of John the Baptist to preach the baptism of repentance for the remission of sins; *Mark* 1. 4.

On the day of Pentecost, the Apostle Peter very earnestly exhorted the multitude, "Repent, and be baptized every one of you in the name of Jesus Christ for the remission of sins;" *Acts* 2. 38.

The Apostle Paul says, "Without shedding of blood is no remission;" *Heb.* 9. 22. John the Apostle also asserts the same doctrine: "The blood of Jesus Christ his Son cleanseth us from all sin;" 1 *John* 1. 7. It is evident, from the tenor of the sacred writings, that only by being buried with Christ in water, by baptism, is the shedding of his blood available to man for the remission of sins.

Bible.

Luke 3. 3 John preached the baptism of repentance, for the remission of sins.

Acts 22. 16 arise and be baptized and wash away your sins.

Eph. 5. 26 that he might sanctify and cleanse it with the washing of water.

Titus 3. 5 by the washing of regeneration.

1 *Peter* 3. 21 the like figure whereunto even baptism doth also now save us.

Book of Mormon.

2 *Nephi* 31. 17 after baptism by water, cometh the remission of sins.

Alma 7. 14 be baptized unto repentance, that ye may be washed from your sins.

3 *Nephi* 1. 23 baptism unto repentance, in which there was a remission of sins.

7. 25 baptism by water, a witness of repentance and a remission of sins.

18. 30 the sacrament to be administered only to those who have been baptized.

30. 2 come to me and be baptized, for the remission of sins.

Moroni 8. 11 baptism and fulfilling the commandments bringeth remission of sins.

Doctrine & Covenants.

Sec. 19. 31 Shalt declare repentance and remission of sins by baptism and by fire.

55. 2 repentance and remission of sins by way of baptism.

68. 27 children to be baptized for remission of sins when eight years old.

76. 51, 52 baptism and remission of sins necessary, in order to come forth in the resurrection of the just.

84. 27 the Gospel of repentance, and of baptism, and remission of sins.

74 those not baptized for the remission of sins shall be damned.

Miscellaneous Passages.

Matt. 3. 7 when he saw Pharisees and Sadducees come to his baptism.

20. 22 are ye able to be baptized with the baptism I am baptized with? *Mark* 10. 39.

21. 25 the baptism of John, was it from heaven or of men? *Mark* 11. 30. *Luke* 20. 4.

28. 19 go ye therefore, and teach all nations, baptizing them.

Mark 1. 8 I, indeed, have baptized you with water.

Luke 3. 7 said he to the multitude that came to be baptized of him. 12.

16 John answered, I indeed baptize you with water. 21.

7. 29 the publicans justified God, being baptized with the baptism of John. 30.

12. 50 I have a baptism to be baptized with.

John 1. 25 why baptizest thou, if thou be not the Christ?

26 1 baptize with water, but there standeth one among you. 28.

33 he that sent me to baptize with water, said to me;

3. 22 there he tarried with them and baptized. 23.

4. 1 that Jesus made and baptized more disciples than John.

Acts 1. 5 John baptized with water, but ye shall be baptized with the Holy Ghost. 22.

2. 41 then they that gladly received his word were baptized.

8. 12 when they believed Philip they were baptized, both men and women. 13.

16 as yet he was fallen on none of them, only they were baptized.

36 see, here is water, what doth hinder me to be baptized?

9. 18 Saul received sight and arose and was baptized.

10. 37 that word published throughout all Judea, after the baptism John preached. 47.

16. 15 Lydia, when she was baptized, and her household, besought us. 33.

18. 8 many of the Corinthians believed and were baptized. 25.

1 *Cor.* 1. 13 or were ye baptized in the name of Paul? 14, 16, 17.

12. 13 for by one spirit are we all baptized into one body.

Gal. 3. 27 as many as have been baptized into Christ, have put on Christ.

Eph. 4. 5 one Lord, one faith, one baptism.

Heb. 6. 2 of the doctrine of baptism and laying on of hands.

Book of Mormon.

1 *Nephi* 10. 9 my father said, he should baptize in Bethabary beyond Jordan; also, that he should baptize the Messiah with water. 10.

2 *Nephi* 31. 4 the prophet the Lord showed me should baptize the Lamb of God. 6-10, 13.

14 if ye should deny me after being baptized with water and the Holy Ghost, better if ye had not known me.

Mos. 18. 10 what have you against being baptized in the name of the Lord?

21. 33 many desirous of being baptized, but there was none having authority. 35.

25. 17, 18 Alma baptized the people of Limhi.

Alma 7. 15 baptism a witness that we covenant with God to keep his commandments.

15. 13 Alma consecrated priests and teachers, to baptize unto the Lord.

19. 35 the Lamanites that believed were baptized, and became a righteous people. 36.

Hel. 16. 1 when they found Nephi they desired to be baptized. 3.

3 *Nephi* 11. 21, 22 the Lord gave Nephi, and others, power to baptize.

12. 1 Jesus called twelve and gave them authority to baptize.

19. 10-13 Nephi, and all those whom Jesus had chosen, were baptized.

26. 17 the disciples whom Jesus had chosen began to baptize as many as came to them.

27. 1 as the disciples were journeying and baptizing in the name of Jesus.

28. 18 uniting to the church those who believed on their preaching, baptizing them.

Mormon 7. 10 are first baptized with water, following the example of our Savior.

9. 29 see that ye are not baptized unworthily.

Moroni 6. 1-4 explains who are fit subjects for baptism.

8. 4-22 why little children are not fit subjects for baptism.

Doctrine & Covenants.

Sec. 18. 7 as thou hast been baptized by my servant, J. Smith, Jun.

20. 37 qualifications necessary for baptism and reception into the church.

38-58 duties of the Priesthood in connection with baptism.

68 duty of members after they receive baptism.

22. 1, 2 old covenants of no avail; necessary to be baptized to enter the new covenant.

39. 20 go forth baptizing with water, preparing the way. 23.

52. 10 let them go, two by two, baptizing by water and laying on hands.

134. 12 not lawful to baptize bond servants, without consent of their masters.

See Testimonies of ancient and modern authors in relation to baptism, Mil. Star, Vol. 21, pages 687, 721, 754, 768, 801, 833, and Vol. 22, pages 44, 142, 491.

O. Spencer's Letters to Rev. Wm. Crowel, No 4.

A Pamphlet by O. Pratt.

History of J. Smith, Mar. 20, 1842.

Mil. Star, Vol. 33, pages 65, 82.

Article by N. Williams, Mil. Star, Vol. 41, page 84.

*   *   *   *   *

BAPTISM FOR THE DEAD.

A prominent feature in the plan of redemption is the vicarious nature of the labors of Christ, and his ministers, for the salvation of men. In his death and resurrection, Christ did that for men which they could not do for themselves. In all dispensations of the Priesthood, it has been the duty of those officiating in its ordinances to act for others, when they could not act for themselves.

Under the Mosaic law, the tribe of Levi was set apart, to make it the special business of their lives, in all their generations, to understand its ordinances and ceremonies that they might be capable of acting in behalf of the people, who were engaged in the ordinary avocations of life. This labor was accepted by the Lord, in behalf of the people, as though they had done it for themselves.

The ordinances described in the 16th *chap.* of *Lev.*, which the High Priest was required to perform as an atonement for the sins of the house of Israel, clearly illustrates this principle. It is said of the scapegoat, "And Aaron shall lay both his hands upon the head of the live goat, and confess over him all the iniquities of the children of Israel, and all their transgressions in all their sins, putting them upon the head of the goat, and shall send *him* away by the hand of a fit man into the wilderness;" 16. 21. This confession of the sins of the people, by the High Priest, was a vicarious work, and was accepted by the Lord as though they had confessed their own sins, with their hands upon the head of the goat—a work evidently impracticable for them to do.

The vicarious nature of the sufferings of Christ are clearly foretold in the prophetic vision of Isaiah: "Surely he hath borne our griefs, and carried our sorrows: yet we did esteem him stricken, smitten of God, and afflicted. But he *was* wounded for our transgressions, *he was* bruised for our iniquities: the chastisement of our peace *was* upon him; and with his stripes we are healed;" 53. 4, 5. The same prophet speaking further of Christ says, that he should be "For a covenant of the people, for a light of the Gentiles;" 42. 6. Evidently referring to his earthly mission in which this was literally fulfilled.

At the time when this should take place, there was another labor which he was to perform. He was "To open the blind eyes, to bring out the prisoners from the prison, and them that sit in darkness out of the prison house;" *verse* 7. This passage informs us that there was a class of persons who were confined in a dark, benighted prison, who were to be delivered when Christ should be "For a covenant of the people, for a light of the Gentiles."

The Apostle Peter informs us that Jesus, between his death and resurrection, when his spirit was free from his body, went and preached to the spirits in prison. "For Christ also hath once suffered for sins, the just for the unjust, that he might bring us to God, being put to death in the flesh, but quickened by the Spirit: By which also he went and preached unto the spirits in prison;" 1 *Pet.* 3. 18, 19. In the context he informs us that these spirits were those, of the people, who were disobedient in the days of Noah.

The Apostle Peter had no narrow views of the plan of salvation, for when he speaks of Christ suffering, "the just for the unjust," he makes no discrimination in favor of the living. For the assertion is sweeping and universal, that Christ died for all; else what profit could there be in Christ's preaching to the spirits in prison, unless the way was opened for them to receive the ordinances and blessings of the Gospel, in common with the living?

Peter positively informs us that the Gospel was preached to the dead, and the reason why, "For, for this cause was the Gospel preached also to them that are dead, that they might be judged according to men in the flesh, but live according to God in the spirit;" 4. 6. If they are judged according to men in the flesh, it would evidently be unjust, if they should not have the benefit of all the ordinances and privileges that pertain to the living. To the question, How can the dead receive the ordinances of the Gospel? there can be but one answer—by proxy; by the vicarious works of the living.

Not only did Peter assert that the Gospel was preached to the spirits in prison, that they might be judged according to men in the flesh, but the Apostle Paul informs us that the first Gospel ordinance, of all dispensations—baptism, was administered by proxy among the former-day Saints.

Speaking of the resurrection, he asks the Corinthian Saints, "Else what shall they do which are baptized for the dead, if the dead rise not at all? why are they then baptized for the dead?" 1 *Cor.* 15. 29. That is, of what utility are baptisms for the dead, if there is no resurrection? This doctrine was evidently neither strange nor new to those to whom the Apostles were writing.

Paul further says, "For to this end Christ both died, and rose, and revived, that he might be Lord both of the dead and living;" *Rom.* 14. 9. If this passage asserts anything, it is that Christ died for the dead as well as the living. Again, there is here no discrimination made in favor of the living.

Jesus gave some light on this subject, when talking with the Jews on marrying and the resurrection: "Neither can they die any more: for they are equal unto the angels; and are the children of God, being the children of the resurrection. * * * For he is not a God of the dead, but of the living: for all live unto him;" *Luke* 20. 36, 38. The following may be inferred from these passages: that notwithstanding men die, they must live unto God through the resurrection, and as myriads have died without a knowledge of the Gospel, they must have an opportunity of enjoying its blessings, in order to live unto God, after they have come forth from the dead.

The prophet Malachi, in vision, saw our day, over 2200 years ago. In the closing chapter of his prophecy and of the Old Testament, he says, "For, behold, the day cometh, that shall burn as an oven; and all the proud, yea, and all that do wickedly, shall be stubble: and the day that cometh shall burn them up, saith the Lord of Hosts, that it shall leave them neither root nor branch;" 4. 1. But there is another important event to take place before that day, as we learn in *verses* 5 & 6: "Behold, I will send you Elijah the prophet before the coming of the great and dreadful day of the Lord: and he shall turn the heart of the fathers to the children, and the heart of the children to their fathers, lest I come and smite the earth with a curse."

Elijah's coming must evidently be to some one who is prepared to receive him, and to labor in the great work he is sent to inaugurate, for the expression, "He shall turn the heart of the fathers to the children, and the heart of the children to their fathers," is very comprehensive. It does not discriminate between the living and the dead, between the past and the future. It pertains to the whole family of Adam.

Moroni, the heavenly messenger who ministered to Joseph Smith, Jun., makes the universality of the work to be accomplished still plainer: "And he shall plant in the hearts of the children, the promises made to the fathers, and the hearts of the children shall turn to their fathers; if it were not so, the whole earth would be utterly wasted at his coming;" *P. of G. P.*, p. 50.

"It is sufficient to know, in this case, that the earth will be smitten with a curse, unless there is a welding link of some kind or other, between the fathers and the children, upon some subject or other, and behold what is that subject? It is the baptism for the dead. For we without them cannot be made perfect; neither can they without us be made perfect.

"Neither can they nor we be made perfect, without those who have died in the Gospel also; for it is necessary in the ushering in of the dispensation of the fulness of times; which dispensation is now beginning to usher in, that a whole and complete and perfect union, and welding together of dispensations, and keys, and powers, and glories should take place, and be revealed from the days of Adam even to the present time; and not only this, but those things which never have been kept hid from the foundation of the world, but have been kept hid from the wise and prudent, shall be revealed unto babes and sucklings in this the dispensation of the fulness of times;" *Doc. & Cov., sec.* 128. 18.

The time came for Elijah to appear and fill his great and glorious mission. The place was prepared, and the men were there who had the faith to receive him, and the authority and power he was to bring to men in the flesh, to administer in the ordinances of the Gospel for the dead.

He appeared to Joseph, the Seer, and O. Cowdery, in the Kirtland Temple, April 3d, 1836, and said, "Behold, the time has fully come, which was spoken of by the mouth of Malachi, testifying that he (Elijah) should be sent before the great and dreadful day of the Lord come, to turn the hearts of the fathers to the children, and the children to the fathers, lest the whole earth be smitten with a curse. Therefore the keys of this dispensation are committed into your hands, and by this ye may know that the great and dreadful day of the Lord is near, even at the doors;" *Doc. & Cov., sec.* 110. 14, 15, 16.

Ordinances for the salvation of the dead require temples, or sacred places especially constructed for their administration. The former-day Saints usually remained in the same scattered condition in which they received the Gospel. For these reasons, it is probable that the doctrines pertaining to the salvation of the dead were imperfectly taught. This may account for so little being said in the New Testament on this subject.

The prophet Joseph has given special instructions on this subject in *secs.* 127 & 128, *Doc. & Cov.*

See Sermon by B. Young, J. of D., Vol. 3, page 362.

See Sermon by J. Smith, J. of D., Vol. 6, page 1.

See Sermon by Jos. Young, J. of D., Vol. 6, page 226.

See Sermon by G. Q. Cannon, J. of D., Vol. 14, page 310.

See Sermon by J. Taylor, J. of D., Vol. 15, page 284.

See Sermon by W. Woodruff, J. of D., Vol. 16, page 263.

See Sermon by O. Pratt, J. of D., Vol. 18, page 41.

See Sermon by B. Young, J. of D., Vol. 18, page 235.

History of J. Smith, Oct. 18, 1840.

History of J. Smith, Oct. 31, 1841.

History of J. Smith, Dec. 13, 1841.

History of J. Smith, March 27, 1842.

History of J. Smith, April 15, 1842.

History of J. Smith, Jan. 21, 1844.

History of J. Smith, April 8, 1844.

History of J. Smith, May 12, 1844.

REMISSION OF SINS.

This subject is closely connected with the fall of man and the atonement of our Savior. The fall was brought about by a law being given to him, in the Garden of Eden. He broke that law, and the fall was the penalty of transgression.

The atonement opens up the way for the removal of that penalty; and also for the removal of the effects of men's individual sins through repentance. It is through obedience to certain laws and ordinances, deriving their efficacy from the atonement of Christ, that men's sins are remitted.

Man, in his weak and fallen state, is ever prone to sin. God, in his great love and mercy, has provided a way through which his sins may be forgiven. Besides the outward ordinances of the Gospel, there are three general conditions which the sinner must fulfil, in order to have his sins remitted. He must confess them and ask forgiveness; *Doc. & Cov.*, 64. 7. He must forgive others of their trespasses. Christ taught his disciples, "For if ye forgive men their trespasses, your Heavenly Father will also forgive you: but if ye forgive not men their trespasses, neither will your Heavenly Father forgive your trespasses;" *Matt.* 6. 14, 15.

The Lord said to his prophet Joseph, "Ye ought to forgive one another, for he that forgiveth not his brother his trespasses, standeth condemned before the Lord, for there remaineth in him the greater sin;" *Doc. & Cov*, 64. 9. The third condition is, men must continually bear in mind the atonement of Christ. The Nephite Saints continually looked forward to the atonement of Christ, "Thus retaining a remission of their sins;" *Alma* 4. 13, 14. We are often taught in the sacred writings to make our supplications to the Father, in the name of his Son Jesus Christ, who has become a propitiation for sin. The works necessary to attain to a remission of sins, and the results of that remission, are well expressed by the Nephite prophet, Moroni:

"And the first fruits of repentance is baptism; and baptism cometh by faith, unto the fulfilling the commandments; and the fulfilling the commandments bringeth remission of sins; and the remission of sins bringeth meekness, and lowliness of heart, and because of meekness and lowliness of heart, cometh the visitation of the Holy Ghost, which Comforter filleth with hope and perfect love, which love endureth by diligence unto prayer, until the end shall come, when all the Saints shall dwell with God;" *Moroni* 8. 25, 26.

Bible.

Exo. 23. 21 provoke him not, for he will not pardon your transgressions.

32. 32 Moses said, yet now if thou wilt forgive their sin.

34. 7 forgiving transgression and sin, and that will by no means clear the guilty.

Josh. 24. 19 is a holy a jealous God, he will not forgive your sins.

1 *Kings* 8. 30 hear thou in heaven, and when thou hearest forgive.

2 *Chron.* 7. 14 then will I hear from heaven and will forgive their sin.

Neh. 9. 17 thou art a God ready to pardon, slow to anger.

Psalm 32. 1 blessed is he whose transgression is forgiven, whose sin is covered *Rom.* 4. 7.

86. 5 for thou, Lord, art good and ready to forgive.

103. 3 who forgiveth all thine iniquities, who healeth all thy diseases.

130. 4 but there is forgiveness with thee that thou mayest be feared.

Jer. 31. 34 for I will forgive their iniquity and remember their sin no more.

Dan. 9. 9 to the Lord belong mercies and forgiveness. 19.

Mic. 7. 18 who is a God like unto thee that pardoneth iniquity.

Matt. 6. 12 forgive us our debts as we forgive our debtors. *Luke* 11. 4.

9. 2 son, be of good cheer, thy sins be forgiven thee.

18. 21 how oft shall my brother sin against me and I forgive him?

35 if ye forgive not every one his brother their trespasses.

Mark 2. 7 who can forgive sins but God only?

11. 25 forgive, that your Father in heaven may forgive you.

Luke 6. 37 condemn not; forgive, and ye shall be forgiven.

17. 3, 4 if thy brother trespass against thee seven times.

23. 34 Jesus said, Father, forgive them for they know not what they do.

John 20. 23 whosoever sins ye remit they are remitted.

Acts 26. 18 turn them from the power of Satan to God, that they may receive forgiveness of sins.

Eph. 4. 32 forgiving one another as God hath forgiven you

Heb. 9. 22 without shedding of blood there is no remission.

1 *John* 2. 12 because your sins are forgiven, for his name's sake.

Book of Mormon.

Mos. 26. 30 as often as my people repent will I forgive them. 31.

Moroni 10. 33 shedding of the blood of Christ, which is in the covenant of the Father unto the remission of your sins.

Doctrine & Covenants.

Sec. 62. 3 angels rejoice over you and your sins are forgiven.

64. 7 I the Lord forgive sins unto those who confess their sins before me.

8 the former-day disciples were afflicted because they forgave not one another. 9.

10 I forgive whom I will, but of you it is required to forgive all men.

82. 1 inasmuch as you have forgiven one another, so I the Lord forgive you.

110. 5 your sins are forgiven you: you are clean before me.

LAYING ON OF HANDS.

FOR ORDINATION.

Ordinations to offices in the holy Priesthood are sometimes mentioned in both the Old and New Testaments, when it is not stated in the context that it was by the imposition of hands. The apostle Paul exhorted Timothy, "Neglect not the gift that is in thee, which was given thee by prophecy, with the laying on of the hands of the presbytery;" 1 *Tim.* 4. 14. The inference is reasonable, that Paul here refers to an ordination to some office in the Priesthood.

Paul again said to Timothy, "Stir up the gift of God, which is in thee by the putting on of my hands;" 2 *Tim.* 1. 6.

The Lord revealed to Joseph the prophet, that the Priesthood descended from Adam to Noah under the HANDS OF THE FATHERS; *Doc & Cov.* 107. 40-52.

We are further informed that "Abraham received the Priesthood from Melchisedek, who received it through the lineage of his fathers, even till Noah;" 84. 14. Esaias, who lived in the days of Abraham, "received it under the hands of God;" from him it descended under the hands of the fathers to Moses; 6-13.

In this dispensation all the offices and authority of the Priesthood are conferred by the laying on of hands. The first ordination to the Priesthood, in this dispensation, was under the hands of John the Baptist; *Doc. & Cov., sec.* 13. The angel, John the Baptist, commanded Joseph Smith and O. Cowdery to baptize each other. The prophet says: "Accordingly we went and were baptized, I baptized him first, and afterwards he baptized me, after which I laid my hands upon his head and ordained him to the Aaronic Priesthood, afterwards he laid his hands on me and ordained me to the same Priesthood—for so were we commanded;" *His. of J. Smith, May* 15, 1829.

The same order as was observed in the ordination to the Aaronic Priesthood, was also observed by Joseph Smith and O. Cowdery in their ordination to the Melchisedek Priesthood; *Doc. & Cov.* 20. 3, 4, *sec.* 21. 10-12.

*   *   *   *   *

FOR THE GIFT OF THE HOLY GHOST.

The laying on of hands for the reception of the Holy Ghost, characterized the primitive Gospel dispensation, as recorded in the New Testament. Peter and John laid their hands on the people of Samaria, who had been baptized, and they received the Holy Ghost; *Acts* 8. 17.

Ananias laid hands on Saul, by special commandment, before he was baptized, that he might receive his sight and be filled with the Holy Ghost; 9. 17.

Paul found some people at Ephesus, that claimed to be disciples of John the Baptist, who had not even heard of the Holy Ghost. When he had baptized them, "and when he had laid his hands upon them, the Holy Ghost came on them; and they spake with tongues and prophesied;" 19. 2-6.

The laying on of hands for the reception of the Holy Ghost characterized both the Mosaic and Gospel dispensations among the Nephites. "Now it came to pass that when Alma had said these words, that he clapped his hands upon all them who were with him. And behold, as he clapped his hands upon them, they were filled with the Holy Spirit;" *Alma* 31. 36. We are informed that the Nephites, at this time, were very strict in observing the ordinances of God according to the law of Moses; 30. 3.

When our Savior organized the Council of Twelve Apostles among the Nephites, he touched them with his hand and gave them power to give the Holy Ghost. "And it came to pass that when Jesus had made an end of these sayings, he touched with his hand the disciples whom he had chosen, one by one, even until he had touched them all, and spake unto them as he touched them; and the multitude heard not the words which he spake, therefore they did not bear record; but the disciples bear record that he gave them power to give the Holy Ghost;" 3 *Nephi* 18. 36, 37.

The Apostles of this dispensation are especially instructed to lay hands on those who have been baptized into the church, "For the baptism of fire and the Holy Ghost, according to the scriptures;" *Doc. & Cov.* 20. 41.

When the few who had received the Gospel first met to organize the church, the prophet Joseph laid his hands on O. Cowdery and ordained him an elder in the church, after which O. Cowdery ordained the prophet Joseph to the same office. They then administered the sacrament to the Saints. Afterwards they laid their hands "on each individual member of the church present, that they might receive the gift of the Holy Ghost, and be confirmed members of the Church of Christ;" *His. of J. Smith, April* 6, 1830. This was the first time in this dispensation that hands were publicly laid on for the bestowal of the Holy Ghost, and for confirmation.

*   *   *   *   *

FOR HEALING THE SICK.

Jesus Christ has left us his example for laying hands on the sick, that they might be healed. He touched the hand of Peter's wife's mother, and the fever left her; *Matt.* 8. 15. "He laid his hands upon a few sick folk, and healed them;" *Mark* 6. 5.

About the close of his earthly mission, Jesus said to his disciples, "Go ye into all the world, and preach the Gospel to every creature;" and promised them that if they would lay hands on the sick, they should recover; 16. 15, 18.

"By the hands of the apostles were many signs and wonders wrought among the people;" *Acts* 5. 12.

The Lord, through his prophet, Joseph, has commanded his people to administer to the sick by the laying on of hands. "And whosoever among you are sick, and have not faith to be healed, but believe, shall be nursed with all tenderness, with herbs and mild food, and that not by the hand of an enemy. And the elders of the church, two or more, shall be called, and shall pray for and lay their hands upon them in my name; and if they die they shall die unto me, and if they live they shall live unto me;" *Doc. & Cov.*, 42. 43, 44.

The ordinance of laying on of hands for the bestowal of authority, power and blessing has characterized all the dispensations of the holy Priesthood. But it does not necessarily follow that the Creator may not bestow these favors in other ways.

Before the flood, the Lord said to Enoch, "Anoint thine eyes with clay, and wash them, and thou shalt see;" and the spiritual creations were opened to his vision; *P. of G. P., p.* 15.

Naaman, the Syrian, was cleansed of his leprosy by washing seven times in Jordan; 2 *Kings* 5. 10-14.

The blind man, after Jesus had anointed his eyes with clay, received his sight by washing them in the pool of Siloam; *John* 9. 7. Contrary to the usual custom, Ananias laid hands on Saul, before he was baptized, that he might be filled with the Holy Ghost; *Acts* 9. 17.

Bible.

Num. 27. 18 take thee Joshua, the son of Nun, and lay thine hand upon him.

2 *Kings* 5. 11 I thought he would strike his hand over the place.

Mark 7. 33 put his finger into his ears, and touched his tongue.

8. 23 he took the blind man and put his hands on him. 25.

Acts 4. 30 stretching forth thy hand to heal, that signs and wonders be done.

14. 3 granted signs and wonders to be done by their hands.

Doctrine & Covenants.

Sec. 20. 58 teachers and deacons have no authority to lay on hands.

25. 8 by his hands you shall receive the Holy Ghost.

33. 15 by the laying on of hands I will bestow the Holy Ghost.

36. 2 will lay my hands upon you, by the hand of my servant.

39. 23 by your hands they shall receive the Holy Ghost, and know me.

42. 43, 44 the elders shall lay hands on the sick.

49. 14 receive the Holy Ghost by the laying on of hands. *Sec.* 52. 10. *Sec.* 53. 3. *Sec.* 55. 1.

66. 9 lay your hands upon the sick and they shall recover.

68. 25 children should be taught baptism, and the Gift of the Holy Ghost by laying on hands.

27 and their children shall be baptized for the remission of their sins when eight years old, and receive the laying on of the hands.

See Mil. Star, Vol. 3, page 59.

History of J. Smith, March 20, 1842.

THE RESURRECTION.

What little knowledge we have of this doctrine we have received from Jesus Christ, the author of it, and from those whom he has sent to teach mankind. From these we learn that a resurrection has occurred, and that there will be others at different periods of time, as well as under different circumstances.

The resurrection is predicated on the death or dissolution of the earth, and all organizations pertaining to it. As the fall of Adam brought death or dissolution, so the death and resurrection of Christ will bring to pass a restoration to life, of all creatures that have been affected by the fall.

AT CHRIST'S RESURRECTION.

That Christ well understood the great object of his earthly mission, is evident from many of his sayings previous to his death and resurrection. Early in his ministry he said to Nicodemus, "As Moses lifted up the serpent in the wilderness, even so must the Son of Man be lifted up: that whosoever believeth in him should not perish, but have eternal life;" *John* 3. 14, 15.

On another occasion Jesus said to Martha the sister of Lazarus, "I am the resurrection, and the life: he that believeth on me, though he were dead, yet shall he live;" *John* 11. 25. At another time, in talking with the Pharisees, he said, "Therefore doth my Father love me, because I lay down my life, that I might take it again. No man taketh it from me, but I lay it down of myself. I have power to lay it down, and to take it up again;" *John* 10. 17, 18.

We are informed that one resurrection has already taken place, and that it occurred at the resurrection of our Savior. "And the graves were opened; and many bodies of the Saints which slept arose, and came out of the graves after his resurrection, and went into the holy city, and appeared unto many;" *Matt.* 27. 52, 53.

The following indicates that the prophet Isaiah had a prophetic glimpse of this resurrection; "Thy dead *men* shall live, *together* with my dead body shall they arise. Awake and sing, ye that dwell in dust: for thy dew is as the dew of herbs, and the earth shall cast out the dead;" *Isa.* 26. 19.

It would appear that the Psalmist, David, looked forward for redemption from the dead, at the resurrection of Christ. "My flesh also shall rest in hope. For thou wilt not leave my soul in hell; neither wilt thou suffer thine Holy One to see corruption;" *Psalm* 16. 9, 10.

The Book of Mormon is much more definite and comprehensive on this subject than the Bible. "And there cometh a resurrection, even a first resurrection; yea, even a resurrection of those that have been, and who are, and who shall be, even until the resurrection of Christ: for so shall he be called. And now, the resurrection of all the prophets, and all those that have believed in their words, or all those that have kept the commandments of God, shall come forth in the first resurrection; therefore, they are the first resurrection * * * And these are those who have part in the first resurrection; and these are they that have died before Christ came in their ignorance, not having salvation declared unto them. And thus the Lord bringeth about the restoration of these; and they have a part in the first resurrection, or have eternal life, being redeemed by the Lord. And little children also have eternal life;" *Mos.* 15. 21-25.

This declaration of the prophet-king, Mosiah, was made about 100 B. C. Alma, who lived and prophesied a few years later, says, "And behold, again it hath been spoken, that there is a first resurrection; a resurrection of all those who have been, or who are, or who shall be, down to the resurrection of Christ from the dead;" *Alma* 40. 16.

From these passages quoted from the Book of Mormon, and their contexts, it is evident that the Nephite Saints looked forward to the resurrection of Christ from the dead, for their deliverance from the grave, with the same assurance that the Latter-day Saints anticipate their resurrection at his second coming.

By way of explanation, the prophet Alma adds, "The resurrection meaneth the re-uniting of the soul with the body of those from the days of Adam, down to the resurrection of Christ;" 40. 18, 19.

The Lamanite prophet, Samuel, speaking of the resurrection of Christ, says, "And many graves shall be opened, and shall yield up many of their dead; and many Saints shall appear unto many;" *Hel.* 14. 25. During Christ's ministry among the Nephites, his disciples testified that this prophecy was fulfilled; 3 *Nephi* 23. 10.

Bible.

Job 19. 25 for I know that my Redeemer liveth, and that he shall stand at the latter day upon the earth.

Matt. 17. 9 until the Son of Man be risen from the dead. *Mark* 9.9. 27. 64 and the people say he is risen from the dead.

28. 6 he is not here, for he is risen as he said. *Mark* 16. 6, 9, 14.

Luke 24. 34 the Lord is risen, indeed, and hath appeared to Simon.

John 2. 19-21 destroy this temple and in three days I will raise it up.

5. 25 the hour is coming, and now is, when the dead shall hear the voice of the Son of God.

26 the Father gave to the Son to have life in himself.

8. 28 when ye have lifted up the Son of Man, then shall ye know that I am he.

12. 32 if I be lifted up I will draw all men to me.

Acts 1. 22 must one be ordained to be a witness of his resurrection.

2. 31 David spake of the resurrection of Christ. 32.

26. 23 that he should be the first that should rise from the dead.

Rom. 8. 34 is risen again, who is even at the right hand of God.

14. 9 died and rose that he might be Lord of the dead and living.

Col 1. 18 who is the beginning, the first born from the dead.

Rev. 1. 18 I am he that liveth and was dead.

Book of Mormon.

2 *Nephi* 2. 8, 9 he layeth down his life and taketh it again, that he may bring to pass the resurrection of the dead. *Mos.* 13. 35.

Mos. 16. 9 he is a life that is endless, that there can be no more death. 10.

3 *Nephi* 6. 20 testifying of the death of Christ and of his resurrection, in all the land.

Doctrine & Covenants.

Sec. 18. 12 he hath risen from the dead, that he might bring all men to him.

Pearl of Great Price.

Page 21. the Saints arose at the resurrection of Christ. The spirits that were in prison came forth.

AT THE SECOND COMING OF CHRIST.

Those who have lived and died since the resurrection of Christ, in the hope of a resurrection from the dead, are looking forward to the time of his coming, in the latter days, for their redemption from the grave. "Even so them also which sleep in Jesus will God bring with him. For this we say unto you by the word of the Lord, that we which are alive and remain unto the coming of the Lord shall not prevent them which are asleep. For the Lord himself shall descend from heaven with a shout, with the voice of the archangel, and with the trump of God: and the dead in Christ shall rise first: Then we which are alive *and* remain shall be caught up together with them in the clouds, to meet the Lord in the air;" 1 *Thess.* 4. 14-17.

Christ said to his Nephite disciples who were to remain until his coming, "When I shall come in my glory, ye shall be changed in the twinkling of an eye from mortality to immortality;" 3 *Nephi* 28. 8.

The Lord said to Joseph Smith, the Seer, "Behold, I will come; and they shall see me in the clouds of heaven, clothed with power and great glory, with all the holy angels; and he that watches not for me shall be cut off; * * and the Saints that have slept shall come forth to meet me in the cloud;" *Doc. & Cov.*, 45. 44, 45.

We have seen by previous reference to the Book of Mormon, that the heathen nations, and those who knew no law, should be resurrected when Christ arose from the dead. The Lord revealed to Joseph, the Seer, that this should also take place when he comes in his glory. "And then shall the heathen nations be redeemed, and they that knew no law shall have part in the first resurrection;" *verse* 54.

The Lord gave Joseph, the Seer, a further description of this glorious event. "And immediately after shall the curtain of heaven be unfolded, as a scroll is unfolded after it is rolled up, and the face of the Lord shall be unveiled; and the Saints that are upon the earth, who are alive, shall be quickened, and be caught up to meet him. And they who have slept in their graves shall come forth; for their graves shall be opened, and they also shall be caught up to meet him in the midst of the pillar of heaven: They are Christ's, the first fruits: they who shall descend with him first, and they who are on the earth and in their graves, who are first caught up to meet him;" 88. 95-98.

Then comes the redemption of those who have received their part in that prison that is prepared for them; *verse* 99. "Then cometh the spirits of men who are to be judged, and are found under condemnation; and these are the rest of the dead, and they live not again until the thousand years are ended, neither again, until the end of the earth;" *verses* 100 and 101. These appear to be the only ones of the family of man whose bodies remain in their graves until the last resurrection.

Bible.

Dan. 12. 2 many of them that sleep in the dust of the earth shall awake.

Luke 14. 14 for thou shalt be recompensed at the resurrection of the just.

Rev. 11. 18 the time of the dead, that they should be judged.

20. 5, 6 blessed and holy is he that has part in the first resurrection.

Doctrine & Covenants.

Sec. 29. 13 the dead who have died in Christ shall come forth.

63. 18 they shall not have part in the first resurrection. 49, 51.

76. 50-70 concerning those who shall come forth in the resurrection of the just.

71-80 concerning those of the terrestrial world who shall rise in the first resurrection.

88. 100 then cometh the spirits of men who are still under condemnation.

RESURRECTION AT THE END OF THE WORLD.

John, the Revelator, has left us a short description of this resurrection, and of the judgment connected with it. "And I saw the dead, small and great, stand before God; and the books were opened: and another book was opened, which is *the book of life*: and the dead were judged out of those things which were written in the books, according to their works. And the sea gave up the dead which were in it; and death and hell delivered up the dead which were in them; and they were judged every man according to their works;" *Rev.* 20. 12, 13.

At that time, the earth, having filled the measure of its creation, in this order of things, will undergo a change that will fit it for the residence of exalted, celestial beings; "And I saw a new heaven and a new earth: for the first heaven and the first earth were passed away;" 21. 1.

The Book of Mormon, also gives some account of this final resurrection; "And they shall come forth, both small and great, and all shall stand before his bar, being redeemed and loosed from the eternal band of death;" *Mormon* 9. 13.

The Jaredite prophet, Ether, who lived on the American continent 600 years before the Savior was born, predicted this great change in the earth; "And there shall be a new heaven and a new earth; and they shall be like unto the old, save the old have passed away, and all things shall become new;" *Ether* 13. 9.

Joseph, the Seer of the present dispensation, has given us a more comprehensive view of this subject than has come down from other dispensations; "And the end shall come, and the heaven and the earth shall be consumed and pass away, and there shall be a new heaven and a new earth, for all old things shall pass away, and all things shall become new, even the heaven and the earth, and all the fulness thereof, both men and beasts, the fowls of the air, and the fishes of the sea; and not one hair, neither mote, shall be lost;" *Doc. & Cov.*, 29. 23-25.

Both the wicked and the righteous will be resurrected; *verses* 26, 27. That the final change in the earth will be equivalent to a resurrection is evident from the following: "Wherefore it shall be sanctified; yea, notwithstanding it shall die, it shall be quickened again, and shall abide the power by which it is quickened;" 88. 26.

Bible.

Matt. 25. 32 all nations to be gathered before the Son of Man.

Rev. 20. 15 those not found written in the book of life, were cast into the lake of fire.

8 the wicked had their part in the lake of fire.

22. 11 he that is unjust, let him be unjust still. 12.

15. without are dogs, sorcerers and whoremongers.

Book of Mormon.

3 *Nephi* 26. 4 when all people and nations shall stand before God.

Mormon 9. 2 when the earth shall be rolled together as a scroll, when ye shall be brought to stand before the Lamb of God.

13 when all, both small and great, shall be loosed from the bands of death.

Ether 4. 19 he that is faithful at the last day shall be lifted up.

5. 6 when we shall stand before God at the last day.

Doctrine & Covenants.

Sec. 76. 39 for all the rest shall be brought forth by the resurrection of the dead.

81-89 concerning those of the telestial world who will come forth in the last resurrection.

* * * * *

RESURRECTION OF THE BODY THAT IS LAID DOWN.

When Job said, "Though after my skin *worms* destroy this body, yet in my flesh shall I see God;" 19. 26; it is evident that he believed that though his body should be disorganized, yet, in his own flesh, and not in that of another, he should see God. As if to confirm his assertion, he further adds, "Whom I shall see for myself, and mine eyes shall behold, and not another;" *verse* 27.

A literal resurrection was manifested to Ezekiel in his vision of the resurrection of the house of Israel; 37. 1-14.

When Herod the tetrarch heard of the fame of Jesus, and said, "This is John the Baptist; he is risen from the dead;" *Matt.* 14. 1, 2; he probably, in common with the Jews, believed in a literal resurrection.

Jesus said to his disciples, "Behold my hands and my feet, that it is I myself: handle me, and see; for a spirit hath not flesh and bones, as ye see me have;" *Luke* 24. 39; *John* 20. 27; *Acts* 10. 41. "He that raised up Christ from the dead shall also quicken your mortal bodies;" *Rom.* 8. 11. That is, their bodies that died, and not some other bodies.

The apostle Paul gives us some light on this subject: "But some *man* will say, How are the dead raised? and with what body do they come? *Thou* fool, that which thou sowest is not quickened, except it die; * * thou sowest not that body that shall be. * * But God giveth it a body as it hath pleased him, and to every seed his own body. All flesh is not the same flesh: but *there is one kind of* flesh of men, another flesh of beasts, another of fishes, and another of birds;" 1 *Cor.* 15. 35-39.

The apostle evidently considers the old body the germ of a new body, which will be like the old, but a new growth, even as new grain is produced from that which is sown.

It is also evident that the apostle considered it impossible for one kind of flesh to mingle with another in the resurrection, as they widely differ, from different combinations of the elements, in their organization. As well might we expect the different grades of spiritual organizations, to intermingle, as the different kinds of flesh of which their material bodies are composed.

The following is from the *Times and Seasons, vol. 5, page* 617: "Mothers, you shall have your children, for they shall have eternal life: for their debt is paid, there is no damnation awaits them, for they are in the spirit. As the child dies, so shall it rise from the dead and be forever living in the learning of God; it shall be the child, the same as it was before it died out of your arms. Children dwell and exercise power in the same from as they laid them down."

In the *History of Joseph Smith*, under date of April 7, 1843, we find the following very pointed assertion on this subject: "There is no fundamental principle belonging to a human system that ever goes into another in this world or in the world to come: I care not what the theories of men are. We have the testimony that God will raise us up, and he has the power to do it. If any supposes that any part of our bodies, that is the fundamental parts thereof, ever goes into another body, he is mistaken."

See a Sermon by J. Smith, Jun., Times and Seasons, Vol, 5, page 612.

Also a Pamphlet published the same year in which the above Discourse was delivered.

Book of Mormon.

2 Nephi 9. 4 must waste away, but in our bodies we shall see God.

6 as death has passed on all men, there must be a power of resurrection.

8. 9 if the flesh should rise no more, our spirits must become subject to the devil.

12 the bodies and spirits of men will be restored, the one to the other.

Alma 11. 43-45 the spirit and the body shall be reunited in perfect form.

40. 23 not a hair of the head shall be lost.

Mormon 6. 21 day soon cometh that your mortal must put on immortality.

Miscellaneous Passages.

Matt. 22. 28 therefore in the resurrection whose wife shall she be, *Luke* 20. 33.

31, 32 God is not the God of the dead but of the living.

Mark 12. 25 rise from the dead, they neither marry nor are given in marriage.

Luke 20. 36 are the children of God, being the children of the resurrection.

John 5. 21 the Father raiseth up the dead; the Son quickeneth whom he will.

28 all that are in their graves shall hear his voice.

11. 24 I know he shall rise again in the resurrection at the last day. 25, 26.

Acts 4. 2 and preached through Jesus the resurrection from the dead. 10, 33.

24. 15 a resurrection of both the just and unjust.

26. 8 thought a thing incredible with you, that God should raise the dead.

Rom. 4. 17 even God who quickeneth the dead.

6. 5 we shall be also in the likeness of his resurrection.

1 *Cor.* 3. 22 life or death, things present or to come, all are yours.

15. 40-44 bodies are raised in different degrees of glory, according to their order.

45 first man, Adam, was made a living soul, the last a quickening spirit.

Col. 3. 1 ye then be risen with Christ, seek those things which are above.

2 *Tim.* 1. 10 who hath brought life and immortality to light through the Gospel.

Heb. 6. 2 of the resurrection of the dead, and of eternal judgment.

11. 35 not accepting deliverance, that they might obtain a better resurrection.

1 *Peter* 1. 3 hath begotten us again unto a lively hope of the resurrection.

Rev. 1. 5 first begotten of the dead, and king of the princes of the earth.

14. 13 blessed are the dead that die in the Lord. Their works follow them.

Book of Mormon.

Alma 11. 41 the wicked remain as though there had been no redemption made, except the loosing of the bands of death.

12. 7 been spoken concerning the resurrection of the dead, that all shall rise. 16, 18, 24.

Chap. 40. no resurrection until after the coming of Christ. A time appointed that all shall rise. Must needs be a space between death and the resurrection. State of the soul during that time.

3 *Nephi* 28. 36-40 concerning the change wrought in the disciples who were to tarry.

Doctrine & Covenants.

Sec. 42. 45 especially for those that have not hope of a glorious resurrection.

43. 18 say to the sleeping nations, ye Saints arise, ye sinners stay and sleep.

32 he that liveth in righteousness shall be changed in the twinkling of an eye.

88. 14 through the redemption that is made for you, is brought to pass the resurrection of the dead.

101. 31 not sleep but shall be changed in the twinkling of an eye.

130. 18 whatever knowledge we attain to in this life, will rise with us in the resurrection.

132. 13 all things not ordained of God, shall not remain after the resurrection.

133. 55 Moses, Elijah and John with Christ in his resurrection.

See a Pamphlet by B. Young.

Sermon by J. Smith, J. of D., Vol. 6, page 1.

Sermon by B. Young, J. of D., Vol. 15, page 139.

Sermon by Geo. Q. Cannon, J. of D., Vol. 17, page 134.

Article by P. P. Pratt, Mil. Star, Vol. 2, page 97.

Key to Theology, Chapter 15.

Sermon by J. Smith, Mil. Star, Vol. 3, page 59.

Article by C. W. Penrose, Mil. Star, Vol. 30, page 65.

History of J. Smith, April 16, 1843.

THE HOLY PRIESTHOOD.

"There are, in the church, two Priesthoods, namely, the Melchisedek and Aaronic, including the Levitical Priesthood. Why the first is called the Melchisedek Priesthood, is because Melchisedek was such a great High Priest. Before his day it was called *the Holy Priesthood, after the Order of the Son of God.* * * * All other authorities or offices in the church are appendages to this Priesthood;" *Doc. & Cov.* 107. 1-5.

In the ordinances of this Priesthood "The power of Godliness is manifest; and without the ordinances thereof, and the authority of the Priesthood, the power of Godliness is not manifest unto men in the flesh;" 84. 20, 21.

This Priesthood, or *Order of the Son of God.* is "Without father, without mother, without descent, having neither beginning of days, nor end of life;" *Heb.* 7. 3. Its authority and powers have ever existed, and there has never been wanting intelligences to manifest them through its ordinances.

"This greater Priesthood administereth the Gospel and holdeth the key of the mysteries of the kingdom even the key of the knowledge of God;" *Doc. & Cov.* 84. 19. That this passage refers to a personal knowledge of God is evident from *verse* 22, "For without this no man can see the face of God, even the Father, and live." This is a distinct line drawn between the two Priesthoods.

That man could not attain to the knowledge which would admit him to the presence of God, without the Melchisedek Priesthood, "Moses plainly taught to the children of Israel in the wilderness, and sought diligently to sanctify his people that they might behold the face of God; but they hardened their hearts and could not endure his presence, therefore the Lord in his wrath (for his anger was kindled against them) swore that they should not enter into his rest while in the wilderness, which rest is the fulness of his glory. Therefore he took Moses out of their midst, and the Holy Priesthood also;" *verses* 23-25.

The Latter-day Saints have this Priesthood, with its authority, ordinances and blessings. How they have obtained it, is a very important question. Peter was the chief of the apostles, in the Gospel dispensation, from which we understand that the Presidency of the Melchisedek Priesthood, in that dispensation, was vested in him, and that it was through him that its succession could be again restored to the earth. We find that in June, 1829, a revelation was given, making known the calling of a Council of Twelve Apostles; *Doc & Cov.* 18. 27.

It is evident that between the fifteenth of May, 1829, and the time when this revelation was given, in June following, Joseph Smith, Jun., O. Cowdery, and D.

Whitmer were called to the Melchisedek Priesthood. For the Lord, speaking to O. Cowdery and D. Whitmer, said, "I speak unto you, even as unto Paul mine apostle, for you are called even with the same calling with which he was called;" *verse* 9.

While Joseph Smith, Jun., is not mentioned here as an apostle, we have the information in a revelation given April, 1830, that he was the first apostle and elder of this church, "Which commandments were given to Joseph Smith, Jun., who was called of God, and ordained an APOSTLE of Jesus Christ, to be the FIRST ELDER of this church; and to Oliver Cowdery, who was also called of God, an apostle of Jesus Christ, to be the SECOND ELDER of this church, and ordained under his hand;" *Doc. & Cov*. 20. 2, 3.

We are informed in *sec*. 27. 12, under date of September, 1830, who ordained them; "And also with Peter, and James, and John, whom I have sent unto you, by whom I have ordained you and confirmed you to be apostles, and especial witnesses of my name, and bear the keys of your ministry, and of the same things which I revealed unto them."

The presidency of Peter, James and John are plainly asserted in the above passages; the thirteenth verse, with the context, informs us that they bestowed the presidency of this dispensation on Joseph Smith and others: "Unto whom I have committed the keys of my kingdom, and a dispensation of the Gospel for the last time; and for the fulness of times, in the which I will gather together in one all things, both which are in heaven, and which are on earth." We are informed that these primitive apostles also testified that they held this presidency of the Melchisedek Priesthood: "The voice of Peter, James and John in the wilderness between Harmony, Susquehanna County, and Colesville, Broome County, on the Susquehanna river, declaring themselves as possessing the keys of the kingdom, and of the dispensation of the fulness of times;" 128. 20.

In the thirty-seventh verse of *sec*. 18, the Lord designated O. Cowdery and D. Whitmer as two men he had chosen to search out the then future Twelve, whom the Lord declares, in the twenty-seventh verse were already called. This selection, of the Council of Twelve Apostles, was not made until February 14, 1835, over five years afterwards.

The most comprehensive evidence that Joseph Smith. Jun., received the authority and power of the Holy Priesthood, is that the works of John the Baptist, of Jesus and his apostles, are being again done on the earth by his administration. To receive the powers of this Priesthood, it is necessary that men should obey the laws and ordinances of the Gospel.

The Lord has personally appeared to some men, and covenanted with them as he did with Abraham; *Gen*. 12. 1-3. *chap*. 13. 14-17. The Lord also personally called and authorized his twelve Jewish apostles. So fully were they authorized to labor for him, and act in his name, that he said to them, "He that receiveth you receiveth me; and he that receiveth me receiveth him that sent me;" *Matt*. 10. 40.

More generally, it is from the prophets and apostles of Christ that men receive the Priesthood. Many received it under the hands of the apostles of the first Gospel dispensation. Those who have received it in this latter-day dispensation, have received it from Joseph Smith, Jun., and O. Cowdery, and, in doing so, have received it through a legitimate channel from God the Father, and his Son Jesus Christ. Those who have received this Priesthood have covenanted with God the Father, and he with them. This is evidently the view taken of the subject in the above passage quoted from Matthew.

The doctrine is more fully illustrated in *Doc. & Cov.*: "All they who receive this Priesthood receiveth me, saith the Lord; for he that receiveth my servants receiveth me; and he that receiveth me receiveth my Father; and he that receiveth my Father, receiveth my Father's kingdom; therefore all that my Father hath shall be given unto him; and this is according to the oath and covenant which belongeth to the Priesthood;" 84. 35-39.

Bible.

Gen. 14. 18, 20 Melchisedek, king of Salem, blessed Abraham. *Heb.* 7. 1, 2.

Psalm 110. 4 thou art a priest forever after the order of Melchisedek. *Heb.* 5. 6, 10. *Chap.* 6. 20.

Acts 14. 23 and when they had ordained them elders in every church.

20. 17 sent to Ephesus and called the elders of the church.

Titus 1. 5 and ordain elders in every city.

Heb. 2 17 a faithful High Priest, to make reconciliation for the sins of the people.

3. 1 the Apostle and High Priest of our profession.

4. 14 a great high priest, Jesus the Son of God.

15 not an high priest who cannot be touched with the feeling of our infirmities.

5. 1 every high priest taken from among men is ordained. 8. 3.

8. 1, 2 Jesus Christ an high priest, and minister of the sanctuary. 3, 5.

10. 19-21 boldness to enter into the holiest by the blood of Jesus.

Book of Mormon.

Mos. 29. 42 the office of high priest conferred on Alma by his father.

Alma 4. 4 Alma high priest over the church. 20. *Chap.* 5. 3, 49, 51.

6. 1 ordained priests and elders according to the holy order of God. 8.

13. 1, 2. ordained priests after the order of his Son, that the people might know how to look forward to the redemption of his Son.

3 *Nephi* 18. 5 one ordained to bless bread, and break it.

Doctrine & Covenants.

Sec. 18. 27-39 duty of the Twelve Apostles to preach the Gospel.

21. 1 J. Smith, Jun., to be called a seer, translator, prophet and apostle.

10, 11 J. Smith, Jun., and O. Cowdery ordain each other.

27. 5-11 personages who held important keys of the Priesthood, in former dispensations.

28. 2 none to receive revelations for the church but J. Smith, Jun.

Sec. 102. organization of the first High Council of the church.

106. 1 W. A. Cowdery appointed and ordained a presiding high priest.

107. 33 the Twelve are a traveling presiding High Council, to officiate in the name of the Lord under the direction of the Presidency of the church agreeable to the institution of heaven to build up the church, and regulate all the affairs of the same in all nations; first unto the Gentiles, and secondly unto the Jews.

Pearl of Great Price.

Page 26. Abraham became a high priest, holding the right belonging to the fathers.

28. Pharaoh was of that lineage which could not have the right of Priesthood.

Miscellaneous Passages.

John 15. 16 ye have not chosen me, but I have chosen you.

1 *Cor.* 5. 5 offenders to be delivered to Satan by the Priesthood.

2 *Cor.* 5. 20 now then we are embassadors for Christ.

Heb. 5. 4 no man taketh this honor, but he that is called of God.

7. 15-28 another priest who is made after the power of endless lives.

9. 11-28 Christ the great sacrifice, the Mediator of the New Testament.

10. 19-21 boldness to enter into the holiest, by the blood of

Jesus.

1 *Peter* 2. 5 an Holy Priesthood to offer up spiritual sacrifices. 25.

Rev. 1. 6 and hath made us kings and priests unto God. 5. 10. *Chap.* 20. 6.

7. 3 sealed the servants of God in their foreheads.

Book of Mormon.

2 *Nephi* 6. 2 called of God and ordained after his holy order.

Mos. 3. 23 I have spoken what the Lord hath commanded me.

23. 16, 17 none received authority to teach except from God.

Alma 7. 22 ye may walk after the holy order of God. *Chap* 8. 4.

13. 3 being called and prepared, from the foundation of the world.

5-20 calling, foreordination and eternal duration of the Priesthood.

17. 3 they taught with power and authority from God.

18 Ammon imparted the word of God to his brethren.

49. 30 word of God declared by those ordained after the holy order of God.

Hel. 8. 18 many before Abraham who were called by the order of God. *Ether* 12. 10.

Doctrine & Covenants.

Lecture on Faith, Sec. 2. genealogy of the Priesthood from Adam to Abraham.

Sec. 1. 17, 18 J. Smith, Jun., authorized to declare the Gospel, that the prophets might be fulfilled.

30 that they might have power to organize the true church.

2. 1, 2 the Priesthood to be revealed by Elijah.

19. 9 I speak unto you that are chosen in this thing.

29. 4 ye are chosen out of the world to declare my Gospel.

35. 18 the keys of those things that have been sealed, given to J. Smith, Jun.

42. 11 ordination to be done by one having authority.

65 unto you is given to know the mysteries of the kingdom. 69.

64. 5 the keys of the kingdom not to be taken from J. Smith,

Jun.

68. 2 this is an ensample to all who were ordained to this Priesthood.

72. 1 the kingdom and power given to the high priests of the church.

77. 11 those to be sealed out of the tribes of Israel are high priests. *Rev.* 7. 4-8.

78. 1 hearken to me you who are ordained to the High Priesthood.

84. 6-16 lineage of the Priesthood from the sons of Moses back to Adam.

25, 26 the Lord took Moses and the Holy Priesthood from the midst of Israel.

29 offices of elder and bishop necessary appendages to the Melchisedek Priesthood.

33, 34 those faithful to the obtaining of these two Priesthoods, become the sons of Moses and Aaron.

86. 8 saith the Lord to you with whom the Priesthood hath continued. 10, 11.

113. 8 the strength of Zion is the power of the Priesthood.

121. 21 neither they nor their posterity shall have a right to the Priesthood.

36-45 the necessity of exercising the powers of the Priesthood in meekness.

124. 33, 34 temples necessary for the purposes of the holy Priesthood.

91-95 H. Smith clothed with the same Priesthood and gifts as were once bestowed on O. Cowdery.

123 the offices and keys of the Priesthood, on J. Smith, Jun.

124 H. Smith holds the sealing blessings of the church.

135-145 instructions concerning various quorums.

127. 8 the Lord about to restore many things pertaining to the Priesthood.

128. 8 nature of this ordinance consists in the power of the Priesthood.

132. 44 then shall you have power by my Holy Priesthood to take her.

58 many things pertaining to the law of the Priesthood.

Pearl of Great Price.

Page 13. the same Priesthood, in the beginning and end of the world.

17. thou art after the order of him who was without beginning of days.

23. and the Lord ordained Noah after his order.

29. the seed of Abraham to bear this mission and Priesthood to all nations.

*   *   *   *   *

THE AARONIC PRIESTHOOD.

John the Baptist was the acknowledged forerunner of Christ, and, as such, he preached the preparatory Gospel of repentance, and baptism for the remission of sins. His father, Zacharias, was a priest of the course of Abia, and his mother was of the daughters of Aaron; *Luke* 1. 5.

Thus the Aaronic Priesthood was the heritage of John the Baptist. His ministry evidences that he was clothed with its authority. That the chain of evidence might be complete, regarding this fact, the Lord revealed to Joseph Smith, Jun., that he was ordained to the Aaronic Priesthood by an angel; *Doc. & Cov.* 84. 28. Being the first man ordained to it in the former Gospel dispensation, he holds the presidency of that Priesthood in all subsequent dispensations.

As a sequence, the man who should open up the last dispensation must receive it from him. We have the testimony of Joseph Smith, Jun., and Oliver Cowdery, that John the Baptist did ordain them to this Priesthood, using the following words, "Upon you my fellow servants, in the name of Messiah, I confer the Priesthood of Aaron, which holds the keys of the ministering of angels, and of the Gospel of repentance, and of baptism by immersion for the remission of sins; and this shall never be taken again from the earth, until the sons of Levi do offer again an offering unto the Lord in righteousness;" *Doc. & Cov., sec.* 13.

"The messenger who visited us on this occasion, and conferred this Priesthood upon us, said that his name was John, the same that is called John the Baptist in the New Testament, and that he acted under the direction of Peter, James and John, who held the keys of the Priesthood of Melchisedek, which Priesthood he said should in due time be conferred on us, and that I should be called the first Elder, and Oliver the second. It was on the fifteenth day of May, 1829, that we were ordained under the hand of the messenger and baptized;" *His. of J. Smith, Jun., May 15, 1829.*

Thus was the succession of the Lesser Priesthood again restored to the earth.

Bible.

Gen. 29. 34 Levi was the third son of Jacob and Leah.

50. 7 all the elders of his house, and of the land of Egypt.

Exo. 3. 16 go and gather the elders of Israel together.

6. 16 names of the sons of Levi.

17. 5 take with thee of the elders of Israel.

18. 1 Jethro, the priest of Midian.

19. 7 Moses called for the elders. 22.

28. 1 Aaron and his sons set apart to minister in the priest's office. *Chap.* 29. 44. *Chap.* 30. 30. *Chap.* 40. 13, 15.

Lev. 7. 35, 36 Aaron and his sons anointed priests by a statute throughout all their generations. 4. 15.

Chap. 8. Aaron and his sons anointed and clothed in their priestly garments.

Chap. 16. an enumeration of many of the duties of Aaron.

Num. 3. 1-10 Aaron and his sons appointed to the priest's office.

3. 12 the Levites taken in place of the first-born of Israel.

Chap. 4. an enumeration of some of the duties of the priests and Levites.

11. 25 the Lord gave his Spirit unto the seventy elders.

16. 10 seek ye the Priesthood also?

Chap. 18. the Lord's charge to Aaron and his sons.

35. 2-8 the cities of refuge the inheritance of the Levites.

Deut. 10. 8, 9 Levi had no inheritance with his brethren.

21. 5 the Priesthood of Levi had authority to try all manner of controversy.

31. 28 go gather all the elders of your tribes.

2 *Chron.* 29. enumerates several duties of the Priesthood.

31. 4-11 tithing to be received by the Aaronic Priesthood.

Psalm 99. 6 Moses and Aaron among his priests.

107. 32 praise him in the assembly of the elders.

132. 9 let thy priests be clothed with righteousness.

Isa. 61. 6 ye shall be named the priests of the Lord.

66. 21 I will take of them for priests and Levites, saith the Lord.

Ezek. 8. 1 I sat in mine house, and the elders of Israel before me.

45. 4 Levitical Priesthood the ministers of the sanctuary.

Joel 1. 14 gather the elders and all the inhabitants of the land.

Mal. 2. 4-6 God's covenant with Levi for his righteousness.

3. 3 he shall purify and purge the sons of Levi.

Phil. 1. 1 to the Saints, bishops and deacons.

1 *Tim.* 3. 1-13 qualifications and duties of bishops and deacons.

Doctrine & Covenants.

Sec. 20. 38-71 the duties of elders, priests, teachers, deacons and members of the church of Christ.

41. 9 E. Partridge ordained first bishop to the church.

42. 12-14 instructions to elders, priests and teachers.

68. 14, 15 bishops to be high priests, unless literal descendants of Aaron.

16, 17 the first born held the right of presidency in the Aaronic Priesthood.

22-24 a bishop can be tried only by the First Presidency of the church.

72. 18-20 N. K. Whitney ordained. Duties of bishops.

84. 18 the Lord confirmed a Priesthood on Aaron and his sons for ever.

107 the lesser Priesthood to go before and prepare the way.

Sec. 107. the higher and lesser Priesthoods, their organizations, the duties pertaining to their various offices, and the lineage of the Priesthood.

*   *   *   *   *

EVANGELISTS OR PATRIARCHS.

In the *History of Joseph Smith*, under date of June 27, 1839, will be found the following: "An Evangelist is a Patriarch, even the oldest man of the blood of Joseph or of the seed of Abraham. Whenever the Church of Christ is established in the earth, there should be a Patriarch for the benefit of the posterity of the Saints, as it was with Jacob in giving his patriarchal blessing unto his sons," etc.

As the singular number is here used, exclusively, doubtless the Prophet Joseph, in the above passage, speaks of then Patriarch of the whole church.

In the *History of Joseph Smith*, under date of September 14, 1840, we are informed that Joseph Smith, Sen., Patriarch of the Church of Jesus Christ of Latter-day Saints, died at Nauvoo. In a biographical sketch of him, of the same date, we are informed that he was ordained to this office, on the eighteenth of December, 1833.

The distinguishing feature between his calling and that of other patriarchs is, that he was patriarch of the whole church, while others were ordained patriarchs in the church. Of the latter was John Young, Sen., who was ordained a patriarch in the church by the Prophet Joseph Smith, in 1834; *His. of J. Smith, under date of Aug. 8, 1844.*

"It is the duty of the Twelve, in all large branches of the church, to ordain evangelical ministers, (or patriarchs), as they shall be designated unto them by revelation;" *Doc. & Cov.* 107. 39.

"The order of this (patriarchal) Priesthood was confirmed, to be handed down from father to son, and rightly belongs to the literal descendants of the chosen seed, to whom the promises were made. This order was instituted in the days of Adam, and came down by lineage;" *verses* 40-57.

From the last quotation it is evident that if a man holds the High Priesthood, by virtue of that Priesthood he is patriarch over his own posterity, and as such has a right to bestow upon them patriarchal blessings.

A little more than four months after the death of the Patriarch, Joseph Smith, Sen., in a revelation given to his son Joseph, occurs the following: "That my servant Hyrum may take the office of Priesthood and Patriarch, which was appointed unto him by his father, *by blessing and also by right*, that from henceforth he shall hold the keys of the patriarchal blessings upon the heads of all my people, that whoever he blesses shall be blessed, and whoever he curses shall be cursed; that whatsoever he shall bind on earth shall be bound in heaven; and whatsoever he shall loose on earth shall be loosed in heaven;" *Doc. & Cov.* 124. 91-93.

From this we learn, that Joseph Smith, Sen., inherited the Patriarchal Priesthood, by right from the fathers over the house of Israel in this dispensation. For this right to have descended to him, by lineage, he must of necessity be an Ephraimite, for Ephraim, by the right of appointment and ordination by his father Jacob, is the head of Israel. This fact is plainly stated in the Scriptures: "Now the sons of Reuben the firstborn of Israel, for he was the firstborn; but, forasmuch as he defiled his father's bed, his birthright was given unto the sons of Joseph the son of Israel: and the genealogy is not to be reckoned after the birthright;" 1 *Chron.* 5. 1.

Just before his death, in blessing Ephraim and Manasseh, Jacob adopted the sons of Joseph as his own. Said he, "Let my name be named on them, and the name of my fathers Abraham and Isaac;" *Gen.* 48. 16. For this reason, these two sons of Joseph, each, had a name as the head of tribes in Israel, "and he set Ephraim before Manasseh;" *Gen.* 48. 20.

The Lord further declared through his prophet Jeremiah, "I am a father to Israel, and Ephraim is my firstborn;" 31. 9.

By virtue of this adoption of Ephraim, as the head of the house of Israel, and Joseph Smith, Sen., being the oldest son of Ephraim, holding the Priesthood in this dispensation, he is Patriarch of the whole church, by right. This right should be perpetuated in his family, as the oldest branch of the tribe of Ephraim.

If, from any cause, there should be failure of a son to exercise this right, then the office would be filled from the next eldest branch of the family.

This has been the case in the short history of the church. When Joseph and Hyrum were martyred, the latter had no son old enough to fill the office of patriarch, and John, his eldest living brother, was ordained to the office vacated by his death.

After the death of father John Smith, the office reverted back to the family of Hyrum Smith, for his oldest son John had grown to manhood, and was ordained Patriarch of the whole church.

Bible.

Gen. 8. 21, 22 God covenanted with Noah, that he would not again destroy all flesh.

9. 1 God blessed Noah and his sons, and said, be fruitful and multiply.

24-27 Noah cursed Canaan, and blessed Shem and Japhet.

12. 1-3 the Lord promised Abraham that in his seed all the families of the earth should be blessed. 26. 4.

7 the land of Canaan promised to Abraham and his seed.

13. 15-17 I will make thy seed as the dust of the earth.

14. 18, 19 Melchisedek took bread and wine and blessed Abraham.

16. 10 the angel said to Hagar, I will multiply thy seed exceedingly.

17. 6 I will make nations of thee, and kings shall come out of thee.

7 God covenants to be a God to Abraham and his seed.

16 Abraham is promised that Sarah should be a mother of nations.

19 the Lord promised to establish his covenant with Isaac.

20 Ishmael to become a great nation.

22. 17 the seed of Abraham to possess the gate of their enemies.

24. 60 Rebecca to be the mother of thousands of millions.

25. 23 Rebecca is promised that she should be the mother of two nations.

27. 28, 29 Isaac's blessing on his son Jacob.

39, 40 Jacob's blessing on Esau.

28. 1-4 Isaac sends Jacob to Padan-aram and blesses him.

31. 55 Laban kissed and blessed his sons and daughters.

32. 12 Jacob claims the blessings of Abraham and Isaac.

24-29 the Lord wrestles with and blesses Jacob at Peniel.

35. 10-12 the Lord names Jacob Israel, and declares that a company of nations shall come of him.

46. 2-4 Jacob is promised that he should be made a great nation in Egypt, and be brought out again.

48. 15-20 Jacob's blessings on the sons of Joseph.

49 1 Jacob called his sons together to bless them.

22-24 Joseph a fruitful bough by a well, whose branches run over the wall; * * * from thence is the shepherd, the stone of Israel.

Book of Mormon.

1 *Nephi* 5. 5 I have attained a land of promise.

2 *Nephi* 1. 31, 32 the seed of Zoram to be blessed with the seed of Nephi.

3. 3 Lehi promised Joseph that his seed should not be utterly destroyed. 25.

5 a righteous branch to be raised up from the loins of Joseph.

24 a mighty man to be raised up among the seed of Joseph the son of Lehi.

4. 9 the blessing of the children of Laman left on the children of Lemuel.

Ether 1. 43 none greater than the nation I will make of thee.

2. 7, 15 but they shall come forth to a land of promise choice above all other lands.

Pearl of Great Price.

Page 26. Abraham sought for the blessings of the fathers, and obtained his right to the office of high priest, which came down to him through the fathers from Adam.

See sermon by P. P. Pratt, J. of D., Vol. 1. page 256.

See sermon by J. Smith, J. of D., Vol. 6, page 237.

See sermon by B. Young, J. of D., Vol. 9, page 86, at Mill Creek.

See sermon by B. Young, J. of D., Vol. 9, page 279.

See sermon by B. Young, Des. News, Vol. 11, page 68.

See sermon by B. Young, Des. Eve. News, June 2, 1877, at Logan.

See sermon by B. Young, Mil. Star, Vol. 15, page 493.

Article, Mil. Star, Vol. 4, page 1.

Article, Mil. Star, Vol. 15, page 486.

Article, J. A. Little, Mil. Star, Vol. 18, page 145.

Article, Geo. Taylor, Mil. Star, Vol. 19, page 796.

Article, C. W. Penrose, Mil. Star, Vol. 29, page 177.

O. Spencer's Letters to Rev. Wm. Crowel, No. 9.

A pamphlet, Items on Priesthood, by John Taylor.

A Pamphlet, Succession in the Priesthood, by John Taylor.

History of J. Smith, June 1829.

History of J. Smith, April 13, 1833.

History of J. Smith, May 2, 1835.

History of J. Smith, July 2, 1839.

History of J. Smith, April 28, 1842.

History of J. Smith, May 1, 1842.

CHRIST'S FIRST COMING.

The oldest Bible prophecy, of the coming of Christ, is in Jacob's blessing on Judah: "The sceptre shall not depart from Judah, nor a lawgiver from between his feet, until Shiloh come;" *Gen.* 49. 10.

When Christ was born, the sceptre had not wholly departed from Judah, for Herod the king, who reigned at the time of his birth, was virtually king of Judea. Christ was condemned to be crucified by Pontius Pilate, a Roman governor. The Shiloh had come and the sceptre had entirely departed, for Judah was under Gentile rule.

The records of three dispensations assert that Christ came to his own, and they did not receive him; *John* 1. 11. 3 *Nephi* 9. 16. *Doc. & Cov.* 6. 21. He came to his own covenant people, the house of Israel, and, though they still retained most of the forms of the Mosaic ritual, they had apostatized from the faith of their fathers, had drank deep into pagan philosophy, had become wicked and corrupt, and, when the Shiloh came, they new him not, rejected him, and were the means of his death.

The numerous prophecies of the first coming of Christ, in both the Jewish and Nephite records, had a veritable fulfilment in his birth, life, sufferings, death and resurrection, and furnish overwhelming testimony of the Divine inspiration of those records. That Jesus Christ was the same being who called Abraham from his native country, who led Israel out of the land of Egypt with mighty miracles and wonders, who made known to them his law amid the thunderings of Sinai, who delivered them from their enemies, who chastened them for their disobedience, who inspired their prophets, and whose glory filled Solomon's temple, is evident from all the inspired writings, and in none more so than in the Bible.

His lamentation over Jerusalem evidences that, in his humanity, he had not forgotten his former exalted position: "O Jerusalem, Jerusalem, thou that killest the prophets, and stonest them that are sent unto thee, how often *would I have gathered* thy children together, * * and ye would not;" *Matt.* 23. 37. It was this creator of the world, this mighty ruler, this controller of the destinies of the human family, who, in his last moments, cried out in the agony of his soul, "My God, my God, why hast thou forsaken me?" *Mark* 15. 34.

He was the great sacrifice for the world's redemption. It was a sacrifice worthy of Deity. How grandly, how nobly it was made! It was made in the meridian of time, and it changed the character of dispensations. Israel ceased to be a nation, and the Gentile rule was ushered in, to continue for many long centuries, in which God's chosen people were to suffer terrible persecutions. We must look at Jesus Christ in his true character of God and Savior, in order to form a proper conception of the great sacrifice which has opened, to the human family, the way to immortality.

Bible.

Deut. 18. 15-19 a prophet to be raised up in Israel like unto Moses.

Psalm 22. several prophecies concerning Christ.

69. 20, 21 in my thirst they gave me vinegar to drink.

118. 22, 23 the stone which the builders rejected. 26.

Isa. 7. 14 a virgin shall conceive and bear a son.

9. 2 the people that sat in darkness have seen a great light. 6, 7

42. 1 he shall bring forth judgment to the Gentiles. 3, 4.

53. 3 he is despised and rejected. 4, 5, 7, 8, 9, 11, 12.

Mic. 5. 2 of thee shall he come forth that is to be ruler in Israel.

Zech. 9. 9 just and lowly and sitting on an ass. 10.

11. 12 so they weighed for my price thirty pieces of silver.

Acts 3. 22, 23 he that will not hear that prophet shall be cut off.

Book of Mormon.

1 *Nephi* 10. 4, 5 six hundred years after Lehi left Jerusalem Messiah should come.

12. 4-4 a great destruction to take place before Christ should appear to the Nephites.

19. 10 the God of Abraham yieldeth himself up.

11, 12 at his death Christ shall manifest himself to the house of Israel.

2 *Nephi* 9. 5 he suffered himself to become subject to men in the flesh, that all men might be subject to him.

10. 3 expedient that Christ should come among the more wicked part of the world.

25. 26 we talk of Christ, rejoice in Christ, prophesy of Christ, preach of Christ.

26. 24 he layeth down his life that he may draw all men to him.

Mos. 3. 5-10 the Lord came among the children of men, was crucified and rose from the dead, that a righteous judgment might come on them. 13, 15.

4. 2 Jesus, the Creator of heaven and earth, who shall come

among men.

13. 33-35 Moses and all the prophets since the world began, prophesy of Christ.

15. 1-11 God, himself, shall come down among the children of men.

Alma 39. 18, 19 as necessary that the plan of salvation should be known before, as well as after the coming of Christ.

Hel. 14. 12 Jesus Christ, the Son of God, the Creator of heaven and earth.

3 *Nephi* 1. 9-14 Christ made known to Nephi, that, on the morrow he would come into the world.

20. 23 the prophet of whom Moses spake was Jesus Christ.

Ether 3. 16 Christ said to the brother of Jared, as I appear to thee in the spirit, so will I appear to my people in the flesh.

Doctrine & Covenants.

Sec. 20. 26, 27 not only those who believe after he comes, but all those from the beginning, as well as those who shall come after.

76. 39 who was in the bosom of the Father before the worlds were made.

CHRIST'S SECOND COMING.

Christ's first coming attracted comparatively little attention. He was born a helpless infant, under very humble circumstances. Through the ministration of an angel, a few shepherds rejoiced over his advent, and some wise men, who must have known of, and believed in prophecies concerning him, visited and made presents to him. They were warned to leave the country in a private manner, on account of the evil designs of Herod. He grew up in obscurity, performed his labors in the ministry, in affliction and persecution and apparently, to men, died the death of a malefactor.

At his second appearance he will come "With clouds; and every eye shall see him, and they also which pierced him; and all kindreds of the earth shall wail because of him;" *Rev.* 1, 7. "Behold the Lord cometh with ten thousand of his saints, to execute judgment upon all;" *Jude* 14, 15. "He shall have dominion from sea to sea, and from the river unto the ends of the earth;" *Psalm* 72. 8. "Yea, all kings shall fall down before him; all nations shall serve him;" *verse* 11. "The Son of Man shall come down in heaven, clothed in the brightness of his glory, to meet the kingdom of God which is set up on the earth;" *Doc. & Cov.* 65. 5.

When will Christ come in his glory and power? This question many millions of the human family have asked, and the query still remains unanswered. Jesus said to his disciples, "Be ye therefore ready also: for the Son of Man cometh at an hour when ye think not;" *Luke* 12. 40. "But the day of the Lord will come as a thief in the night;" 2 *Pet.* 3. 10. "But the hour and the day no man knoweth, neither the angels in heaven, nor shall they know until he comes;" *Doc. & Cov.* 49. 7.

The Lord has not told us that there shall be no period of time designated in which he will come, but that neither the day nor the hour shall be known. Had we a correct chronology we might, perhaps, approximate very closely to the year, for according to *Sec.* 77. 12, it will be in the beginning of the seventh thousand years. It will be a time of destruction for the wicked; "The Lord shall punish the host of the high ones *that are* on high, and the kings of the earth upon the earth;" *Isa.* 24. 21. "The Lord who shall come down upon the world with a curse to judgment; yea, upon all the nations that forget God, and upon all the ungodly among you;" *Doc. & Cov.* 133. 2.

There will be great commotion and changes in the elements; "The foundations of the earth do shake. The earth is utterly broken down, the earth is clean dissolved, the earth is moved exceedingly. The earth shall reel to and fro like a drunkard, and shall be removed like a cottage; and the transgressions thereof shall be heavy upon it; and it shall fall, and not rise again;" *Isa.* 24. 18-20.

The fulfilment of the prophecies and the signs of the times indicate that the coming of the Son of Man is nigh at hand. The Lord through Joseph, the Seer, also informs us that this is the case. "Not many days hence and the earth shall tremble and reel to and fro as a drunken man, and the sun shall hide his face, and shall refuse to give light, and the moon shall be bathed in blood, and the stars shall become exceeding angry, and shall cast themselves down as a fig that falleth from off a fig tree;" *Doc. & Cov.* 88. 87.

Israel requested Moses, when around Mount Horeb, that they might no more hear the voice of the Lord, nor see his glory, lest they should die. They had not faith to behold his presence, and the law of carnal commandments was given them. When they were about to enter into the land of their inheritance, Moses rehearsed these things to them, and repeated what the Lord had said to him concerning a future prophet: "I will raise them up a prophet from among their brethren, like unto thee, and will put my words in his mouth; and he shall speak unto them all that I shall command him. And it shall come to pass, that whosoever will not hearken unto my words which he shall speak in my name, I will require it of him;" *Deut.* 18. 18, 19. The Book of Mormon informs us that this prophet was Jesus Christ: "Behold, I am he of whom Moses spake, saying, A prophet shall the Lord your God raise up unto you of your brethren, like unto me;" 3 *Nephi* 20. 23.

Peter, when he reproved the Jews for killing the "Prince of life," repeated this prophecy, rendering the latter part of it a little plainer: "Every soul, which will not hear that Prophet shall be cut off from among the people;" *Acts* 3. 22, 23. It is evident from *verses* 19-21, that the time when those who would not hear that prophet should be cut off, would be at the time of the restitution of all things, when he whose right it is shall reign, and the kingdoms of this world shall become the kingdoms of our Lord and of his Christ.

The prophet Joseph says, "I was once praying very earnestly to know the time of the coming of the Son of Man, when I heard a voice repeat the following—'Joseph, my son, if thou livest until thou art eighty-five years old, thou shalt see the face of the Son of Man: therefore let this suffice, and trouble me no more on this matter.' I was left thus, without being able to decide whether this coming referred to the beginning of the millennium or to some previous appearing, or whether I should die and thus see his face. I believe the coming of the Son of Man will not be any sooner than that time;" *Doc. & Cov.* 130. 14-17.

"I have asked of the Lord concerning his coming; and while asking the Lord, he gave me a sign and said, 'In the days of Noah I set a bow in the heavens as a sign and token that in any year that the bow should be seen the Lord would not come; but there should be seed time and harvest during that year; but whenever you see the bow withdrawn, it shall be a token that there shall be famine, pestilence, and great distress among the nations, and that the coming of the Messiah is not far distant.' * * *

"I also prophesy, in the name of the Lord, that Christ WILL NOT COME IN FORTY YEARS; and if God ever spoke by my mouth, he will not come in that length of time. Brethren, when you go home, write this down, that it may be remembered. * * * Jesus Christ never did reveal to any man the precise time that he would come;" *His. of J. Smith, March* 10, 1844.

Bible.

Job 19. 25 he shall stand in the latter day upon the earth.

Psalm 50. 3-5 our God shall come and shall not keep silence.

Matt. 16. 27 the Son of man shall come in the glory of his Father. *Chap.* 25. 31-46

Acts 1. 11 this same Jesus which is taken up from you into heaven.

1 *Thess.* 3. 13 at the coming of our Lord Jesus Christ with all his Saints.

Heb. 9. 28 shall he appear the second time, without sin unto salvation.

1 *Peter* 4. 13 that when his glory shall be revealed ye may be glad.

1 *John* 2. 28 and not be ashamed before him at his coming.

3. 2 when he shall appear we shall be like him.

Book of Mormon.

3 *Nephi* 26. 3 Christ expounded all things from the beginning to the time he shall come in his glory.

28. 7 the three disciples to remain until Christ come in his glory.

29. 2 ye need not say that the Lord delays his coming.

Doctrine & Covenants.

Sec. 33. 17, 18 verily, I say unto you, that I come quickly.

34. 6 preparing the way of the Lord for his second coming.

35. 15 the poor and the meek shall be looking for my coming.

45. 38-44 shall be looking to the coming of the Son of Man.

74, 75 all nations shall be afraid because of the glory of the Lord.

See Sermon by O. Pratt, J. of D., Vol. 18, page 57.

See Sermon by O. Pratt, J. of D., Vol. 15, page 53.

See Sermon by W. Woodruff, J. of D., Vol. 15, page 275.

History of J. Smith, April 6, 1843.

THE SCATTERING OF ISRAEL.

During the administration of Moses, the Lord promised Israel, conditionally, many blessings and curses. The former if they were obedient to his commandments, the latter if they were rebellious. These promises were, in their nature, prophetic. Evidently, no man, unless inspired by the Holy Ghost, as was Moses, could have thought of blessings and curses so varied and comprehensive in their nature, much less have spoken and recorded them.

The subject of the scattering of Israel is historical, and needs to be well understood, in order to comprehend the great work of their gathering in the latter times. A moderate comprehension of the scattering of Israel requires much careful study of their history in the Old Testament, and as written by that eminent Jewish historian, Josephus, a general knowledge of history, and of the many prophecies yet to be fulfilled concerning them.

If a complete history of the house of Israel were written, it would be the history of histories, the key of the world's history for the past twenty centuries. The student is particularly recommended to study the last chapters of *Deuteronomy*, from the beginning of the twenty-seventh to the end of the book.

The scattering of the seed of Joseph, among all nations, was foreshadowed in the blessing of his father, Jacob: "Joseph is a fruitful bough, even a fruitful bough by a well, whose branches run over the wall;" *Gen.* 49. 22.

A terrible prophetic picture of the afflictions which the Lord would heap upon Israel, is drawn by Moses in the twenty-sixth chapter of *Leviticus*. If persistently disobedient, they were to be scattered among all nations and suffer great afflictions in the lands of their enemies.

The prophet Abijah said to the wife of Jeroboam, "The Lord shall smite Israel, as a reed is shaken in the water, and he shall root up Israel out of this good land, which he gave to their fathers, and shall scatter them beyond the river;" 1 *Kings* 14. 15. This prophecy was fulfilled when the ten tribes were carried into captivity by the king of Assyria 721, B. C.; 2 *Kings* 17. In the Apocrypha, the prophet Esdras states that these ten tribes went a year and a half journey into the north country; 2 *Esdras* 13. 39-45. That many remained is evident from *verses* 48 and 49 of the same chapter.

The great historian of Israel, Josephus, who wrote nearly 800 years after the captivity of the ten tribes, corroborates this view of the subject. Speaking of the return of the Jews under Esdras, he says: "Many of them took their effects with them, and came to Babylon, as very desirous of going down to Jerusalem, but then the entire body of the people of Israel remained in that country, wherefore there are but two tribes in Asia and Europe subject to the Romans, while the ten tribes are beyond the Euphrates till now, and are an immense multitude, and not to be estimated by numbers;" *Ant. B*. 11. *C*. 5. Over twenty-six centuries these scattered tribes of Israel, which Josephus declared, 1800 years ago, were an immense multitude in Asia, have continued to mix up with the nations of the earth.

The second great scattering of Israel was brought about by the Babylonish captivity. The Lord said through the prophet Jeremiah, "I will give all Judah into the hand of the king of Babylon;" 20. 4. There is an account of the fulfilment of this prophecy in 2 *Kings, chapters* 24 and 25. Jerusalem was desolated and only the poor left to till the land.

The Jews, like the ten tribes before them, were scattered among the nations of Asia. In *Ezra, Chap*. 2, we have an account of those who returned to build the waste places of Judah, but multitudes of them remained in their scattered condition, as is evident from the book of Esther. Some nine years after the completion of the term of their captivity, they were scattered from India to Ethiopia, through the 127 provinces of the Persian empire; 8. 9.

Jeremiah prophesied the entire desolation of Judah; "Judah shall be carried away captive all of it, it shall be wholly carried away captive;" 13. 19. It was nearly 600 years from the consummation of the Babylonish captivity to the fulfilment of this prophecy, by the final destruction of the Jews, as a nation, by the Romans, when a remnant of some 97,000 were sold into slavery in the cities of the Roman empire, and were scattered wherever the caprice of their masters led them.

During this period, from the Babylonish captivity to the destruction of Jerusalem, the Jews suffered much from their enemies, and many thousands were sold into slavery. A few references to Josephus will assist to comprehend this subject:

Ant. B. 11. *C*. 5. Miserable condition of the Jews as represented to the prophet Nehemiah.

B. 11. *C*. 6. Haman said to the king of Persia, "There is a certain wicked nation (the Jews), and it is dispersed over all the habitable earth that is under thy dominion."

B. 12. *C*. 1. The first Ptolemy took a great many captives in Judea and carried them into Egypt.

B. 12. *C*. 2. The second Ptolemy liberated 120,000 Jews who where in bondage in Egypt.

B. 12. *C*. 3. Antiochus set free all the Jews who had been carried captive.

B. 12. *C*. 4. The Samaritans were in a flourishing condition, and much distressed the Jews, cutting off parts of their land, and carrying off slaves.

B. 12. *C*. 5. The daily sacrifice was taken away, and 10,000 Jews carried captive.

B. 14. *C*. 7. The Jews were scattered over the habitable earth. Cassius, the Roman general, carried 30,000 Jews captive.

B. 14. *C*. 11. Four Jewish cities sold into slavery for taxes.

B. 15. *C*. 3. Not a few ten thousands of Jews that dwelt about Babylonia.

B. 16. *C*. 2. A great multitude of Jews dwelt in the cities of Ionia.

B. 16. *C*. 6. The cities of Asia and Lybia ill-treated the Jews. The northern part of Africa was then called Lybia.

These references to Josephus, and their contexts, well considered, will greatly assist the student in forming a proper idea of the scattered condition of the Jews about the commencement of the Christian era.

We have no knowledge of the location or condition of that part of the ten tribes who went into the north country.

B. C. 600, a colony left Jerusalem, under one Lehi, to people the western hemisphere. Eleven years after, it was followed by another under the direction of Mulek. Their descendants have scattered over the American continent from Cape Horn to the Arctic Sea.

This branch of the house of Israel may truly be said to be scattered over half the globe. The Book of Mormon, and the monumental ruins they have left on the land, give us all the information we have of them down to the year 1492, A. D., when Christopher Columbus discovered America.

Since that time, their history forms a part of the general history of the continent, which is a record of the fulfilment of many of the prophecies, in the Bible and Book of Mormon, concerning the scattering of Israel.

Bible.

Deut. 28. 37 thou shalt become a proverb and a by-word.

64 Israel to be scattered from one end of the earth even unto the other. *Chap*. 32. 26.

Psalm 106. 27 to overthrow their seed also among the nations.

Isa. 5. 13 my people have gone into captivity.

10. 3 what will ye do in the day of visitation?

32. 14 the multitude of the city shall be left.

42. 24 who gave Jacob for a spoil and Israel to the robbers.

64. 10 Zion is a wilderness, Jerusalem a desolation.

Jer. 5. 15-18 I will bring a nation upon you from afar. *Deut*. 28. 49-57.

6. 8-12 their houses, fields and wives shall be turned to others.

7. 15 and I will cast you out of my sight.

8. 3 which remain in all the places whither I have driven them.

9. 11 I will make the cities of Judah desolate. 16.

10. 22 to make the cities of Judah desolate. 25.

15. 4 I will cause them to be removed into all kingdoms of the earth.

34. 17 to be removed into all the kingdoms of the earth.

Ezek. 20. 23 I would disperse them through the countries. *Chap.* 22. 15. *Chap.* 34. 6. *Chap.* 36. 19.

Hos. 7. 8. Ephraim hath mixed himself among the people.

Joel 3. 2 the Lord will plead with all nations who have scattered his people.

Amos 7. 17 Israel shall surely go into captivity.

9. 9 I will sift the house of Israel among all nations.

Mic. 3. 12 Zion shall be ploughed as a field.

Zach. 7. 14 I scattered them with a whirlwind among all nations.

10. 9 I will sow them among the people.

Matt. 23. 38 your house is left unto you desolate. *Luke* 13. 35.

James 1. 1 to the twelve tribes which are scattered abroad.

Book of Mormon.

1 *Nephi* 10. 12-14 the house of Israel to be scattered over all the face of the earth. *Chap.* 14. 14. *Chap.* 22. 3.

13. 14 the seed of the brethren of Nephi to be scattered and smitten of the Gentiles.

39 other books to come forth to the convincing of the Jews who were scattered over the face of the whole earth.

19. 14 they shall wander in the flesh, and perish, and become a hiss and a by-word.

22. 4 the more part of all the tribes have been led away and are scattered, to and fro, on the isles of the sea.

5 the Jews to be scattered among all nations, because they hardened their hearts against the Holy One of Israel. 2 *Nephi* 10. 5, 6, 22.

7 the Lord shall raise up a mighty nation in this land, and by them shall our seed be scattered.

2 *Nephi* 6. 8 the Lord showed Jacob that those at Jerusalem had been slain and scattered. 11.

25. 14, 15 the final destruction of Jerusalem foretold.

16 the Jews to be scourged until they believe in the Messiah.

Hel. 15. 12 the Lamanites to be hunted, and smitten, and scattered.

3 *Nephi* 10. 7 the places of your dwellings shall become desolate, until the time of the fulfilling of the covenant to your fathers.

16. 4 the remnant of their seed who shall be scattered on the face of the earth.

20. 27 which blessings upon the Gentiles shall make them mighty, unto the scattering of my people. *Mormon* 5. 9, 20.

Mormon 5. 15 this people shall be scattered and become dark.

Ether 13. 11 they are they who were scattered and gathered from the four quarters of the earth, and from the north country.

GATHERING OF ISRAEL.

It will appear to the most casual reader, that the Gathering of Israel is predicated on its having been scattered. That part of the subject needs to be well studied, to obtain a proper conception of the great work of gathering in the latter times.

As general as was the scattering of Israel so must the gathering be. If the dispersion was over all the earth, and among all nations, so the gathering must be out of all nations, and from all parts of the earth.

When we reflect that it is thirty-two centuries since the enemies of Israel began to oppress them in the land of Canaan, that about one-third of the time they were a people in that land, they were, more or less, in bondage to their enemies; that seven hundred years before the coming of Christ the ten tribes were scattered throughout western Asia; that we have no record that any have as yet returned to the land of their inheritance; that nearly 600 years before Christ the Babylonish captivity took place, and that, according to the Book of Esther only a part of the Jews ever returned, but were scattered through the 127 provinces of the Persian empire; that Asia was the hive from which swarmed the nomadic tribes who overran Europe; that at the destruction of Jerusalem by the Romans the Jews were scattered over the known world; we may well ask the question, Does not Israel today constitute a large proportion of the human family? With this comprehensive view of the subject of the scattering, we the better understand such passages as the following, "I will gather the remnant of my flock out of all countries whither I have driven them;" *Jer*. 23. 3. "Wherefore, he will bring them again out of captivity, and they shall be gathered together to the lands of their inheritance; and they shall be brought out of obscurity, and out of darkness;" 1 *Nephi* 22. 12.

Our Savior had a clear conception of the magnitude of this gathering when he said, "He shall send his angels with a great sound of a trumpet, and they shall gather together his elect from the four winds, from one end of heaven to the other;" *Matt*. 24. 31.

"And Jerusalem shall be trodden down of the Gentiles, until the times of the Gentiles be fulfilled;" *Luke* 21. 24. That is until the Gentile rule shall wane before the growing power of Israel, when, "Israel shall be saved in the Lord with an everlasting salvation;" *Isa*. 45. 17. When "They shall take them captives, whose captives they were; and they shall rule over their oppressors;" 14. 2.

Then will the promise made to Abraham be fully realized by his children, "And thy seed shall possess the gate of his enemies;" *Gen*. 22. 17. Then will Abraham be the heir of the world, "Through the righteousness of faith;" *Rom* 4. 13.

It is evident from the Book of Mormon, that the Jews, as well as other portions of the house of Israel, will believe in Jesus Christ and accept the Gospel, before they are gathered to the land of their inheritance.

The first Nephi, about 600 years before the final dispersion of the Jews, recorded the following very comprehensive prophecy about their gathering: "And after they have been scattered, and the Lord God hath scourged them by other nations, for the space of many generations, yea, even down from generation to generation, until they shall be persuaded to believe in Christ, the Son of God, and the atonement, which is infinite for all mankind; and when that day shall come, that they shall believe in Christ, and worship the Father in his name, with pure hearts and clean hands, and look not forward any more for another Messiah, then, at that time. The day will come that it must needs be expedient that they should believe these things, and the Lord will set his hand again the second time to restore his people from their lost and fallen state. Wherefore, he will proceed to do a marvellous work and a wonder among the children of men;" 2 *Nephi* 25. 15, 16, 17.

Bible.

Deut. 30. 3 Lord will gather Israel from all nations whither he has scattered them.

Neh. 1. 9 the Lord will gather those that are scattered from the uttermost part of heaven.

Psalm 50. 5 gather my Saints together who have made a covenant with me by sacrifice.

Isa. 2. 2 in the last days the mountain of the Lord's house shall be established in the tops of the mountains.

5. 26, 27 he will lift up an ensign to the nations.

10. 20, 22 the remnant shall return, even the remnant of Jacob.

11. 11-16 set his hand the second time to recover the remnant.

18. 1-3 see ye when he lifteth up an ensign on the mountains.

27. 12, 13 ye shall be gathered one by one.

29. 22, 23 Jacob shall not now be ashamed.

35. 10 the ransomed of the Lord shall return and come to Zion.

40. 2 speak ye comfortably to Jerusalem. 9, 11.

43. 5, 6 I will bring thy seed from the east.

9 let all nations be gathered together, let the people be assembled.

49. 12 these shall come from far, from the north and from the west.

22 lift up my hand to the Gentiles, and set up my standard to the people.

23 kings shall be thy nursing fathers.

51. 3 the Lord will comfort Zion.

11 the redeemed of the Lord shall return.

52. 9-12 the Lord hath comforted his people, he hath redeemed Jerusalem.

54. 7 with great mercies will I gather thee.

56. 1-8 the stranger that keepeth his hand from doing evil, will the Lord gather with the outcasts of Israel.

60. 3 the Gentiles shall come to thy light.

4 thy sons shall come from far. 5, 6, 10, 16.

61. 4 they shall repair the desolations of many generations.

62. 7 till he make Jerusalem a praise in the earth.

66. 20 they shall bring your brethren out of all nations.

Jer. 3. 14 take one of a city and two of a family.

17 all nations shall be gathered to Jerusalem.

18 the house of Judah shall walk with the house of Israel.

16. 14-16 it shall no more be said, the Lord liveth that brought up the children of Israel out of Egypt. I will send for many fishers.

23. 8 Lord liveth which led the children of Israel out of the north country.

25. 34 the days of your dispersions are accomplished.

30. 3 I will bring again the captivity of my people. 10, 18.

31. 8-14 I will bring them from the north country and gather them from the coasts of the south. They shall come with weeping.

32. 37-44 I will give them one heart, I will make an everlasting covenant with them.

33. 9 Israel shall be an honor to me before all the nations of the earth. 14, 16.

50. 4, 5 they shall ask the way to Zion, with their faces thitherward.

Ezek. 11. 17 I will assemble you out of the countries.

20. 34-42 in my holy mountain shall the house of Israel serve me.

28. 25 when I shall be sanctified in Israel, in the sight of the heathen.

34. 11-31 Lord will deliver his sheep out of all places where they have been scattered in a cloudy and dark day.

37. 21-28 Israel shall be one nation, and one king shall reign over them.

Joel 2. 15, 16 blow ye the trumpet in Zion, gather the people.

Zeph. 3. 19, 20 I will make you a praise among all people.

Book of Mormon.

1 *Nephi* 10. 14 the house of Israel to be gathered in.

19. 15-17 then will he remember the isles of the sea.

2 *Nephi* 6. 11 when the Jews shall come to a knowledge of their Redeemer, they shall be gathered again to the lands of their inheritance.

9. 2 when they shall be restored to the true church, they shall be established in their lands of promise.

10. 7 when they believe that I am Christ, I have covenanted with their fathers that they shall be restored to the lands of their inheritance.

30. 7 8 the Jews shall begin to believe in Christ, and to gather.

Jacob 6. 2 he shall set his hand the second time to recover his people.

3 *Nephi* 5. 26 then shall they know their Redeemer, and be gathered from the four quarters of the earth.

20. 29-33 the Jews shall believe in Jesus Christ, then will the Father gather them together again.

21. 1 a sign that I will gather in my people from their long dispersion.

26-28 at that day shall the work of the Father commence among all the dispersed of my people.

Mormon 5. 14 the record of the Nephites to go to the Jews, that they may believe in Christ.

Doctrine & Covenants.

Sec. 29. 7, 8 be gathered in one place, and be prepared against the day of tribulation.

42. 36 be gathered in one when I shall come to my temple.

45. 17 day of redemption shall come, and the restoration of scattered Israel.

25 but shall remain until the time of the Gentiles be fulfilled.

43 and the remnant shall be gathered unto this place.

69 there shall be gathered unto it out of every nation.

57. 1, 2 the land of Missouri consecrated for the gathering of the Saints.

58. 56 let the work of the gathering not be in haste.

63. 36 I will that my Saints should be assembled upon the land of Zion.

101. 13 and they that have been scattered shall be gathered.

20-22 the Lord will appoint the places for the gathering of his Saints.

64-69 must gather my people, according to the parable of the wheat and tares.

105. 24 boast not of faith or mighty works, but carefully gather together.

110. 11 Moses delivered the keys of the gathering of Israel.

125. 2 let them gather to places I shall appoint, by my servant Joseph.

133. 7 go ye out from Babylon, gather ye out from the nations.

See Sermon by J. Smith, J. of D., Vol. 6, page 237.

See Sermon by B. Young, J. of D., Vol. 2, page 266.

See Sermon by B. Young, J. of D., Vol. 12, page 161.

See Sermon by B. Young, J. of D., Vol. 12, page 226.

See Sermon by J. Taylor, J. of D., Vol. 19, page 150.

See Sermon by O. Pratt, J. of D., Vol. 18, page 16.

See Sermon by G. Q. Cannon, J. of D., Vol. 15, page 202.

O. Spencer's Letters to Rev, Wm. Crowel, No. 10.

Article, Mil. Star, Vol. 4, pages 161 and 177.

Article, Mil. Star, Vol. 22, pages 321, 339, 362, 379.

Article, by J. J., Mil. Star, Vol. 33, pages 209, 294, 325, 449.

Article, by D. McK., Mil. Star, Vol. 38, page 296.

History of J. Smith, April 21, 1834.

BOOK OF MORMON—EVIDENCES OF ITS DIVINE AUTHENTICITY.

In order that the predictions of the ancient prophets might be fulfilled, it was necessary that a book should be brought forth to the world which should be a record of truth. This book must also come forth from the earth.

The prophet Enoch, according to Bible chronology, lived 969 years before the flood.

On a certain occasion, the Lord made known to him many things that should transpire a short period before his latter-day coming. He said, "Great tribulation shall be among the children of men, but my people will I preserve; and righteousness will I send down out of heaven; and truth will I send forth out of the earth, to bear testimony of mine Only Begotten; and righteousness and truth will I cause to sweep the earth as with a flood, to gather out mine own elect from the four quarters of the earth." *P. of G. P., page* 21.

The Book of Mormon, in every particular, fulfils this very ancient prediction of Enoch's. It is a record of truth; it was brought forth from the earth; it bears testimony of the Only Begotten Son of God; of his birth, death, resurrection, teachings, and ministrations among the Nephites. Righteousness has been sent down out of heaven by the restoration of the Priesthood, with all its authority, ordinances, and blessings, through which, alone, righteousness can be made manifest.

The latter-day gathering of Israel has been inaugurated, and righteousness, and truth are sweeping the earth as with a flood, and gathering the elect from the four quarters of the earth.

This wonderful prophecy of Enoch's was reiterated by prophets who lived many centuries after him. The Psalmist David, who lived until 1015 B. C., mentions this event in connection with the latter days: "Truth shall spring out of the earth; and righteousness shall look down from heaven;" *Psalms* 85. 11.

The prophet Isaiah, also, saw in prophetic vision these great events of the latter days, when he said: "Let the skies pour down righteousness; let the earth open and let them" — that is, the earth and the skies together — "bring forth salvation;" 45. 8.

According to the twenty-ninth chapter of *Isaiah*. there was to be a people who like Ariel, or Jerusalem, were to be brought down and they should speak out of the ground, their speech was to be low out of the dust.

The predictions in *verses* 1-6 of this chapter have been fulfilled in every particular, in the history of the Nephites and in the coming forth of their record, the

Book of Mormon.

For an account of the fulfilment of many of the predictions in this chapter, see *P. of G. P., pages* 49-54.

Ezekiel's prophecy, in *chapter* 37, *verses* 16-20, concerning the sticks of Judah and Joseph, is literally fulfilled in this generation. The most of the Latter-day Saints are of the tribe of Ephraim, the son of Joseph. There can be but one conclusion with regard to the Bible, and that is, that it is the stick of Judah referred to by Ezekiel.

The stick or record of Joseph, is fitly represented by the Book of Mormon, which is a record of the Nephites, who are descendants of Joseph who was sold into Egypt. They are both, to-day, in the hands of Ephraim.

A very good explanation of this subject is contained in 2 *Nephi, chapter* 3. Lehi was rehearsing to his son Joseph, some important promises which the Lord made to their father, Joseph, who was sold into Egypt. The special promise to which we refer is in the twelfth verse.

"Wherefore, the fruit of thy loins shall write; and the fruit of the loins of Judah shall write; and that which shall be written by the fruit of thy loins, and also that which shall be written by the fruit of the loins of Judah, shall grow together, unto the confounding of false doctrines, and laying down of contentions, and establishing peace among the fruit of thy loins, and bringing them to the knowledge of their fathers in the latter-days; and also to the knowledge of my covenants, saith the Lord."

The following from the writings of O. Pratt, is very appropriate to this subject.

"If the historical parts of the Book of Mormon be compared with what little is known from other sources, concerning the history of ancient America, there will be found much evidence to substantiate its truth; but there cannot be found one truth among all the gleanings of antiquity that clashes with the historical truths of the Book of Mormon.

"If the prophetical part of this wonderful book be compared with the prophetical declarations of the Bible, there will be found much evidence in the latter to establish the truth of the former. But though there are many predictions in the Book of Mormon, relating to the great events of the last days, which the Bible gives us no information about, yet there is nothing in the predictions of the Bible that contradicts in the least, the predictions of the Book of Mormon.

"If the doctrinal part of the Book of Mormon be compared with the doctrines of the Bible, there will be found the same perfect harmony which we find on the comparison of the prophetical parts of the two books. Although there are many points of the doctrine of Christ that are far more plain and definite in the Book of Mormon than in the Bible, and many things revealed in relation to doctrine that never could be fully learned from the Bible, yet there are not any items of doctrine in the two sacred books that contradict each other, or clash in the least.

"If the various books which enter into the collection, called the Book of Mormon, be carefully compared with each other, there will be found nothing contradictory in history, in prophecy, or in doctrine.

"If the miracles of the Book of Mormon be compared with the miracles of the Bible, there cannot be found in the former anything that would be more difficult to believe, than what we find in the latter.

"If we compare the historical, prophetical, and doctrinal parts of the Book of Mormon, with the great truths of science and nature, we find no contradictions—no absurdities—nothing unreasonable. The most perfect harmony, therefore, exists between the great truths revealed in the Book of Mormon, and all other known truths, whether religious, historical, or scientific." *Divine Authenticity of B. of M., page* 56.

A person educated in the doctrines and traditions of modern Christianity, could not have written the Book of Mormon, for many of its important doctrines do not agree with those of the Christian sects.

They do not believe in the ministry of angels, in miracles, in signs, in dreams and in visions. The book had its origin in those things, much of it is made up of an account of them.

Lehi, the most prominent patriarch of the aboriginal American race, was warned by an angel that Jerusalem would be destroyed; 1 *Nephi* 1. 11, 13. That he might not be destroyed with it, the Lord warned him in a dream to take his family and depart into the wilderness; 2. 2. In the nineteenth verse of this last chapter, the Lord spake to Nephi, and blessed him on account of his great faith.

Nephi, who wrote the first two books of the Book of Mormon, had wonderful visions and manifestations. An infidel, or deist, having no faith in manifestations from God, could not have written the book; equally impossible that it could have been written by a sectarian Christian.

Was the Book of Mormon written for a romance? It would spoil the interest of a work of fiction, for the writer to commence it with a sketch of the plan of his story. Yet the two books of Nephi, which commence the Book of Mormon, are a very plain, prophetic sketch of the then future history of the people of America.

Besides, what writer of fiction could expect to interest the literary world of the nineteenth century, with an account of the organization of a church, on the American continent, exactly after the pattern of the primitive church in Asia, with advocating baptism by immersion for the remission of sins, the gift of the Holy Ghost by the laying on of hands, and with an almost verbatim repetition of Christ's sermon on the Mount. Such a fiction would be wanting in all the elements of modern romance.

Skeptics, Christian divines, and writers of romance are not the men to stake their reputation on the enunciation of such principles as the following: "He that believeth and is baptized shall be saved, and he that believeth not and is not baptized shall be damned." "Harlotry is the most abominable of all sins in the sight of God, except it be the sin against the Holy Ghost." In fact, it is the teaching of such pure principles in the Book of Mormon that makes it so very unpopular with a large portion of mankind.

The Book of Mormon, as a whole, must be either true or false. If false, the Bible is equally so, for there is no antagonism between the two.

The former states that it and the Bible shall grow together for the confounding of false doctrine in the latter times. The writer of a book of errors would hardly have staked his reputation on the fact that his book was an evidence of the truth of the Bible, and *vice versa*. That one is a witness of the truth of the other is readily evident to any one who will honestly compare them.

Written by different authors, under very different circumstances, and on opposite sides of the globe, such perfect concordance would have been impossible, unless the authors had all been actuated by the same Spirit of divine inspiration.

The admission is general that the Bible was written and compiled on the Eastern hemisphere, and, more or less continuously through a period of some 1500 years. The fact is generally recognized that the Book of Mormon was written on the Western hemisphere, and by those who had nothing to do in getting up the Bible.

The chain of history it has recorded; the principles it teaches; its anomalous style as a literary production, and its truthfulness as a prophetic record, are all against its being a production of modern times.

As an ancient record, it contains many predictions of prophets and seers which have been realized, and many others which are now having a remarkable fulfilment. It has these facts in favor of its divine origin, as well as the Bible.

Not the least remarkable of its prophecies are those declaring how it should be written, and why. How it should be hid up in the earth for many generations, and how it should come forth in the latter times; every particular of which has been realized.

Bible.

Isa. 29. 10-12 the vision of all is become as the words of a book.

13, 14 and their fear towards me is taught by the precepts of men.

18 in that day shall the deaf hear the words of the book.

43. 19 I will do a new thing, now it shall spring forth.

Ezek. 37, 15-28 the sticks of Judah and Ephraim.

Hos. 8. 12 I have written to him the great things of my law.

Hab. 1. 5 I will work a work in your days which you will not believe.

2. 3 for the vision is yet for an appointed time, but at the end it shall speak.

Doctrine & Covenants.

Sec. 3. 16-20 the records of the Book of Mormon preserved, that the promises of the Lord might be fulfilled.

5. 11-15 the testimony of three witnesses to the Book of Mor-

mon.

10. 1-52 concerning that portion of the Book of Mormon which Martin Harris had permitted to pass into the hands of wicked men.

20. 8 gave him power from on high to translate the Book of Mormon.

9-16 the purposes of God in bringing forth the Book of Mormon.

24. 1 thou wast called and chosen to write the Book of Mormon.

27. 5 and with Moroni, whom I have sent to reveal the Book of Mormon.

33. 16 Book of Mormon and Holy Scriptures given for instruction.

42. 12 elders to teach the principles contained in the Bible and Book of Mormon.

124. 119 unless he be a believer in the Book of Mormon and the revelations.

135. 3 J. Smith, Jun., brought forth the Book of Mormon by the power of God.

6 Book of Mormon and Doctrine and Covenants cost the best blood of the nineteenth century.

Pearl of Great Price.

44-57 an account of the coming forth of the Book of Mormon in fulfilment of prophecy.

See Sermon by O. Pratt, J. of D., Vol. 15, page 178.

See Sermon by O. Pratt, J. of D., Vol. 16, page 209.

A series of six pamphlets, by O. Pratt, on the Divine Authenticity of the Book of Mormon.

Public Discussion between J. Taylor and Rev'ds C. W. Cleeve, James Robertson and Phillip Cater.

An account of several remarkable visions, by O. Pratt.

JOSEPH SMITH, JUN., AS A FULFILLER OF BIBLE PROPHECIES.

The mission of Joseph Smith, Jun., is the key of the dispensation of the fulness of times. If he was not sent of God, the pretentions of the Latter-day Saints to be the true Gospel church are without foundation, and their labors for the redemption of the world must prove a failure.

If, in his life's labors, and their results, the predictions of the ancient prophets are being fulfilled, it should be satisfactory evidence of the divinity of his mission. For unless a man have the spirit of the prophets, he can neither understand their predictions, nor the nature of the events that would fulfil them.

John, the Revelator, in his vision of the latter times, saw another "Angel fly in the midst of heaven, having the everlasting Gospel to preach unto them that dwell on the earth, and to every nation, and kindred, and tongue;" *Rev.* 14. 6.

On page 49, *P. of G. P.*, Joseph Smith, Jun., states that a glorious personage appeared to him and said that his name was Moroni. This angel told Mr. Smith one thing concerning his own future, that, since that time, 1823, has had a remarkable fulfilment. This was that his name "should be had for good or evil among all nations, kindreds and tongues."

He also informed him that there was a record on gold plates, deposited in the earth, which gave an account of the ancient inhabitants of this continent, and of the source from which they sprang.

A book containing such information, as the angel said, was engraven on the plates, was produced by Mr. Smith, with competent witnesses that it was a translation from certain plates of gold which were shown to them by an angel. (*See Book of Mormon for the historical account, and the third page for the testimony of the witnesses.*)

The angel Moroni further stated, that the record contained the fulness of the everlasting Gospel. Here we have all the conditions necessary for the fulfilment of the prophetic vision of St. John, regarding the restoration of the Gospel in the latter times.

The angel repeated to Mr. Smith the fifth verse of the last chapter of Malachi, thus: "Behold, I will reveal unto you the Priesthood, by the hand of Elijah the prophet, before the coming of the great and dreadful day of the Lord." In *Doc. & Cov.*, 110. 13, 14, we find an account of the fulfilment of this prophecy, by the appearance of Elijah to Mr. Smith. He stated that he had come in fulfilment of this prediction of Malachi's.

The angel Moroni quoted the sixth verse as follows: "And he shall plant in the hearts of the children, the promises made to the fathers, and the hearts of the children shall turn to their fathers; if it were not so, the whole earth would be utterly wasted at his coming." "Therefore," said the prophet Elijah to Joseph Smith, "The keys of this dispensation are committed into your hands."

After receiving authority from the prophet Elijah, Mr. Smith made it the business of his life to lay the foundation for accomplishing the great work committed to him. He has left the world most important instructions on this subject, in *Doc. & Cov. sec.* 128.

After referring to the prophecy of Malachi, he says "It is sufficient to know, in this case, that the earth will be smitten with a curse, unless there is a welding link of some kind or other, between the fathers and the children, upon some subject or other, and behold, what is that subject? It is baptism for the dead. For we without them cannot be made perfect; neither can they without us be made perfect. Neither can they nor we, be made perfect, without those who have died in the Gospel also;" *verse* 18. It is necessary that all things be connected and welded together in one glorious and complete union, from Adam down to the present time.

To accomplish this it is necessary that the hearts of the fathers and children be turned towards each other, by understanding the promises made in the Gospel. We have no information that the Christian world has had any knowledge of these glorious principles for the universal redemption of man, from the time of the primitive church until they were revealed through Joseph Smith, Jun.

In the bringing forth of the Book of Mormon, through the agency of an angel, we find the fulfilment of *Psalm* 85. 11, "Truth shall spring out of the earth; and righteousness shall look down from heaven;" and also of a parallel prophecy of Enoch's, *P. of G. P. page* 21. "Righteousness will I send down out of heaven; and truth will I send forth out of the earth." What for? "To bear testimony of mine Only Begotten."

Truth came forth out of the earth, in the Book of Mormon, through the ministration of the angel Moroni, and righteousness came down out of heaven through the blessings and ordinances of the holy Priesthood, as restored to the earth by John the Baptist, when he appeared to J. Smith, Jun., and O. Cowdery, and conferred upon them the Priesthood of Aaron, "Which holds the keys of the ministering of angels, and of the Gospel of repentance, and of baptism by immersion for the remission of sins;" *Doc. & Cov.* 13.

And by Peter, James and John, who were sent to Jos. Smith, Jun., and others, and who ordained them to be apostles and especial witnesses of Christ. 27. 12. Through these ordinances and blessings came the power to work righteousness on the earth.

Here we have all the conditions for the fulfilment of the prophecies of Enoch and David, through the agency of Mr. Smith. We find, by comparison, that there is no antagonism in doctrine between the Book of Mormon and Bible. Christ said, "This Gospel of the kingdom shall be preached in all the world for a witness unto all nations; and then shall the end come;" *Matt.* 24. 14.

Joseph Smith, Jun., reiterates this prediction of our Savior's nearly 1800 years after its utterance: "For verily the voice of the Lord is unto all men;" *Doc. & Cov.* 1. 2; "And the voice of warning shall be unto all people;" *verse* 4. "Wherefore the voice of the Lord is unto the ends of the earth;" *verse* 11.

Joseph Smith, Jun., spent the labors of his life, for the accomplishment of the great work of preaching the Gospel to all the world, and it has been the great object of the labors of the Latter-day Saints for more than fifty years. Considering the magnitude of the work it is being rapidly accomplished.

Jesus called the Gospel, the "Gospel of the kingdom." Of what kingdom did he speak, unless of a kingdom of God on the earth which this Gospel was to establish? Even the kingdom which Daniel speaks of: "And in the days of these kings shall the God of heaven set up a kingdom, which shall never be destroyed: * * and it shall stand forever;" *Dan.* 2. 44. "And there was given him (the Son of Man) dominion, and glory, and a kingdom, that all people, nations, and languages, should serve him;" 7. 14; "And the kingdom and dominion, and the greatness of the kingdom under the whole heaven, shall be given to the people of the Saints of the Most High;" *verse* 27. The kingdom which this Gospel was to build up, is the great object for which all Latter-day Saints labor.

One of the great burdens of the ancient prophets was the gathering of Israel in the latter days, that Jerusalem might be established, and Zion built up, that the law might go forth from Zion, "And the word of the Lord from Jerusalem;" *Isa.* 2. 3.

It is evident from the tenor of the inspired writings, that this kingdom is to consist of gathered Israel, and therefore the gathering of Israel must be a part of "This Gospel of the kingdom." Some one must receive authority to organize the means for accomplishing this great gathering of the latter days.

The former great gatherer and deliverer of Israel was Moses, and he, very naturally, was the one to restore that authority to the earth after the fulness of the Gentiles should come in.

Through the inspiration of the Holy Ghost, Jos. Smith, Jun., understood this, and had the faith to receive the administrations of Moses, and he has left the fact on record. "And Moses appeared before us, and committed unto us the keys of the gathering of Israel from the four parts of the earth, and the leading of the ten tribes from the land of the north;" *Doc. & Cov.* 110. 11.

He preached "This Gospel of the kingdom," the obedient received the Holy Ghost, and it moved them to gather together, and Israel, for over fifty years, has been gathering to form that kingdom in fulfilment of the predictions of the ancient prophets.

Joseph Smith, Jun., is the first man of whom we have any record, for some 1800 years, that has labored for the fulfilment of the predictions of the ancient prophets; *Doc. & Cov.* 1. 18.

The Lord said, through his prophet Micah, "In the last days it shall come to pass, that the mountain of the house of the Lord shall be established in the top of the mountains, and it shall be exalted above the hills; * * and many nations shall come, and say, Come, and let us go up to the mountain of the Lord, and to the house of the God of Jacob; and he will teach us of his ways, and we will walk in his paths: for the law shall go forth of Zion, and the word of the Lord from Jerusalem;" *Mic.* 4. 1, 2.

For many years there has been a "House of the Lord" in Salt Lake City, in the top of the mountains, and for more than thirty years, the people of many nations have been saying, "Come and let us go up to the mountain of the Lord."

That there will be a place called Zion from which "The law shall go forth," distinct from Jerusalem, is evident from Isaiah, "When the Lord of Hosts shall reign in Mount Zion, and in Jerusalem;" 24. 23.

How is it that Joseph Smith, Jun., first organized the means for the partial fulfilment of this prophecy, and left, at his death, the authority and instructions necessary to complete its fulfilment, by the building of a great city to be called Zion, in the state of Missouri, which in fulfilment of the prophecy, shall become the capital of this western hemisphere, if he did not obtain his knowledge of the whole matter through Divine inspiration?

The Jaredite prophet, Ether, some 2500 years ago, foretold "That a New Jerusalem should be built up upon this land (America), unto the seed of Joseph;" *Ether* 13. 4, 6.

There is a wonderful connection between this passage in the Book of Mormon, and the prophecies of Isaiah and Micah, the result of one spirit of inspiration, acting upon different men, in countries, long distances apart, and at different periods of time.

It is quite as unaccountable on any other grounds than that of inspiration, that Joseph Smith, Jun., after many centuries had elapsed since these predictions of the prophets, should declare to the world that the time was at hand for their fulfilment, and that he should have the confidence to indicate the identical spot, on this great land of North America, where this city of Zion is to be built. "This is the land of promise, and the place for the city of Zion. * * * Behold, the place which is now called Independence, is the center place, and a spot for the temple is lying westward;" *Doc. & Cov.* 57. 2, 3.

JOSEPH SMITH AS A FULFILLER OF BOOK OF MORMON PROPHECIES.

The first Nephi, 2400 years before the days of Joseph Smith, the Prophet, had a vision of the discovery and colonization of America by Europeans. He also saw the record of the Jews (the Bible) come forth from the Gentiles to the remnant of the seed of his brethren (the American Indians). He says, "After it had come forth unto them, I beheld other books, which came forth by the power of the Lamb, from the Gentiles unto them:" 1 *Nephi* 13. 38, 39.

Admitting that this prophecy has been partly fulfilled, by Christian denominations who have sent missionaries and the Bible among the Indians, it remained for Joseph Smith, Jun., to initiate the fulfilment of the second part of the prophecy, that other books, besides the Bible, should come forth to the children of Lehi, which should bear testimony of the truth of the Bible.

The Book of Mormon was the first of this series of books, which were to be carried forth among the American Indians, after the Bible. It has been followed by the book of Doctrine and Covenants, containing revelations and instructions concerning the latter-day work, and by inspired translations from the writings of Enoch, Abraham and Moses, which all bear record of the truth of the Jewish prophets, and of the teachings of Jesus and his apostles, as foretold they would do by the prophet Nephi.

This same prophet further says, "There is nothing which is secret, save it shall be revealed; * * * there is nothing which is sealed upon the earth, save it shall be loosed. Wherefore, all things which have been revealed unto the children of men, shall at that day be revealed;" 2 *Nephi* 30. 17, 18. The context of this passage shows that it speaks of the latter days.

The following is nearly a parallel passage in meaning: "And he shall send Jesus Christ which before was preached unto you: whom the heaven must receive until the times of restitution of *all things*, which God hath spoken by the mouth of all his holy prophets *since the world began;*" *Acts* 3. 20, 21.

That is, all the knowledge that has ever been revealed to man will be restored to the earth. All that was revealed to Adam and the ante-diluvian prophets; to Noah and the Jaredite prophets; to Abraham; to Moses and the Jewish prophets; to the Nephite prophets; to the primitive apostles of our Savior, and many others, to whom the Lord has shewn all things from the beginning of the world to the end thereof.

After many centuries had passed, in which man's wisdom had failed to comprehend the meaning of the phrase, "The restitution of all things," or the grand fulfilment of prophecy comprehended in a "Dispensation of the fulness of times"—a time in which all the knowledge and power of all times will be gathered into one—Jos. Smith, Jun., appears in the United States of America, and claims that the Lord has authorized him to open up this grand dispensation of a fulness, and that for this purpose he has bestowed upon him first, and then through him upon others, all the keys and powers of the Priesthood which had been held in former dispensations.

"For unto you, (the twelve) and those (the first presidency) who are appointed with you, to be your counselors and your leaders, is the power of this Priesthood given, for the last days and for the last time, in the which is the dispensation of the fulness of times, which power you hold in connection with all those who have received a dispensation at any time from the beginning of creation;" *Doc. & Cov.* 112. 30-32.

In *sec.* 110 we are informed that Jesus Christ, Elias, Moses, and Elijah the prophet, appeared to Jos. Smith, Jun., and others, and bestowed upon them the keys of the holy Priesthood, held in other dispensations, that they might be concentrated in this.

In these last two quotations, from *Doc. & Cov.*, we have an account of the bestowal of the necessary authority upon certain persons, for the opening up of the gathering dispensation of the latter times, that is perfectly consistent with the Book of Mormon and the Bible.

No man, unless endowed by Divine inspiration, could have conceived of such a sacramental feast as is represented in the following, to which will be gathered in the latter times, the great dignitaries of all dispensations, with Jesus Christ at their head, together holding all the keys, authority and powers of the holy Priesthood, pertaining to the redemption of man and of the earth.

"For the hour cometh that I will drink of the fruit of the vine with you on the earth, and with Moroni, whom I have sent unto you to reveal the Book of Mormon, containing the fulness of my everlasting Gospel, * * * and also with Elias, to whom I have committed the keys of bringing to pass the restoration of all things," and with John the Baptist, "whom I have sent unto you, my servants, Jos. Smith, Jun., and Oliver Cowdery, to ordain you unto this first Priesthood which you have received. * *

"And also Elijah, unto whom I have committed the keys of the power of turning the hearts of the fathers to the children, * * * and also with Joseph and Jacob, and Isaac, and Abraham, your fathers, * * and also with Michael, or Adam, the father of all, the prince of all, the ancient of days.

"And also with Peter, and James, and John, * * * by whom I have ordained you and confirmed you to be Apostles, and especial witnesses of my name, and bear the keys of your ministry, and of the same things which I have revealed unto them: unto whom I have committed the keys of my kingdom, and a dispensation of the Gospel for the last times; and for the fulness of times, in the which I will gather together in one all things, both which are in heaven, and which are on earth;" 27.

5-13.

On a certain occasion, when the Nephite disciples of our Savior were engaged "in mighty prayer and fasting," he appeared in their midst and asked them, "What will ye that I shall give unto you? And they said unto him, Lord, we will that thou wouldst tell us the name whereby we shall call this church; for there are disputations among the people concerning this matter.

"And the Lord said unto them, Verily, verily I say unto you, why is it that the people should murmur and dispute because of this thing? Have they not read the scriptures, which say ye must take upon you the name of Christ, which is my name? For by this name shall ye be called at the last day. * * * Therefore whatsoever ye shall do, ye shall do it in my name; therefore ye shall call the church in my name;" 3 *Nephi* 27. 2-7.

In the above Jesus plainly told his disciples that his name was Christ, and that his church should be called Christ's Church, not Christian, Catholic, Campbellite or Episcopalian.

When Jos. Smith, Jun., organized this church, on the 6th of April, 1830, it was organized as the Church of Jesus Christ, in obedience to the instructions of Jesus Christ, some 1800 years before.

The prophet Nephi, speaking of the gathering of Israel, says, that the Lord "Will bring them again out of captivity, and they shall be gathered together to the lands of their inheritance; and they shall be brought out of obscurity, and out of darkness;" 1 *Nephi* 22. 12.

The Book of Mormon, brought forth through the agency of Jos. Smith, Jun., reveals to the world the fact that the millions of aboriginal Americans scattered over the American continent, from Cape Horn to the Arctic Ocean, are of the house of Israel.

The keys of the Patriarchal Priesthood enable those on whom they are bestowed, to know, by revelation, the lineage of the Latter-day Saints, and tens of thousands of Ephraim, and thousands of Manasseh, are being gathered, who were not known before the days of Jos. Smith, Jun., as portions of the house of Israel. Thus the great work of bringing the tribes of Israel, out of obscurity and darkness, and of developing their existence to themselves, and to the world, has been inaugurated by Jos. Smith, Jun. The work must continue until they are gathered from all parts of the earth, in fulfilment of the words of the prophets, and of the promises made to their fathers.

The following promise was made to Joseph who was sold into Egypt, "The fruit of thy loins shall write; and the fruit of the loins of Judah shall write;" and that which shall be written, "Shall grow together, unto the confounding of false doctrines, and laying down of contentions, and establishing peace among the fruit of thy loins, and bringing them to the knowledge of their fathers in the latter-days; and also the knowledge of my covenants, saith the Lord;" 2 *Nephi* 3. 12. Jos. Smith, Jun., has brought forth the Book of Mormon, the writing of the fruit of the loins of Joseph through Ephraim and Manasseh, and has placed it, side by side, with the writing of the fruit of the loins of Judah—the Bible—the one establishing the truth of the other, and thus has literally fulfilled this prophecy.

The Lord further said to Joseph who was sold into Egypt, "I will raise up unto the fruit of thy loins; and I will make for him a spokesman. And I, behold, I will give unto him, that he shall write the writing of the fruit of thy loins (the Nephites), unto the fruit of thy loins (the American Indians); and the spokesman of thy loins shall declare it;" *verse* 18.

In *Doc. & Cov.*, we are informed of the fulfilment of this prophecy. The Lord said to Joseph the prophet and S. Rigdon, "It is expedient in me that you, my servant Sidney, should be a spokesman unto this people; yea, verily, I will ordain you unto this calling, even to be a spokesman unto my servant Joseph;" 100. 9.

"And it shall be as if the fruit of thy loins had cried unto them from the dust;" 2 *Nephi* 3. 19. Jos. Smith, Jun., was of the lineage of Joseph who was sold into Egypt, to whom these promises were made. The Nephites were also his descendants, and they wrote and hid up the plates of the Book of Mormon, with the assurance that, in after years, the writing should be brought forth to their descendants and others of the house of Israel; *Mormon* 8. 14-16. The record was engraved on plates in a language known only to the Nephites; *Mormon* 9. 34.

Of necessity there were some means provided for interpreting and re-writing the record in a modern language, before it could benefit those for whom it was designed. With the plates of the Book of Mormon was found a Urim and Thummim, by means of which, through the power of God, Jos. Smith, Jun., was enabled to translate the Nephite record for the benefit of the descendants of Lehi, and any others of the human family who would receive it; *Doc. & Cov.* 10. 1. "And it shall be as if the fruit of thy loins had cried to them from the dust," was fulfilled in taking the writing out of the earth, where it had been deposited for 1400 years.

In *Mormon* 8. 13, 14, we are informed that the record was hid up in the earth by Moroni, the son of Mormon, and it remained under his care until he delivered it to Joseph Smith, Jun., *P. of C. P. page* 49. The Lord said, "And it shall come to pass that my people which are of the house of Israel, shall be gathered home unto the lands of their possessions; and my word also shall be gathered in one;" 2 *Nephi* 29. 14.

In fulfilment of this prophecy, Jos. Smith, Jun., during the short period of his ministry, not only inaugurated the great work of gathering Israel, but also of gathering together sacred writings, which at this time consist of the unsealed portion of the record of Mormon; the Book of Doctrine and Covenants, and of important portions of the writings of Enoch, of Abraham, and of Moses. He also declared that more sacred writings would come forth, as fast as the people were prepared to receive them.

Moroni, who completed and hid up the record of Mormon in the earth, says, of the plates, "Unto three shall they be shown by the power of God; wherefore they shall know of a surety that these things are true. And in the mouth of three witnesses shall these things be established;" *Ether* 5. 3, 4. We find that the Lord repeated this prediction to Jos. Smith, Jun.; *Doc. & Cov.* 5. 11-15. On the second page, after the title page of the Book of Mormon, we find the testimony of three men, Oliver Cowdery, David Whitmer and Martin Harris, that an angel appeared to them and showed them the plates, "Which is a record of the people of Nephi, and also of the Lamanites their brethren, and also of the people of Jared, who came from the tower" of Babel.

It was made manifest to them that they had been translated by the gift and power of God, and the voice of the Lord commanded that they should bear record of the things that had been shown them.

JOSEPH SMITH, JUN., AS A PROPHET, AND FULFILLER OF HIS OWN PROPHECIES.

"And the voice of warning shall be unto all people, by the mouths of my disciples, whom I have chosen in these last days;" *Doc. & Cov.* 1. 4. This was one of the first prophetic commandments given to the Latter-day Saints, through Jos. Smith, Jun.

Many hundreds of the Elders of the Church have traveled to and fro in the earth, regardless of exposure to the elements, of fatigue, or of pecuniary considerations, warning the people to repent of their sins, for the day of the Lord was near.

There are now but few nations who are prepared to receive the word, that have not had the Gospel of this dispensation preached to them. With a constantly increasing number of Elders, the labor will continue until the Gospel is preached "as a witness to all nations." The quorums of the Priesthood were organized and set in order, by Jos. Smith, Jun., with this great work especially in view.

In *sec*. 3. 16-20, it is predicted that a knowledge of the Savior, and also of their fathers, should come to the descendants of Lehi, the American Indians. Through the ministry and teachings of Jos. Smith, Jun., thousands of the Lamanites have come to a knowledge of their fathers, and many "Believe the Gospel and rely upon the merits of Jesus Christ," of which many of the Latter-day Saints are witnesses.

"Behold, a marvellous work is about to come forth among the children of men;" 4. 1. This declaration was made in February, 1829; before the organization of the Church. The organization of the Church, the teachings, unity, energy, and progress of the Latter-day Saints, have ever been a marvel to the world, and are daily becoming more so, in fulfilment of this often repeated prediction in the book of *Doc. & Cov.*

In March, 1829, the Lord said to Jos. Smith, Jun., "For hereafter you shall be ordained and go forth and deliver my words unto the children of men;" 5. 6. On the 15th of May following, John the Baptist laid his hands upon the heads of Jos. Smith, Jun., and O. Cowdery, and ordained them to "The Priesthood of Aaron, which holds the keys of the ministering of angels, and of the Gospel of repentance, and of baptism by immersion for the remission of sins;" *sec*. 13.

It is evident that, previous to this time, Jos. Smith, Jun., had foreseen by the spirit of prophecy, that it was necessary he should be called of God as was Aaron, and for this reason was prepared to receive a proper ordination by the hands of an authorized messenger from God. We have no record of such previous ordination to the Priesthood, since the days of the primitive apostles.

The Lord said to Joseph Smith, Jun., "There are many that lie in wait to destroy thee from off the face of the earth;" 5. 33. The whole life of Jos. Smith, Jun., and his death, evidence the truthfulness of this prophecy. Some forty times was he brought before the courts by his enemies, and they failed to substantiate the charges preferred against him, and, on the 27th of June, 1844, he, and his brother Hyrum, were assassinated in Carthage jail, by a mob, when under the pledged protection of the Executive of the state of Illinois.

"And the poor and the meek shall have the Gospel preached unto them, and they shall be looking forth for the time of my coming;" 35. 15. Not only has the Gospel been preached to the poor and the meek, but they are the ones who have received it, and are looking and preparing for the coming of our Lord, "For it is nigh at hand."

"Inasmuch as my people shall assemble themselves to the (state of) Ohio, I have kept in store a blessing such as is not known among the children of men, and it shall be poured forth upon their heads;" 39. 15. This prophetic promise was given through Joseph Smith, Jun., in Fayette, New York, January 5, 1831. In 1836, a temple was completed in the town of Kirtland, Ohio. It was the first temple of modern times, dedicated to that Priesthood of which Jesus Christ is the acknowledged head.

In this temple the Elders of the Church received endowments and great blessings, of which the world generally were entirely ignorant. The Lord said through J. Smith, Jun., "The sound must go forth from this place into all the world, and unto the uttermost parts of the earth—the Gospel must be preached unto every creature, with signs following them that believe;" 58. 64.

This prophecy was literally fulfilled by the Elders scattering from Kirtland, after receiving their endowments, to all parts of the United States and the Canadas, and by the first European Mission being established soon after.

At this time thousands of Latter-day Saints can testify that the Gospel has been preached in a large portion of the world, and that the signs of faith, gift of tongues, healing, etc., have followed the believer.

The following remarkable prophecy was delivered Dec. 25th, 1832. "Thus saith the Lord, concerning the wars that will shortly come to pass, beginning at the rebellion of South Carolina, which will eventually terminate in the death and misery of many souls. The days will come that war will be poured out upon all nations, beginning at that place; * * and it shall come to pass, after many days, slaves shall rise up against their masters, who shall be marshalled and disciplined for war;"

In 1861, twenty-nine years after this prophecy was recorded, the war between the North and South commenced in South Carolina. It continued for several years and was very destructive. In the latter part of it many thousands of slaves deserted their masters and were marshalled and disciplined for war, and formed a part of the armies of the Northern States.

During the contest the Southern States called upon the nation of Great Britain for assistance. "And it shall come to pass also, that the remnants who are left of the land (the Indians) will marshal themselves, and shall become exceeding angry, and shall vex the Gentiles with a sore vexation;" *Sec.* 87.

Never before, since the United States have been a nation, has the Indian question been so complicated and vexatious as now. That a part of this prophecy has been so literally fulfilled would seem a guarantee that the whole will be realized.

The delivery of the keys of the holy Priesthood unto the Prophet Joseph Smith, by Elias, by Moses, by Elijah, their ordination to the Priesthood of Aaron by John the Baptist, to the Melchisedek Priesthood by Peter, James and John, the building of temples, the ordinances and endowments for the living and for the dead, received in them; the preaching of the Gospel to all the world, the gathering of Israel; and all the varied labors of the Latter-day Saints in order to establish a veritable kingdom of God on the earth, and to prepare for the coming of our Savior in his glory, are the direct results of the personal labors and inspired teachings of Joseph Smith, Jun.

He stands forth, pre-eminently, as the Divinely inspired prophetic leader of the "Dispensation of the fulness of times;" as God's agent for the "Restitution of all things spoken by all holy prophets since the world began." As the great fulfiller of numerous prophecies of both the ancient Jewish and Nephite prophets, as recorded in the Bible and Book of Mormon; as the great prophet of the nineteenth century, and the fulfiller of his own prophecies, showing that he was Divinely inspired to both prophesy and to fulfil.

See a pamphlet by O. Pratt, entitled, "Divine Authority, or, was Joseph Smith sent of God."

A pamphlet entitled, "A Public Discussion, between J. Taylor and C. W. Cleeve, J. Robertson and P. Cater."

"Joseph Smith's Prophetic Calling," Mil. Star, Vol. 42, pages 164, 187, 195, 227.

Epistle of D. W. Patten, History of J. Smith, July 31, 1838.

O. Spencer's Letters to Rev. Wm. Crowel, No. 1.

MARRIAGE—A DIVINE INSTITUTION, AND DESIGNED TO BE ETERNAL.

Marriage is ordained of God unto man, that the earth might answer the end of its creation, and "Be filled with the measure of man, according to his creation before the world was made;" *Doc. & Cov.* 49. 15-17.

Outside of marriage the salvation of man would be incomplete: "Neither is the man without the woman, neither the woman without the man, in the Lord;" 1 *Cor.* 11. 11. All the works of God receive the impress of eternity: "I know that, whatsoever God doeth, it shall be forever: nothing can be put to it, nor anything taken from it;" *Eccl.* 3. 14.

When the Creator joined Adam and Eve together, as the progenitors of the human race, we do not learn that he set any limit to the continuance of their marriage relations. We have no reason to doubt that the gift of Eve, to Adam, was designed to be as eternal as himself.

Man, in his fulness, is a twofold organization—male and female. Either being incapable of filling the measure of their creation alone, it requires the union of the two to complete man in the image of God, for in *Gen.* 1. 27, it expressly says, that he was created male and female in the image of God. Therefore, without the proper union of the sexes, man would be less than what God created him.

There is a comprehensive significance in, "The Lord God said, it is not good that the man should be alone;" *Gen.* 2. 18. It speaks of no particular period of man's life, and has no limit in its application. The entire narrative of the union of Adam and Eve, in the second chapter of Genesis, intimates the designed inseparable relationship between man and wife, in marriage as ordained of God.

Adam said, "This is now bone of my bones, and flesh of my flesh;" 2. 23. He evidently well understood this eternal relationship with Eve, when he answered the Lord's question, "Hast thou eaten of the tree, whereof I commanded thee that thou shouldest not eat?" and he replied, "The woman whom thou gavest to be with me, she gave me of the tree, and I did eat;" *Gen.* 3. 11, 12.

Here Adam tells the Lord, by way of apology, that in order to keep his commandment, that he and the woman should remain together, he was compelled to partake of the forbidden fruit after her. This is evidently the view the apostle Paul took of the subject: "Adam was not deceived, but the woman being deceived was in the transgression;" 1 *Tim.* 2. 14.

This inseparable connection between man and wife, in marriage as ordained of God, is further exemplified by the same apostle in *Eph.* 5. 22-33: "The husband is the head of the wife, even as Christ is the head of the church." That is, as Christ is eternally the head of the church, so is the husband eternally the head of the wife. "Husbands, love your wives, even as Christ also loved the church. * * so ought men to love their wives as their own bodies. He that loveth his wife loveth himself. For no man ever yet hated his own flesh. * * Let every one of you in particular so love his wife even as himself."

The principle of inseparable connection is fully expressed in Adam's answer to the Lord as rendered in the writings of Moses, translated by Joseph, the Seer. "The woman whom thou gavest me, and commanded that she should remain with me, she gave me of the fruit of the tree and I did eat;" *P. of G. P., page* 8.

We further read, on *page* 13, "In the day that God created man, (in the likeness of God made he him), in the image of his own body, male and female, created he them, and blessed them, and called their name Adam." Here we are informed that it required the male and female, united, to make one image of his own body, and that male and female were necessary to form one Adam, who was in the dual image of God his father. We also find by referring again to *Gen.* 1. 27, that it required the male and female to make an image of God.

The Lord has ever manifested a great interest in the marriage relations of his chosen people and Priesthood, and has protected the sexual relations by stringent laws and regulations. The importance of marrying in the same lineage, as themselves, appears to have been well understood by the patriarchs. For this reason, doubtless, Abraham married a near relation, and sent his servant, Eliezer, to his kindred to obtain a wife for his son, and heir, Isaac; *Gen.* 20. 12. *Chap.* 24.

Isaac also commanded Jacob to go to Padanaram, and take one of his cousins to wife; *Gen.* 28. 1-6. Twice the Lord interfered, in a miraculous manner, to prevent the wife of Abraham from being defiled; *Gen.* 12. 17-20. *Chap.* 20. 2, 3. Evidently for the reason that she was the foreordained covenant wife of Abraham, and destined mother of the Lord's chosen people. Israel was forbidden to marry with the Canaanites; *Deut.* 7. 3.

The Lord gave special commandments regarding the marriage of priests and their families. A priest's daughter that profaned herself was to be burned with fire; *Lev.* 21. 9. The High Priest was required to take a virgin of his own people to wife; *verse* 14. The sons of Aaron were commanded not to take a wife that was a whore, or profane, or a woman put away from her husband; *verse* 7.

"If a man be found lying with a woman married to a husband, then they shall both of them die;" *Deut.* 22. 22. If a man lay with a virgin, in the city, that was betrothed to an husband, they were both stoned to death; *verses* 23, 24. If a man lay with a virgin not betrothed, and thereby humbled her, he was required to pay her father fifty shekels of silver, and take her to wife, without the possibility of divorcing her; *verse* 28, 29.

The eighteenth chapter of Leviticus is chiefly occupied with forbidding the unlawful indulgence of the passions. The Nephite prophet, Alma, told his son that harlotry was "most abominable above all sins, save it be the shedding of innocent blood;" *Alma* 39, 5. Jesus told his Nephite disciples "It is better that ye should deny yourselves of these things, wherein ye will take up your cross, than that ye should be cast into hell;" 3 *Nephi* 12. 30.

In *Doc. & Cov.*, the passages are numerous in which adultery is forbidden. The Lord has given much instruction to the Latter-day Saints concerning the intercourse of the sexes. They are required to keep themselves strictly within their marriage covenants.

From the sacred writings, it would appear that in all dispensations of the Priesthood, the laws regulating this matter have been substantially the same, and have been calculated to strictly guard the issues of life; that all those who would keep them might be "perfect in their generations."

If, on the one hand, what the Lord does is eternal, because he is an eternal and infinite being, then what man does of himself, he being finite, must be limited to this life. Therefore, it is necessary that man and wife, to be eternally united, should be married in the way God has appointed, and by a man whom he has authorized to act in his stead.

It would not be consistent with the character of God, as the spiritual and natural father of mankind, to have no law regulating the marriages of his children, that they might be crowned with the blessings of eternal life and increase.

The Lord brought Abraham forth abroad, "And said, Look now toward heaven, and tell the stars, if thou be able to number them: and he said unto him, So shall thy seed be;" *Gen.* 15. 5. This was a promise of infinite and eternal increase. If we could count the stars, and grasp infinitude, we might comprehend the result of the promise.

We find that the Lord confirmed blessings to Abraham, and to his seed, by recorded ordinance and covenant. For this reason it is not probable that a blessing of such magnitude, as the sealing upon man and wife the power of eternal increase, is an exception. Abraham, in his own record, translated by Joseph the Seer, says, "I sought for the blessings of the fathers, and the right whereunto I should be ordained to administer the same." One of these blessings was, "To be a father of many nations, a prince of peace;" *P. of G. P., page* 26.

Abraham understood that this right could only be bestowed by ordination, by one of the fathers who had received it from the fathers in regular descent from Adam. He states that this right was conferred upon him from the fathers, according to his desire. That this right included the authority to regulate the marriage relations, in the future generations of his children, is evident from the further statement, "I sought for mine appointment unto the Priesthood according to the appointment of God unto the fathers concerning the seed." That is, he sought for that especial authority in the Priesthood, through which he had obtained the power of eternal increase.

The priest's office was bestowed upon Aaron and his posterity forever, by ordinance and covenant; *Exodus* 40. 15. Could this have been the case unless his posterity was made an eternal heritage through the everlasting covenant of marriage?

This power of uniting husband and wife by an everlasting covenant of marriage, and by that ordinance giving them an eternal right over their posterity, descended from Abraham through the fathers, until Israel, by transgression, forfeited the blessing.

From the sharpness with which the prophet Nathan reproved David, and the statement that the Lord had given him the wives of his master Saul; 2 *Sam.* 12. 1-12, it is probable that the prophet held this authority.

The great sin of David, apart from the murder of Uriah, was, that he had taken from another man that which the Lord had given him, and stepped outside of his own covenant limits.

Whether the prophet Malachi held the keys of this power or not, he evidently saw in prophetic vision, that it would be taken from the earth, and be restored again, that the broken links of past generations might be welded together. For the Lord said, through him, "I will send you Elijah the prophet before the coming of the great and dreadful day of the Lord: and he shall turn the heart of the fathers to the children, and the heart of the children to their fathers, lest I come and smite the earth with a curse;" 4. 5, 6. Or as it is rendered in *P. of G. P., page* 50, "And he shall plant in the hearts of the children, the promises made to the fathers, and the hearts of the children shall turn to their fathers; if it were not so, the whole earth would be utterly wasted at his coming."

Evidently a very important part of these promises was, that the children would open up the way of salvation to the fathers, through the ordinances of the Gospel, and through them the broken links of past generations would be connected.

Centuries of darkness passed away in which we hear nothing of the order of the holy Priesthood, or of any saving ordinances for the dead, when an obscure man, Joseph Smith, Jun., appeared in the United States of America, and claimed that to him was committed the authority to open up the Dispensation of the fulness of times, in which all the keys and powers of the holy Priesthood should be restored to the earth.

He professed to be a fulfiller of prophecy, and numerous facts, which have become a part of history, prove him to be what he professed. He asserts that in the temple in Kirtland, Ohio, Elias appeared and committed the dispensation of the "Gospel of Abraham," "Saying, that in us, and our seed, all generations after us should be blest." In this we see the needed preparatory work for sealing, upon men the power of eternal lives, through the everlasting covenant of marriage, through which Abraham sought "To be a father of many nations."

Then at the same place appeared Elijah, and said, "Behold, the time has fully come, which was spoken of by the mouth of Malachi, testifying that he (Elijah) should be sent before the great and dreadful day of the Lord come, To turn the hearts of the fathers to the children, and the children to the fathers, lest the whole earth be smitten with a curse. Therefore the keys of this dispensation are committed into your hands;" *Doc. & Cov.* 110. 11-16. Thus we see that the way has been opened for the complete reunion and salvation of all the generations or men, through the keys of the Holy Priesthood which have been bestowed upon Joseph

Smith, Jun. This is the designed glorious culmination of the New and Everlasting Covenant of Marriage—the eternal union of the generations of the righteous in bonds never to be broken.

In *Doc. & Cov. sec.* 128. Joseph, the Seer, gives instructions for restoring the past; in *sec.* 132, he tells the world how future generations may come forth in unbroken succession, each succeeding intelligence, the heritage of its fathers, worlds without end.

*   *   *   *   *

PLURALITY OF WIVES.

Plural marriage is a very ancient institution. Although generally ignored by peoples professing modern Christianity, it is still customary among a large portion of the family of man. Many customs of modern Europe and America are modeled after those of pagan Greece and Rome, instead of after the primitive patriarchs, or after the examples recorded in the history of ancient Israel.

While these ancient nations were monogamists, the limits of intercourse between the sexes, especially on the part of men, were very indefinite. This phase of society is quite characteristic of the modern nations of Europe and America. While the Christian sects of to-day profess some respect for the patriarchs of Israel, they practically condemn their family relations as corrupt and immoral.

If plural marriage be unlawful, then is the whole plan of salvation, through the house of Israel, a failure, and the entire fabric of Christianity without foundation.

God said to Abraham, "I am the Almighty God; walk before me, and be thou perfect. And I will make my covenant between me and thee, and will multiply thee exceedingly. And Abram fell on his face: and God talked with him, saying, as for me, behold, my covenant is with thee, and thou shalt be a father of many nations;" *Gen.* 17. 1-4.

Here we are informed that God talked with Abraham, told him to be perfect, bestowed upon him the blessings of a numerous posterity, and, as a sequence, future power and glory. If polygamy was contrary to his law, it is remarkable that God should have condescended to talk with and greatly bless a man who had, but a short time before, taken a second wife, while the first was living; a fact of which we are informed in the second and third verses of the previous chapter. If this was criminal, Sarai, the mother of all Israel, was involved in the transgression, for she gave Hagar to her husband for a wife; *Gen.* 16. 3.

The Lord told Joseph, the Seer, that he commanded, "And Sarah gave Hagar to Abraham to wife;" *Doc. & Cov.* 132. 34. This is also the testimony of Josephus, the Jewish historian; *Ant.* B. 1. C. 10.

When Hagar was in distress, on account of difficulty with her mistress, the Lord did not treat her as a profane, cast off woman, but sent an angel to counsel and comfort her, by assuring her that her posterity should not be numbered for multitude; *Gen.* 16. 8-10.

The Lord further promised to bless Ishmael, the fruit of this polygamic marriage, and said, "I will make him fruitful, and will multiply him exceedingly; twelve princes shall he beget and I will make him a great nation;" 17. 20.

We find that this great and good man, Abraham, whom the Lord especially favored, had concubines: for "Unto the sons of the concubines, which Abraham had, Abraham gave gifts, and sent them away from Isaac his son;" 25. 6.

Jacob, the grandson and heir to all the blessings of Abraham, was a polygamist. He served seven years for Rachel the daughter of Laban, but being deceived, and Leah given him instead, he served other seven years for Rachel. Each of these wives had a handmaid, which they gave to their husband for wives; *Gen.* 29. 18-35. *Chap.* 30. 3-12.

Moses was conversant with the Lord, and was the great lawgiver of Israel; in his laws especial provision was made for polygamous children; *Deut.* 21. 15-17. In them polygamy is not mentioned as one of the crimes for which penalties were provided.

Elkanah was a polygamist, yet his son, Samuel, was a great prophet, and judge in Israel. He was born, and lived under the special favor of God.

David, king of Israel, was the chosen of the Lord; 1 *Sam.* 16. 12, 13. He took Abigail and Ahinoam, "And they were also both of them his wives;" 1 *Sam.* 25. 42, 43. He "Took him more concubines and wives out of Jerusalem;" 2 *Sam.* 5. 13.

We are further informed, that "David did that which was right in the eyes of the Lord, and turned not aside from anything that he commanded him all the days of his life, save only in the matter of Uriah the Hittite;" 1 *Kings* 15. 5. In this passage we have an assurance that David did right in taking all his wives and concubines, except in one instance, for which he was severely chastised. When Nathan, the prophet, reproved him for this sin, he said to him, in the name of the Lord, "I gave thee thy master's house, and thy master's wives into thy bosom;" 2 *Sam.* 12. 8.

After having repented and suffered for his sin, Bath-sheba was given him for a wife, and she bare Solomon; *verse* 24. The Lord appeared to this son of a plural wife in a dream, and bestowed upon him great blessings; 1 *Kings* 3. God gave him "Wisdom and understanding exceeding much;" 1 *Kings* 4. 29. He was not reproved for plural marriage but for marrying strange wives, who led him into idolatry and wickedness; 1 *Kings* 11. Many chief men in Israel, to whom the Lord manifested his favor, were polygamists.

The following is sometimes quoted as an argument against plural marriage: "For this cause shall a man leave his father and mother, and cleave to his wife; and they twain shall be one flesh;" *Mark* 10. 7, 8. But "Know ye not that he which is joined to a harlot is one body? for two, saith he, shall be one flesh;" 1 *Cor.* 6. 16, shows that it has no connection with the subject.

"A bishop then must be blameless, the husband of one wife;" 1 *Tim.* 3. 2, and let deacons be the husbands of one wife; *verse* 12, are supposed by some to limit officers in the church, and by inference all men, to one wife. But when the passages are taken in connection with the context, which is an enumeration of several qualifications necessary for bishops and deacons, there is but one reasonable construction—that these officers of the church should be married men.

The Latter-day Saints believe that all men should marry; *Doc. & Cov.* 49. 15-17. The Lord is "of purer eyes than to behold evil, and can not look upon iniquity;" *Hab.* 1. 13; and says, that "A bastard shall not enter into the congregation of the Lord; even to his tenth generation;" *Deut.* 23. 2. Yet the patriarchs of the twelve tribes of Israel were the sons of four wives of Jacob; *Gen.* 35. 22-26.

Joseph, the first son of Rachel, the second wife of Jacob, received especial blessings; *Gen.* 49. 22-26. The Lord called to Samuel, the son of a polygamous father; 1 *Sam.* 3. 4-14. Solomon was the son of a polygamist, yet he was a child of promise; 1 *Chron.* 22. 9, 10. Jesus Christ was descended from David through Solomon the son of her who had been the wife of Uriah; *Matt.* 1. 1-17.

The Lord said to Isaiah, "Lift up thy voice like a trumpet, and show my people their transgressions, and the house of Jacob their sins;" 58. 1. This commission was to be faithfully executed; *Ezek.* 3. 18. Polygamy was common in the Jewish nation, yet none of the prophets reproved them for it; but they were sharply reproved for adultery, whoredom, fornication, and other sins; *Jer.* 5. 7, 8, 23. *Ezek.* 22. *Chap.* 23. 36-44.

History evidences that plurality of wives was generally customary among the nations of Asia, yet it is not condemned in any of the epistles of the apostles, nor does John the Revelator mention it in the letters he was commanded to write to the seven churches of Asia.

Paul mentions nearly every crime, in 1 *Cor.* 6. 9, 10, but, says nothing about plurality of wives. Every species of commerce between the sexes, outside of marriage, is often mentioned in the scriptures as crime, but plural marriage is never, except on the part of the woman, who is forbidden to marry another man during the lifetime of her husband; *Rom.* 7. 3.

Had plurality of wives been sinful in man, the inference is reasonable that it would have been equally condemned. Although plural marriage was customary in the days of the patriarchs, some assert that it was done away in Christ. This would seem very inconsistent when he himself was of a polygamous lineage. He was born and filled his earthly mission among a polygamous people, yet, he never reproved them for their plural marriages. There is nothing in the inspired writings to infer that he reproved or did away with either polygamy or monogamy. The following is from the Book of Mormon on this subject: The Lord, through dreams and visions and the ministry of angels, directed a Jewish prophet by the name of Lehi, to leave Jerusalem, 600 years B. C., with his family and others, for the purpose of colonizing America.

It was then a dark period in the history of Israel, as is evident from the Bible history of the times, and from the opening chapters of the Book of Mormon.

The brilliant reign of Solomon had deeply planted in Israel the sins of idolatry and sexual wickedness. His reign was the pride of Israel, and its effects were deep and lasting. It hastened the destruction of the ten tribes, as a people, some one hundred and twenty years before the exodus of Lehi, and at that time was about to culminate in the destruction of Jerusalem and in the Babylonish captivity.

With all his wisdom, Solomon had disobeyed two very important commandments, one especially to the kings of Israel: "Neither shall he multiply wives to himself, that his heart turn not away;" *Deut.* 17. 17. The other was to all Israel, that they should not marry into the idolatrous nations around them: "Neither shalt thou make marriages with them; thy daughter thou shalt not give unto his son, nor his daughter shalt thou take unto thy son;" *Deut.* 7. 3. *Ezra, chapters* 9. 10.

Through disobedience to these injunctions, his heart had turned away from the Lord, and he had been led into idolatry and wickedness. At his death he not only left the influence of his personal example, but, also, a numerous family who, from their great wealth and high social position, must have exercised a powerful and lasting influence for evil, which, with other causes, resulted, in less than three hundred years, in the scattering of the ten tribes among the nations of Asia, and the occupation of their country by strangers, and in less than four hundred years, in the destruction of Jerusalem, and in the Babylonish captivity.

The sexual wickedness which had become prevalent in Israel, and the consequent abuse of the marriage relations, was, evidently, the reason why the Lord commanded that the children of Lehi should have but one wife, for he said to the Nephites, through his prophet Jacob, "This people begin to wax in iniquity; they understand not the scriptures; for they seek to excuse themselves in committing whoredoms, because of the things which were written concerning David, and Solomon his son;" 2. 23.

That is, they excused themselves with the example of these kings for breaking the special command of God to them, that they should have but one wife, and like those eminent persons, ran into excess and wickedness, as their fathers had done before them.

To neutralize the evil effects of the bad example of their fathers was evidently the reason why the Lord commanded the Nephites, "For there shall not any man among you have save it be one wife; and concubines he shall have none;" *verse* 27. Plural marriage would have been whoredom to the Nephites, because the Lord had forbidden it.

That the prophet Jacob foresaw, prophetically, that at some future period this restriction would be taken off is evident from *verse* 30, "For if I will, saith the Lord of hosts, raise up seed unto me, I will command my people; otherwise they shall hearken unto these things." That is, they were required to limit themselves to one wife, until the Lord should order it otherwise, and by implication, when he instructed them to take more than one wife, it would be justifiable.

In the thirty-first verse the Lord gives a reason for forbidding plural marriage among the Nephites, "For behold, I, the Lord, have seen the sorrow, and heard the mourning of the daughters of my people in the land of Jerusalem; yea, and in all the lands of my people, because of the wickedness and abominations of their husbands."

These teachings of the prophet Jacob cannot be presumed, even by opposers of plural marriage, to do away with the tenor of the Jewish Scriptures, for we are informed in 2 *Nephi* 3. 12, that the record of the Jews and of the Nephites, should grow together unto the confounding of false doctrine in the latter-days.

The prophet Jacob could not have intended to condemn a principle on which is based the legitimacy of our Savior, of prophets and patriarchs, and indeed of the whole house of Israel. The words "multiply," and "greatly," in *Deut.* 17. 17, evidently imply excess and unreasonable indulgence, as in the case of David and Uriah, and in taking strange women, as in the case of Solomon.

The absurdity of the argument that these passages imply that a man should have but one wife, is evident from the previous verse, that the kings of Israel should "not multiply horses to themselves." No one would be so unreasonable as to suppose that the Lord designed to limit the kings of Israel to one horse.

The Lord gave Joseph Smith a very important revelation on this subject. It is contained in *Sec.* 132, *Doc. & Cov.* It is entitled a "Revelation on the Eternity of the Marriage Covenant, Including Plurality of Wives."

It commences by stating that the prophet Joseph Smith, Jun., inquired of the Lord, how it was that his servants anciently were justified in having many wives and concubines. The Lord did not answer his question at once, but tells him, in the third verse, to prepare his heart to receive and obey the instructions he was about to give him.

In the fourth verse the Lord said to him, "I reveal unto you a new and an everlasting covenant." We find the general principle involved in that covenant, directly stated in the seventh, thirteenth and fourteenth verses:

"And verily I say unto you, that the conditions of this law are these:—All covenants, contracts, bonds, obligations, oaths, vows, performances, connections, associations, or expectations, that are not made, and entered into, and sealed, by the Holy Spirit of promise, of him who is anointed, both as well for time and for all eternity, and that too most holy, by revelation and commandment through the medium of mine anointed, whom I have appointed on the earth to hold this power, (and I have appointed unto my servant Joseph to hold this power in the last days, and there is never but one on the earth at a time, on whom this power and the Keys of this Priesthood are conferred,) are of no efficacy, virtue or force, in and after the resurrection from the dead; for all contracts that are not made unto this end, have an end when men are dead. * * * * And everything that is in the world, whether it be ordained of men, by thrones, or principalities, or powers, or things of name, whatsoever they may be, that are not by me, or by my word, saith the Lord, shall be thrown down, and shall not remain after men are dead, neither in nor after the resurrection, saith the Lord your God; for whatsoever things remain, are by me; and whatsoever things are not by me, shall be shaken and destroyed." We find a direct application of this law to the marriage relations in *verses* 15 and 19: "If a man marry him a wife in the world, and he marry her not by me, nor by my word; and he covenant with her so long as he is in the world, and she with him, their covenant and marriage are not of force when they are dead, and when they are out of the world; therefore, they are not bound by any law when they are out of the world.

* * * And again, verily I say unto you, if a man marry a wife by my word, which is my law, and by the new and everlasting covenant, and it is sealed unto them by the Holy Spirit of promise, by him who is anointed, unto whom I have appointed this power, and the keys of this Priesthood; and it shall be said unto them, ye shall come forth in the first resurrection; and if it be after the first resurrection, in the next resurrection; and shall inherit thrones, kingdoms, principalities, and powers, dominions, all heights and depths—then shall it be written in the Lamb's Book of Life, that he shall commit no murder whereby to shed innocent blood, and if ye abide in my covenant, and commit no murder whereby to shed innocent blood, it shall be done unto them in all things whatsoever my servant hath put upon them, in time, and through all eternity, and shall be of full force when they are out of the world; and they shall pass by the angels, and the Gods, which are set there, to their exaltation and glory in all things, as hath been sealed upon their heads, which glory shall be a fulness and a continuation of the seeds forever and ever."

The above quotations evidence, that only those who comply with the law will continue in the marriage relations after death; consequently only those who comply with the law can expect a continuation of posterity in the world to come, and the consequent glory and power pertaining to that condition.

The law of the Lord is very plain on this subject. Who can question his right to dictate the marriages of his sons and daughters, that they and their generations may be fitted for his presence?

In *verse* 29, the Lord begins to answer the question in the first verse: "Abraham received all things, whatsoever he received, by revelation and commandment." "God commanded Abraham, and Sarah gave Hagar to Abraham to wife;" *verse* 34. That is, God commanded Abraham to receive Hagar and commanded his already covenant wife to give her handmaid to him. "And why did she do it? Because this was the law." The reason why Abraham was not under condemnation, is very forcibly expressed in the latter part of *verse* 35: "For I, the Lord, commanded it." In *verses* 36-39, the principle is well elucidated, that, in nothing did the ancients sin except in things which they received not of God.

In *verse* 40, the Lord says to Joseph, the Seer: "I gave unto thee, my servant Joseph, an appointment, and restore all things." And from the tenor of the Revelation, "all things" must include plurality of wives and the eternity of the marriage covenant.

This subject may be readily summed up as follows: If a man has a wife in the world to come, she will be a gift from the Lord, through the covenants he has ordained, and that man is justifiable in receiving all the wives the Lord sees fit to give him, through the authority he has appointed on the earth.

Many elders of the Latter-day Saints have been commanded, as was Abraham, to enter into plural marriage, and disobedience becomes transgression. Hence it involves a religious principle, and becomes a matter of conscience. "Thou shalt love thy wife with all thy heart, and shalt cleave unto her and none else;" *Doc. & Cov.* 42. 22, is sometimes referred to as an argument against plural marriage.

If it would admit of this construction, it would not be valid as an argument, from the fact, that the revelation of which it forms a part was given previous to that on the plurality and eternity of the marriage relations, and consequently, before the church was prepared to receive such a revelation. It evidently admits of the construction, that a man may have more than one wife, and yet cleave to none but his wife. That is, it forbids all sexual commerce outside of the marriage covenant.

Bible.

Gen. 16. 1, 2, 3 Sarai gave Hagar to Abraham.

15 Hagar bare Abraham a son.

20. 17 the Lord healed the wife and maidservants of Abimelech.

36. 2 Esau took wives of the daughters of Canaan.

38. 8 Judah said to Onan, go in unto thy brother's wife.

Exo. 2. 21 Moses married Zipporah, daughter of the priest of Midian.

21. 10 and if he take him another wife.

Num. 12. 1 Moses married an Ethiopian woman.

Judges 7. Gideon delivered Israel from bondage through the favor of God.

8. 30 Gideon had three score and ten sons and many wives.

9. 5 Jerubbaal had seventy sons.

10. 3, 4 Jair, a judge in Israel, had thirty sons.

12. 13, 14 Abdon, a judge in Israel, had forty sons.

2 *Sam.* 19. 5 and the lives of thy wives and the lives of thy concubines.

1 *Kings* 8. 10, 11 the glory of the Lord filled the house.

9. 3 the Lord told Solomon that his prayer was answered.

20. 7 for he sent unto me for my wives.

1 *Chron.* 4. 5 Ashur, the father of Tekoa, had two wives.

7. 4 for they had many wives and sons.

8. 8 Shaharaim had two wives.

2 *Chron.* 11. 21 Rehoboam had eighteen wives and three score concubines.

13. 21 Abijah married fourteen wives.

24. 3 Jehoiada, the priest of God, took two wives.

Psalm 45. 9 king's daughters were among thy honorable women.

Isa. 4. 1 in that day seven women shall take hold of one man.

Hos. 1. 2 go take thee a wife of whoredoms.

See Sermon by O. Pratt, J. of D., Vol. 1, page 53.

See Sermon by B. Young, J. of D., Vol. 1, page 112.

See Sermon by O. Hyde, J. of D., Vol. 2, page 75.

See Sermon by B. Young, J. of D., Vol. 2, page 88.

See Sermon by B. Young, J. of D., Vol. 3, page 264.

See Sermon by O. Pratt, J. of D., Vol. 6, page 349.

See Sermon by Geo. A. Smith, J. of D., Vol. 13, page 37.

See Sermon by O. Pratt, J. of D., Vol. 13, page 183.

See Sermon by G. Q. Cannon, J. of D., Vol. 13, page 197.

Article, by P. P. Pratt, Mil. Star, Vol. 5, page 189.

History of Marriage among the Jews, Mil. Star, Vol. 13, pages 263, 282, 296, 316, 324, 350, 365, 377.

Milton on Polygamy, Mil. Star, Vol. 16, pages 321, 342.

Article, "Marriage Ritual of the Church of England," by J. A. Little, Mil. Star, Vol. 18, page 177.

Address by P. P. Pratt, before joint session of Utah Legislature, Mil. Star, Vol. 18, page 337.

History of J. Smith, May 16, 1843.

A pamphlet entitled, "On Marriage," by John Taylor.

*   *   *   *   *

CONCUBINES.

A concubine "In scripture signifies a wife of the second rank, who was inferior to the matron, or mistress of the house.

"The chief wives differed from the concubines in that they were taken into covenant with their husband by solemn stipulation, and with consent and rejoicing of friends.

"They brought with them dowries to their husbands. They had the government of their families under and with their husbands. The inheritance belonged to the children brought forth by them.

"Though the children of the concubines did not inherit their father's estate, yet the father in his life time provided for them, and made presents to them:

Thus Sarah was Abraham's wife of whom he had Isaac, the heir of all his wealth. But he had besides two concubines, namely, Hagar and Keturah; of these he had children, whom he distinguished from Isaac, and made presents to them;" (see Concubine, Cru.

Concor.)

Although Hagar is considered a concubine in the above quotation, yet, according to Cruden's definition, she was a wife of the second degree. She is nowhere called a concubine in the scripture, but emphatically a wife.

"And Sarai, Abram's wife, took Hagar her maid, the Egyptian, * * and gave her to her husband Abram to be his wife;" *Gen.* 16. 3. That this condition of wifehood did not change the former relations of mistress and servant, between Sarai and Hagar, is evident from *verse* 9. The angel said to Hagar, "Return to thy mistress, and submit thyself under her hands."

That Keturah was Abraham's wife is evident from the fact, that she is called his wife in *Gen.* 25. 1: and that she was also called his concubine, appears from 1 *Chron.* 1. 32. That concubine and wife were synonymous terms, further appears from the declaration of Nathan, the prophet, to David, "I will take thy wives before thine eyes, and give *them* unto thy neighbor, and he shall lie with thy wives in the sight of this sun;" 2 *Sam.* 12. 11. In the account of the fulfilment of this prophecy, these wives are called concubines. "And Absalom went in unto his father's concubines in the sight of all Israel;" 16. 22.

The Nephites, whose ancestors colonized America 600 years before Christ, did not forget the custom of their Jewish fathers; for when they broke the special commandment of the Lord to them, by taking more than one wife, they also added concubines; *Mos.* 11. 2-4.

This custom of taking wives and concubines prevailed among the Jaredites, whose ancestors emigrated to North America from the tower of Babel. It appears to have been abused by a wicked king, called Riplakish, who reigned some 1500 years before Christ; *Ether* 10. 5. From both the Bible and Book of Mormon, it appears that the custom of taking a plurality of wives and concubines prevailed at a very early period after the flood. It was, however, of antediluvian origin: "And Lamech took unto himself two wives, Adah and Zillah;" *Gen.* 4. 19. he lived before the flood. It is evident from the "Revelation on the Eternity of the Marriage Covenant," that the Lord anciently gave concubines to good men, as wives, and that only the custom of the country discriminated between them and others: "Abraham received concubines, and they bare him children, and it was accounted unto him for righteousness, because they were given unto him;" *Doc. & Cov.* 132. 37. "David's wives and concubines were given unto him, of me, by the hand of Nathan, my servant, and others of the prophets who had the keys of this power; and in none of these things did he sin against me, save in the case of Uriah and his wife;" *verse* 39.

We cannot presume that the Lord ever gave women to these men under any title, except for the noble purpose of parentage. Concubinage is unknown among the Latter-day Saints. Wifehood, in the fullest sense of the word, is conferred by the marriage covenant. All a man's children are his legitimate heirs, both by law and custom.

FOREORDINATION—ELECTION.

"Known unto God are all his works from the beginning of the world;" *Acts* 15. 18.

The knowledge that we have of the beginning of the world is principally derived from the history of its creation in the Bible Genesis, and in the writings of Moses and of Abraham, as given in *P. of G. P., pages* 4-7, and 32-36.

Abraham says, "Now the Lord had shewn unto me, Abraham, the intelligences that were organized before the world was; and among all these there were many of the noble and great ones; and God saw these souls that they were good, and he stood in the midst of them, and he said, These I will make my rulers; for he stood among those that were spirits, and he saw that they were good; and he said unto me, Abraham, thou art one of them, thou wast chosen before thou wast born;" *P. of G. P., page* 32.

These writings make it plain that man existed in a spiritual condition prior to coming here, and also quite as evident that in that pre-existence he exercised his free agency. These facts throw much light on the following passages: "Him, being delivered by the determinate counsel and foreknowledge of God, ye have taken, and by wicked hands have crucified and Slain;" *Acts* 2. 23. "For whom he did foreknow, he also did predestinate to be conformed to the image of his Son;" *Rom.* 8. 29.

"Moreover, whom he did predestinate, them he also called;" *verse* 30. "God hath not cast away his people which he foreknew;" 11. 2. "For the gifts and calling of God are without repentance;" *verse* 29.

The last passage explains the previous ones. God may have called and chosen men in their first estate, or spiritual existence, but whether they will accept that call and fill it, by repentance and good works in this life, is a matter in which it is their privilege to exercise their free agency.

This idea is illustrated in the case of the Roman centurion, who had faith that his sick servant would be healed if Jesus would only speak the word. Jesus said to those around him, "That many shall come from the east and west, and shall sit down with Abraham, and Isaac, and Jacob, in the kingdom of heaven: But the children of the kingdom shall be cast out into outer darkness;" *Matt.* 8. 11, 12.

The "Children of the kingdom" evidently refers to Israel, the called and chosen of God. The passages are numerous in which Israel is called the "Chosen of God;" "The elect according to the covenant." "Hearken unto me, O Jacob and Israel, my called;" *Isa.* 48. 12.

Jesus, when he predicted the destruction of Jerusalem, and the scattering of the Jews, declared that for the elect's sake those days should be shortened; *Matt.* 24. 22.

The elect could only mean according to the covenant with Abraham for the remnant who were saved in the flesh were of a wicked generation, and they and their children became a hiss and a by-word among all nations, consequently they could not have been the elect through faith and good works.

David said to the congregation, "Solomon, my son, whom alone God hath chosen;" 1 *Chron.* 29. 1. Yet Solomon did not fully prove himself by good works, for he fell into transgression and corrupted Israel; 1 *Kings* 11. 9-11.

The Book of Mormon is plain on this subject: "Being called and prepared from the foundation of the world, according to the foreknowledge of God, on account of their exceeding faith and good works; in the first place being left to choose good or evil;" *Alma* 13. 3-7.

Their calling and preparation from the foundation of the world were evidently based on their faith and good works, previous to their being called, and not on the possibilities of their future good conduct.

This idea is verified by the apostle who, speaking of Christ, says, "And again, when he bringeth in the first-begotten into the world, he saith, And let all the angels of God worship him. * * * Thou hast loved righteousness, and hated iniquity; therefore God, even thy God, hath anointed thee with the oil of gladness above thy fellows;" *Heb.* 1. 6, 9. "Who verily was foreordained before the foundation of the world, but was manifest in these last times for you;" 1 *Pet.* 1. 20. Christ was chosen before the foundation of the world, because he had already proven himself worthy.

Men exercised their free agency in the first or spiritual estate, as well as in this. That the character of their works in that estate shaped their destiny in this is evident. The Lord said to Abraham, "They who keep their first estate, shall be added upon; and they who keep not their first estate, shall not have glory in the same kingdom with those who keep their first estate;" *P. of G. P., page* 32.

There are some foreordained to condemnation: "There are certain men crept in unawares, who were before of old ordained to this condemnation;" *Jude* 4.

"The angels which kept not their first estate, but left their own habitation, he hath reserved in everlasting chains under darkness unto the judgment of the great day;" *Jude* 6. That is, those angels who, voluntarily, by their own acts, forfeited the glory prepared for them.

The Lord revealed to Joseph, the Seer, that the only ones who should not be redeemed in the due time of the Lord are those who "Having denied the Holy Spirit after having received it, and having denied the Only Begotten Son of the Father—having crucified him unto themselves, and put him to an open shame." *Doc. & Cov.* 76. 31-43. We learn from the Book of Mormon also "The way is prepared for all men from the foundation of the world, if so be that they repent and come unto him." 1 *Nephi* 10. 18.

Bible.

Exo. 33. 19 I will shew mercy on whom I will.

Num. 16. 7 the man whom the Lord shall choose shall be holy.

Deut. 7. 6 the Lord hath chosen thee to be a special people. 14. 2.

18. 5 the Lord hath chosen him out of all thy tribes. 21. 5.

2 *Sam.* 6. 21 it was before the Lord which chose me before thy father.

16. 18 whom the Lord and the men of Israel chose.

Neh. 9. 7 thou art the Lord who did'st choose Abram.

Psalm 33. 12 the people whom he hath chosen for his own inheritance.

89. 3 have made a covenant with my chosen; sworn to David my servant.

105. 6 ye seed of Abraham his servant, ye children of Jacob his chosen. 26.

Isa. 14. 1 Lord will have mercy on Jacob, and will yet choose Israel.

41. 8 Jacob whom I have chosen; the seed of Abraham my friend. 9.

42. 1 my servant whom I uphold, mine elect in whom my soul delighteth.

Matt. 12. 18 behold my servant whom I have chosen.

20. 16 and the first last, for many be called but few chosen. 22. 14.

Luke 18. 7 shall not God avenge his own elect?

John 15. 16 ye have not chosen me, but I have chosen you. 19.

Acts 1. 24 shew whether of these two thou hast chosen.

9. 15 for he is a chosen vessel unto me to bear my name.

22. 14 the God of our fathers hath chosen thee.

Rom. 9. 11-22 Jacob have I loved, and Esau have I hated. 23, 24, 26.

11. 7 but the election hath obtained it.

28 but as touching the election they are beloved.

1 *Cor.* 1. 24, 27 God hath chosen the foolish things of the world.

Eph. 1. 4-11. 18 predestination and adoption set forth.

Col. 3. 12 put on therefore as the elect of God.

2 Thess. 2. 13, 14 because God, from the beginning, hath chosen you to salvation.

Titus 1. 1 an apostle of Jesus Christ according to the faith of God's elect.

James 2. 5 hath not God chosen the poor of this world?

1 Peter 1. 2 elect according to the foreknowledge of God.

Rev. 17. 14 those that are with him are called and chosen.

Book of Mormon.

1 Nephi 1. 20 over all whom he has chosen because of their their faith.

3. 29 know ye not that the Lord hath chosen him?

17. 40 he loved our fathers and covenanted with them.

2 Nephi 9. 18 shall inherit the kingdom of God prepared for them.

Alma 13. 10, 11 were called after his holy order on account of their faith.

Moroni 7. 31 by declaring the word of God unto chosen vessels. 48.

8. 12 little children are alive in Christ from the foundation of the world.

22 they that are without law are alive in Christ.

Doctrine & Covenants.

Sec. 10. 59-62 other sheep I have which are not of this fold.

25. 3 Emma Smith an elect lady.

29. 4 ye are chosen out of the world. 7.

46 little children are redeemed from the foundation of the world. 74. 7.

33. 6 so will I gather mine elect from the four quarters of the earth.

52. 1 the elders whom the Lord hath chosen. 21.

53. 1 concerning your calling and election.

84. 34 become the seed of Abraham and the elect of God. 99.

86. 9-11 for ye are lawful heirs according to the flesh.

88. 4 this comforter is the promise of eternal life.

93. 38 every spirit of man was innocent in the beginning.

95. 5. 6 those not chosen have sinned. 8.

101. 3 they shall be mine in that day when I make up my jewels.

Pearl of Great Price.

Page 26. Abraham became a rightful heir.

27. the Lord took Abraham and put upon him his name.

39. if possible they shall deceive the very elect according to the covenant.

40. shall gather the remainder of mine elect. When mine elect shall see these things.

See Article by B. Young and W. Richards, Mil. Star, Vol. 38, page 145.

History of J. Smith, Jan., 1, 1841.

Sermon by B. Young, J. of D., Vol. 10, page 1.

Article by J. Nicholson, Mil. Star, Vol. 27, Page 739.

DISPENSATION OF THE FULNESS OF TIMES.

A dispensation "is power and authority to dispense the word of God, and to administer in all the ordinances thereof." What the dispensation of the fulness of times is, is well expressed by the apostle Paul in *Eph.* 1. 9, "Having made known unto us the mystery of his will, according to his good pleasure which he hath purposed in himself: that in the dispensation of the fulness of times he might gather together in one all things in Christ, both which are in heaven, and which are on earth, even in him."

It is still more comprehensively expressed by the prophet Joseph. "Now the thing to be known is, what the fulness of times means, or the extent and authority thereof. It means this, that the dispensation of the fulness of times is made up of all the dispensations that ever have been given since the world began, until this time. Unto Adam first was given a dispensation. It is well known that God spake to him with his own voice in the garden, and gave him the promise of the Messiah."

"And unto Noah also was a dispensation given; for Jesus said, 'As it was in the days of Noe, so shall it be also in the days of the coming of the Son of Man;' and as the righteous were saved then, and the wicked destroyed, so will it be now. And from Noah to Abraham, and from Abraham to Moses, and from Moses to Elias, and from Elias to John the Baptist, and from then to Jesus Christ, and from Jesus Christ to Peter, James, and John, the Apostles all having received in their dispensation by revelation from God, to accomplish the great scheme of restitution, spoken by all the holy Prophets since the world began; the end of which is, the dispensation of the fulness of times, in which all things shall be fulfilled that have been spoken of since the earth was made." *Mil. Star, vol.* 16, *page* 220. The apostle Paul further says on this subject, "For I would not, brethren, that ye should be ignorant of this mystery, lest ye should be wise in your own conceits, that blindness in part is happened to Israel, until the fulness of the Gentiles be come in. And so all Israel shall be saved: as it is written, There shall come out of Zion the Deliverer, and shall turn away ungodliness from Jacob;" *Rom.* 11. 25, 26.

These passages make it evident, in connection with other passages, that the dispensation of the fulness of times will commence when the fulness of the Gentiles shall come in, for then will a Deliverer come out of Zion who shall turn away ungodliness from Jacob.

This dispensation of the fulness of times is a period in which all things will be restored to their proper order or condition.

The apostle Peter had a very comprehensive view of this subject when he severely reproved the Jews for killing the "Prince of Life," and said to them, "Repent ye therefore, and be converted, that your sins may be blotted out, when the times of refreshing shall come from the presence of the Lord."

This was evidently to take place when Israel should be gathered and the Gospel restored, in its fulness: "And he shall send Jesus Christ, which before was preached unto you: whom the heavens must receive until the times of restitution of all things, which God hath spoken by the mouth of all his holy prophets since the world began;" *Acts* 3. 19, 21. Peter gave them to understand that not until then could those who killed the "Prince of Life" expect to be restored to the privileges of the Gospel which was preached to them while in the flesh.

In this time of restitution everything in heaven and in earth will find its appropriate place and condition, and good and evil will find their fulness of reward.

The Book of Mormon is very plain on this subject: "The meaning of the word restoration, is to bring back again evil for evil, or carnal for carnal, or devilish for devilish; good for that which is good; righteous for that which is righteous; just for that which is just; merciful for that which is merciful. * * * Deal justly, judge righteously, and if ye do all these things, then shall ye receive your reward; yea, ye shall have mercy restored unto you again; ye shall have justice restored to you again; ye shall have a righteous judgment restored unto you again; and ye shall have good rewarded unto you again; for that which ye do send out shall return unto you again, and be restored; therefore, the word restoration more fully condemneth the sinner, and justifieth him not at all;" *Alma* 41. 13-15.

This principle of restitution has also been further revealed in this dispensation: "Unto the day when the Lord shall come to recompense unto every man according to his works, and measure to every man according to the measure which he has measured to his fellow man;" *Doc. & Cov.* 1. 10. The following passage warns us that the time is near when the evil and the good will each find their own place: "The hour is not yet, but is nigh at hand, when peace shall be taken from the earth, and the devil shall have power over his own dominion; and also the Lord shall have power over his Saints, and shall reign in their midst;" 35, 36.

All the intelligences, of whatever order, pertaining to this earth, will be redeemed from death through the resurrection, except the sons of perdition. The great burden of the ancient prophets was the restoration, in the latter times, of the house of Israel to the lands of their inheritance, and to the favor of God. On the other hand, those who have oppressed and persecuted them must suffer the full reward of their evil works.

This world, in its present condition, is one of antagonisms. When all things are restored to their proper place, these antagonisms will cease, and the good and the evil will be placed in positions where they will harmonize with their surroundings.

The term, "Dispensation of the fulness of times," refers to the latter days, when the fulness of the Gospel will be revealed, and the holy Priesthood be restored to the earth. Under its direction the work of restoration will commence and be fully consummated, through the great plan of redemption for man and the earth, which was decided in the councils of heaven before the foundations of the earth were laid.

Bible.

Isa. 11. 6, 7 animals shall dwell together in peace.

9 the earth shall be full of the knowledge of God.

13. 13, 14 the earth will be moved out of its place.

32. 15 until the Spirit be poured out upon us from on high.

16 then judgment shall dwell in the wilderness.

17, 18 and the work of righteousness shall be peace.

35. 1 the wilderness and the solitary place shall be glad.

7 and the parched ground shall become a pool.

9 no lion shall be there, nor any ravenous beast.

51. 6 the earth shall wax old like a garment.

60. 20 the Lord shall be their everlasting light. 21.

62. 4 thy land shall be married.

65. 17-25 a description of the millennial condition of the earth.

Mic. 4, 4 they shall sit, every man under his own fig tree.

Hab. 2. 14 the earth will be filled with a knowledge of the glory of the Lord.

Zech. 14. 4 and the Mount of Olives shall cleave in the midst thereof.

Matt. 17. 11 Elias truly shall first come and restore all things.

Rom. 11. 25 until the fulness of the Gentiles be come in.

2 *Peter* 3. 11, 12 all these things shall be dissolved.

Rev. 6. 13, 14 the stars of heaven will fall, and the heavens be rolled together.

21. 1 and I saw a new heaven and a new earth.

Book of Mormon.

2 *Nephi* 30. 17, 18, works of darkness to be made manifest; that which is sealed to be loosed; all things which have been revealed to be again revealed.

Hel. 14. 31 good restored to good and evil to evil.

Doctrine & Covenants.

Sec. 1. 22 that mine everlasting covenant might be established.

38 all the word of the Lord to be fulfilled.

Sec. 2. Elijah, the prophet, to reveal the Priesthood.

3. 18-20 the records of the children of Lehi to be restored to

them.

Sec. 13. John the Baptist restored the Aaronic Priesthood.

14. 10 the fulness of the Gospel to be brought forth from the Gentiles to the house of Israel.

22. 1 everlasting covenant, even that which was from the beginning, restored.

3 caused this church to be built up as in days of old.

27. 5 the fulness of the everlasting Gospel—the Book of Mormon.

12 Peter, James and John ordained J. Smith, Jun., to hold the keys of the dispensation of the Gospel, for the last time.

38. 7 the Lord gave J. Smith, Jun., the keys of the mysteries of the things which have been sealed.

86. 10 until the restoration of all things spoken by all the holy prophets.

90. 2 which kingdom is coming forth for the last time.

Sec. 110. Moses, Elias and Elijah appeared in the Kirtland temple, and bestowed keys of former dispensations.

112. 30 power of the Priesthood given, for the dispensation of the fulness of times.

121. 26-32 things to be revealed by the Holy Ghost that have not been revealed—all things to be revealed.

128. 8 in the last dispensation, all dispensations will be welded together.

20 declaring themselves as possessing the keys of the dispensation of the fulness of times.

See Sermon by P. P. Pratt, J. of D. Vol. 3, page 127.

See Sermon by E. Snow, J. of D. Vol. 16, page 200.

History of J. Smith, May 2, 1842.

Epistle by D. W. Patten, History of J. Smith, July, 1838.

Latter-day Kingdom, a pamphlet by O. Pratt.

Article, Mil. Star, Vol. 21, pages 17, 35.

O. Spencer's Letters to Rev. Wm. Crowel, Nos. 12, 13.

Voice of Warning, by P. P. Pratt, Chap. 5.

Pearl of Great Price, pages 21, 22.

THE SPIRIT OF GOD, OR HOLY GHOST.

Whenever the Priesthood has been on the earth, through it, and in various ways, the Lord has revealed his will to man. By his voice: "They heard the voice of the Lord God walking in the garden;" *Gen.* 3. 8. The Lord talked with Abraham; *chap.* 18. And with Moses; *Exo.* 3. He called to young Samuel; 1 *Sam.* 3.

Passages are numerous in the inspired writings in which it says "The Lord hath spoken;" "The Lord spake;" "Thus saith the Lord;" etc. He has often revealed his will through the ministrations of angels, by visions and dreams, by signs and tokens; but the more general way has been through the agency of his Spirit, or the Holy Ghost.

The Prophet Joseph Smith has informed us that "The Holy Ghost has not a body of flesh and bones, but is a personage of Spirit." *Doc. & Cov.* 130, 22, 23.

Its office is to enlighten the understanding and give knowledge and wisdom; *Exo.* 31. 1-11. 1 *Chron.* 28. 12. "But the Comforter, *which* is the Holy Ghost, whom the Father will send in my name, he shall teach you all things, and bring all things to your remembrance, whatsoever I have said unto you;" *John* 14. 26.

It is the Spirit of prophecy, and reveals future events, "For the prophecy came not in old time by the will of man: but holy men of God spake *as they were* moved by the Holy Ghost;" 2 *Pet.* 1. 21.

It is a witness and testifies to man, of God and his attributes. "Even so the things of God knoweth no man, but the Spirit of God:" 1 *Cor.* 2. 11. "We are his witnesses of these things; and so is also the Holy Ghost;" *Acts* 5. 32. *Chap.* 20. 23. "No man can say that Jesus is the Lord, but by the Holy Ghost;" 1 *Cor.* 12. 3. It gives the knowledge that is essential to salvation. "When he, the Spirit of truth, is come, he will guide you into all truth." *John* 16. 13.

Nephite prophets declared, that, after Christ should be slain, "He should rise from the dead, and should make himself manifest, by the Holy Ghost, unto the Gentiles;" 1 *Nephi* 10. 11. 3 *Nephi* 15. 23. "The mysteries of God shall be unfolded unto them, by the power of the Holy Ghost, as well in these times as in times of old, and as well in times of old as in times to come;" 1 *Nephi* 10. 19.

The Holy Ghost bears record of the Father and of the Son; 3 *Nephi* 11. 32. The Holy Ghost and Spirit of God are synonymous. The gifts of the Spirit mentioned in 1 *Cor. chap.* 12, are often mentioned in the inspired writings as gifts of the Holy Ghost.

The Comforter, and the Spirit of Truth are also synonymous with the Holy Ghost. "But the Comforter which is the Holy Ghost;" *John* 14. 26. "But when the

Comforter is come, whom I will send unto you from the Father, *even* the Spirit of Truth;" *John* 15. 26.

The Holy Ghost is the moving power in the salvation of the human family, for faith is one of its gifts; 1 *Cor.* 12. 9. And all intelligences work by faith. *Doc. & Cov., Lec. on Faith*; 1. 11.

The Spirit of God is not only the medium by which knowledge is communicated to man, but it is the power by which all organizations are developed, and by which they exist and move. It is the agent of God's power by which, through faith, the elements are controlled. "And the Spirit of God moved upon the face of the waters;" *Gen.* 1. 2. "By his Spirit he hath garnished the heavens;" *Job* 26. 13. "The Spirit of God hath made me, and the breath of the Almighty hath given me life;" 33. 4. "If he gather unto himself his Spirit and his breath; all flesh shall perish together, and man shall turn again unto dust;" 34. 14, 15. "Thou sendest forth thy Spirit, they are created;" *Psalm* 104. 30. "For by the power of my Spirit created I them; yea, all things both spiritual and temporal;" *Doc. & Cov.,* 29. 31. "The power of my Spirit quickeneth all things;" 33. 16.

By it the Lord works his will among the nations: "I have called upon the weak things of the world, those who are unlearned and despised, to thresh the nations by the power of my Spirit;" 35. 13. "The elements are the tabernacle of God;" 93. 35. Through the power of the Spirit which pervades them, they are organized and disorganized in accordance with the laws by which they are governed. Spirit and element must be inseparably connected, through the resurrection, in order to attain the greatest perfection; *verses* 33, 34.

Man, ignorant of God and his attributes, increases in knowledge by experience and observation, explores the fields of nature, watches and experiments with the elements, acquires, to him, new and grand truths, makes discoveries in science which measurably revolutionize the conditions of human life, and thinks, in his ignorance of the spiritual elements, that he accomplishes these important results by his own unaided wisdom, when they are the effects of the workings of that universal spirit of intelligence which emanates from the Father of light, without which man would be like the blind, who wander about at noonday, unconscious of the light that shines around them.

Man observes a universal energy in nature. Organization and disorganization succeed each other. The thunders roll through the heavens; the earth trembles and becomes broken by earthquakes; fires consume cities and forests; the waters accumulate, flow over their usual bounds and cause destruction of life and property; the worlds perform their revolutions in space with a velocity and power incomprehensible to man, and he, covered with a veil of darkness, calls this universal energy, God, when it is the workings of his Spirit, the obedient agent of his power, the wonder-working and life-giving principle in all nature.

Bible.

Gen. 6. 3 my Spirit shall not always strive with man.

Num. 11. 17 I will take of the Spirit that is on thee, and put it on them,

26 The Spirit rested on Eldad and Medad, and they prophe-sied.

24. 2 and the Spirit of the Lord rested on Balaam.

1 *Sam.* 10. 10 the Spirit of God came on Saul and he prophe-sied.

2 *Kings* 2. 9 let a double portion of thy spirit be on me.

15 the spirit of Elijah rested on Elisha. 16.

Neh. 9. 20 thou gavest also thy good Spirit to instruct them.

30 God for many years testified against Israel by his Spirit.

Job 32. 8 there is a spirit in man, and the inspiration of the Al-mighty giveth them understanding.

Prov. 1. 23 behold I will pour out my Spirit on you.

Isa. 29. 10 the Lord hath poured upon you the Spirit of deep sleep.

42. 1 I have put my Spirit on him, he shall bring forth judg-ment.

44. 3 will pour my Spirit on thy seed, my blessing on thine offspring.

48. 16 the Lord God and his Spirit hath sent me.

61. 1 the Spirit of the Lord God is on me. *Luke* 4. 18.

Ezek. 11. 24 brought me in a vision, by the Spirit of God, into Chaldea.

Dan. 4. 8 in whom is the Spirit of the holy Gods.

Joel 2. 29 upon the servants and handmaids, in those days, will I pour out my Spirit. *Acts* 2. 17, 18.

Matt. 3. 16 he saw the Spirit of God descending on him like a dove.

4. 1 Jesus led up of the Spirit into the wilderness. *Luke* 4. 1.

12. 28 if I cast out devils by the Spirit of God?

Luke 1. 17 he shall go before him in the spirit and power of Elias.

2. 25-27 Simeon came by the Spirit into the temple.

4. 14 Jesus returned in power of the Spirit into Galilee.

11. 13 your Heavenly Father give the Holy Spirit to them that ask him.

John 3. 34 God giveth not the Spirit by measure unto him.

6. 63 it is the Spirit that quickeneth.

16. 13 the Spirit of truth is come, he will guide you into all truth.

Acts 2. 4 began to speak with other tongues, as the Spirit gave them utterance.

8. 29 the Spirit said to Philip, go near and join thyself to this chariot.

39 the Spirit caught away Philip, that the eunuch saw him no more.

10. 19 the Spirit said to Peter, three men seek thee.

Rom. 8. 10 but the Spirit is life, because of righteousness.

11 if the Spirit which raised up Jesus shall also quicken your mortal bodies.

26 the Spirit itself maketh intercession for us.

1 *Cor.* 2. 4 in demonstration of the Spirit and power.

10 the Spirit of God searcheth all things.

15. 45 the first Adam was a living soul, the last Adam a quickening spirit.

2 *Cor.* 3. 6 the letter killeth, but the Spirit giveth life.

17 where the Spirit of God is there is liberty.

18 changed from glory to glory, even as by the Spirit of the Lord.

Gal. 5. 16 walk in the Spirit; ye shall not fulfil the lusts of the flesh.

Eph. 2. 2 the Spirit that now worketh in the children of disobedience.

6. 17 take the sword of the Spirit, which is the word of God. 18.

1 *Thess.* 5. 19. 20 quench not the Spirit, despise not prophesyings.

2 *Thess.* 2. 8 the Lord shall consume with the Spirit of his mouth.

1 *Tim.* 3. 16 God manifest in the flesh, justified in the Spirit.

Rev. 1. 10 I was in the Spirit on the Lord's day.

2. 7 hear what the Spirit saith to the churches. 11. 17, 29.

11. 11 After three days, the Spirit of life, from God, entered into them.

14. 13 blessed are the dead that die in the Lord; yea, saith the

Spirit.

17. 3 so he carried me away in the Spirit, into the wilderness.

19. 10 for the testimony of Jesus is the Spirit of prophecy.

Book of Mormon.

1 *Nephi* 1. 12 as he read he was filled with the Spirit.

4. 6 was led by the Spirit, not knowing the things I should do.

18 I obeyed the voice of the Spirit, and smote off the head of Laban.

11. 1 caught away in the Spirit, into an exceeding high mountain.

6 when I had spoken these words, the Spirit cried with a loud voice.

8 the Spirit said to me, look; I looked and beheld a tree.

11 I knew it was the Spirit of the Lord, and he spake unto me as a man speaketh with another.

19 I beheld that she was carried away in the Spirit.

13. 12 the Spirit of God wrought on the man, and he went forth on the waters.

15 the Spirit of the Lord was on the Gentiles, that they prospered.

14. 30 an end of speaking what I saw, when carried away in the Spirit.

17. 52 lest they wither before me, so powerful was the Spirit.

19. 12 kings of the isles shall be wrought upon by the Spirit.

20 I have workings in the Spirit, for those at Jerusalem.

2 *Nephi* 2. 4 for the Spirit is the same yesterday, to-day and forever.

8 who layeth down his life and taketh it, by the power of the Spirit.

3. 5 Messiah to be manifest in the latter days, in the Spirit of power.

4. 25 on the wings of his Spirit hath my body been carried away.

26. 11 the Spirit of God will not always strive with man.

32. 7 I cannot say more, the Spirit stoppeth mine utterance.

Jacob 4. 13 for the Spirit speaketh the truth, and lieth not.

Enos 1. 10 while struggling in the Spirit, the voice of the Lord came.

Mos. 2. 36 that ye do withdraw yourselves from the Spirit of the Lord.

3. 19 but if he yields to the enticings of the Holy Spirit.

5. 3 through his Spirit have great views of that which is to come.

13. 5 durst not lay their hands on him, for the Spirit was on him.

18. 26 might wax strong in Spirit, having the knowledge of God.

Alma 3. 26 reap happiness or misery according to the spirit they listed to obey.

5. 54 sanctified by the Spirit, bring forth works meet for repentance.

7. 13 the Spirit knoweth all things.

16 have eternal life according to the testimony of the Spirit.

8. 24 been called according to the Spirit of revelation and prophecy.

12. 3 thou seest that thy thoughts are made known by the Spirit.

13. 4 would reject the Spirit, on account of the hardness of their hearts.

16. 16 the Lord poured his Spirit on the face of the land.

17. 3 given themselves to fasting and prayer, therefore they had the Spirit.

18. 16 being filled with the Spirit, perceived the thoughts of the king.

19. 13 the queen sank down, being overpowered by the Spirit.

22. 1 he was led by the Spirit to the land of Nephi.

23. 6 according to the Spirit of revelation and prophecy.

30. 46 resist the Spirit of truth, that thy soul may be destroyed.

34. 35 the Spirit of the Lord has withdrawn, and the devil has power over you.

40. 13 the wicked have no part of the Spirit of the Lord.

61. 15 give them power to conduct the war, according to the Spirit of God.

Hel. 5. 45 the Spirit entered their hearts, and they were filled as with fire.

6. 35 the Spirit of the Lord began to withdraw from the Nephites.

10. 16 Nephi taken by the Spirit and conveyed away.

13. 8 except they repent I will withdraw my Spirit from them.

3 *Nephi* 3. 19 to appoint captains of those who had the Spirit of prophecy.

7. 21 signified they had been visited by the Spirit of God.

18. 7 if ye do always remember me, ye shall have my Spirit. 11.

20. 9 when the multitude had eaten and drank, they were filled with the Spirit.

Mormon 2. 26 the Spirit of God did not abide in us, and we were weak.

3. 16 manifestations of the Spirit which had testified of things to come.

Ether 2. 15 remember that my Spirit will not always strive with man.

Moroni 6. 9 conduct meetings after the manner of the workings of the Spirit.

Doctrine & Covenants.

Lecture on Faith 2. 24, 25 when the plan of redemption was revealed men began to call on God, and the Holy Spirit was given, bearing record of the Father and the Son.

5. 2 possessing the same mind with the Father, which mind is the Holy Spirit, that bears record of the Father and the Son.

3 partaking of the fulness of the Father and Son, through the Spirit.

Sec. 1. 33 my Spirit shall not always strive with man.

8. 3 this is the Spirit of revelation, by which Moses brought Israel through the sea.

18. 47 I am Jesus Christ, by the power of my Spirit I have spoken it.

19. 23 walk in the meekness of my Spirit.

27. 18 the sword of my Spirit, which I will pour out upon you.

29. 30 first shall be last, last first, in all things created by the power of my Spirit.

31 by the power of my Spirit all things, both temporal and spiritual, were created.

33. 16 the power of my Spirit quickeneth all things.

35. 13 I have called on the weak things of the world, to thresh the nations by the power of my Spirit. 133. 59.

42. 13-17 all teachings to be by the Spirit.

45. 57 who have taken the Holy Spirit for their guide, shall abide the day.

50. 10 come saith the Lord, by the Spirit, let us reason together.

17-21 to impart the truth, it must be preached in the Spirit of truth.

27 the light the Spirit sent, through Jesus Christ, by the will of the Father.

61. 27 to whom is given power to command the waters, is given the Spirit to know all his ways. 28.

63. 32 angry with the wicked, holding my Spirit from the inhabitants of the earth.

64. 16 they sought evil in their hearts, and I withheld my Spirit.

67. 11 no man has seen God in the flesh, except quickened by the Spirit.

71. 1 expounding mysteries of the scriptures, according to the Spirit and power given.

72. 24 they that are appointed by the Spirit, to go up to Zion.

76. 11 J. Smith, Jun., and S. Rigdon, being in the Spirit.

12, 13 by the power of the Spirit our eyes were opened to see those things ordained of the Father before the world was. 18.

28 while yet in the Spirit, the Lord commanded us to write the vision. 80, 113.

83 these are they who deny not the Spirit.

86 receive not of his fulness, but of the Holy Spirit.

118 through manifestations of the Spirit in the flesh, be able to bear his presence.

84. 45-47 whatsoever is light is Spirit. The Spirit enlighteneth every man.

93. 9-11 the Spirit of truth who came into the world. 23.

26 the Spirit of truth is of God; I am the Spirit of truth.

95. 4 bring to pass my strange act; pour out my Spirit on all flesh.

97. 1 I speak unto you with my voice, even the voice of my

Spirit.

105. 36 the voice of the Spirit shall manifest those chosen.

121. 37 when compulsion is used, the Spirit is grieved.

131. 5 more sure word of prophecy, means a man's knowing he is sealed up to eternal life, by the Spirit of prophecy.

136. 33 the Spirit sent forth into the world, to enlighten the humble.

*   *   *   *   *

THE HOLY GHOST.

Bible.

Luke 1. 15 John shall be filled with the Holy Ghost.

67 and his father, Zacharias, was filled with the Holy Ghost.

2. 26 it was revealed to Simeon by the Holy Ghost.

4. 1 Jesus, being full of the Holy Ghost, returned from Jordan.

12. 12 Holy Ghost shall teach you, in the same hour, what ye shall say.

John 14. 26 the Holy Ghost shall teach you all things.

20. 22 he breathed on them, and said, receive ye the Holy Ghost.

Acts 1. 8 ye shall receive power, after the Holy Ghost shall come upon you.

5. 3 why hath Satan filled thy heart to lie to the Holy Ghost?

6. 3 look ye out seven men, full of the Holy Ghost.

8. 15 prayed for them that they might receive the Holy Ghost.

10. 44 the Holy Ghost fell on all them that heard the word.

13. 9 Paul, filled with the Holy Ghost, set his eyes on him. 52.

15. 28 for it seemed good to the Holy Ghost and to us.

16. 6 were forbidden by the Holy Ghost to preach in Asia.

21. 11 thus saith the Holy Ghost, so shall the Jews at Jerusalem.

1 *Cor.* 2. 13 not of men's wisdom, but which the Holy Ghost teacheth.

6. 19 your body is the temple of the Holy Ghost.

2 *Cor.* 13. 14 the communion of the Holy Ghost be with you.

Heb. 3. 7 the Holy Ghost saith, to-day if ye will hear his voice.

2 *Peter* 1. 21 holy men of God spake as they were moved by

the Holy Ghost.

Book of Mormon.

1 *Nephi* 10. 11 Christ should make himself manifest, by the Holy Ghost to the Gentiles.

19 the mysteries of God unfolded by the power of the Holy Ghost.

12. 7 bare record that the Holy Ghost fell on twelve others.

18 the Messiah, of whom the Holy Ghost bear record from the beginning.

2 *Nephi* 26. 13 Christ manifesteth himself, by the power of the Holy Ghost.

31. 12 to him that is baptized will the Father give the Holy Ghost.

13 by baptism ye shall receive the Holy Ghost.

17 then cometh a remission of sins, by fire and the Holy Ghost.

32. 2 had received the Holy Ghost, ye could speak with the tongue of angels.

Jacob 6. 8 deny the gift of the Holy Ghost, and quench the Spirit.

7. 17 Sherem confessed the Christ, and power of the Holy Ghost.

Alma 13. 12 after being sanctified by the Holy Ghost, being pure and spotless.

36. 24 they might be born of God, and filled with the Holy Ghost.

3 *Nephi* 9. 20 whoso comes to me with a contrite spirit, will I baptize with the Holy Ghost.

11. 32 the Holy Ghost bears record of the Father and the Son. 35, 36.

15. 23 Christ not manifest to the Gentiles, except by the Holy Ghost.

16. 4 my people, at Jerusalem, receive a knowledge of you by the Holy Ghost.

20. 27 pouring out the Holy Ghost through me upon the Gentiles, makes them mighty to the scattering of my people.

28. 11 the Father giveth the Holy Ghost to men because of me.

4 *Nephi* 1. 48 being constrained by the Holy Ghost, Ammaron hid up the sacred records.

Mormon 7. 7 sing praises to Father, Son and Holy Ghost.

Ether 5. 4 Father, Son and Holy Ghost beareth record. *Chap.* 12. 41.

12. 23 made this people that they could speak much, because of the Holy Ghost.

Moroni 8. 26 of meekness cometh visitation of the Holy Ghost, which filleth with hope.

Doctrine & Covenants.

Sec. 8. 2 will tell you in your heart and mind, by the Holy Ghost.

18. 18 ask and ye shall receive the Holy Ghost, which manifesteth all things.

20. 26-28 who believed in all the holy prophets, who spake as they were inspired by the Holy Ghost.

35 neither adding to nor diminishing from that which has come, or shall come, by the gift and power of the Holy Ghost.

60 ordination is by the power of the Holy Ghost.

34. 10 prophecy, and it shall be given by the Holy Ghost.

39. 6 the baptism of the Holy Ghost, which showeth all things.

68. 4 what they shall speak, when moved by the Holy Ghost, shall be scripture.

100. 8 the Holy Ghost shall bear record of what you say.

107. 56 Adam, full of the Holy Ghost, predicted what should befall his posterity.

109. 15 that they may receive a fulness of the Holy Ghost.

121. 26 God shall give the Saints knowledge by the Holy Ghost.

43 reproving with sharpness, when moved by the Holy Ghost.

124. 5 given you by the Holy Ghost, to know concerning kings and authorities.

Pearl of Great Price.

Page 9. in that day the Holy Ghost fell upon Adam.

10. the Lord God called upon men, by the Holy Ghost, everywhere.

12. the Gospel declared by the gift of the Holy Ghost.

13. it was given to write by the Spirit of inspiration.

15 my Spirit is upon you, wherefore all thy words will I justify.

19. Holy Ghost fell on many, and they were caught up into Zion.

History of J. Smith, June 15, 1842.

NAME OF CHRIST'S CHURCH.

The name, Saint, "Signifies a holy or godly person, one that is so by profession, covenant, and conversation;" *Cru. Con.*

In the Old Testament it means one who worked righteousness, and one in whom the Lord delighted, for that reason. "But to the Saints that *are* in the earth, and to the excellent, in whom is all my delight;" *Psalm* 16. 3. "Gather my Saints together unto me; those that have made a covenant with me by sacrifice;" *Psalm* 50. 5.

While the meaning of the term Saints is not changed in the New Testament, it is used in the epistles of the apostles as a general name of the followers of Jesus Christ; "To the Saints which are at Ephesus, and to the faithful in Christ Jesus;" *Eph.* 1. 1. They are those who have submitted themselves to Jesus Christ, and have become his subjects. "Just and true are thy ways, thou king of Saints;" *Rev.* 15. 3.

Jesus said, "I am come in my Father's name, and ye receive me not: if another shall come in his own name, him ye will receive;" *John* 5. 43. This saying of our Savior's is as applicable to the Christian world to-day, as it was to the people to whom he spake. The Latter-day Saints have come in the name of Jesus Christ, and preached the Gospel of repentance as he preached it, and do all things in his name, and, yet, the most of the world reject them.

Some Christian sects have derived their names from their founders, as Calvanists, Lutherans, Wesleyans. Others have some appellation growing out of a peculiarity of doctrine, or faith, as Baptists, Methodists and Presbyterians. Others again derive their name from historical events connected with their origin, and geographical location, as Roman Catholic Church, Greek Church, Church of England, etc. Not a church in all the world bearing the name of Jesus Christ, except that of the Latter-day Saints.

Sectarians may ask, are we not called Christians? But the name of our Savior was Jesus Christ, not Christian. The early Christians first received that name at the city of Antioch; *Acts* 11. 26.

We find that the apostles, in their epistles, addressed the members of the various churches, as Saints, "Beloved of God, called to be Saints;" *Rom.* 1. 7. "To the Saints and faithful brethren in Christ;" *Col.* 1. 2. We further find that the apostles do not speak of themselves as followers of men; but Paul calls himself, "An apostle of Jesus Christ by the will of God;" *Col.* 1. 1. 1 *Tim.* 1. 1. "Paul, a servant of God, and an apostle of Jesus Christ, according to the faith of God's elect;" *Titus* 1. 1. Not according to the doctrines of Luther, Calvin or Wesley.

The most definite instructions on this subject are found in the Book of Mormon. When the Nephite disciples of Jesus were, at a certain time, united in mighty prayer and fasting, he came and stood in the midst of them, and asked them, "What will ye that I shall give unto you?" "And they said unto him, Lord, we will that thou wouldst tell us the name whereby we shall call this church; for there are disputations among the people concerning this matter.

"And the Lord said unto them, Verily, verily I say unto you, why is it that the people should murmur and dispute because of this thing? Have they not read the scriptures, which say ye must take upon you the name of Christ, which is my name? For by this name shall ye be called at the last day; and whoso taketh upon him my name, and endureth to the end, the same shall be saved at the last day; therefore whatsoever ye shall do, ye shall do it in my name; therefore ye shall call the church in my name; and ye shall call upon the Father in my name, that he will bless the church for my sake; and how be it my church, save it be called in my name? For if a church be called in Moses' name, then it be Moses' church; or if it be called in the name of a man, then it be the church of a man; but if it be called in my name, then it is my church, if so be that they are built upon my Gospel;" 3 *Nephi* 27. 2-8.

In accordance with the spirit of the Old and New Testaments, and with these instructions of Jesus Christ, when the church was organized on Gospel principles, by Joseph Smith, Jun., in 1830, it was named, "The Church of Jesus Christ." The Lord afterwards revealed to his Prophet, Joseph Smith, that it should be called, "The Church of Jesus Christ of Latter-day Saints;" *Doc. & Cov.* 115. 3, 4.

Bible.

Psalm 16 3. but the Saints that are in the earth.

Book of Mormon.

Mos. 5. 7-12 the disciples of Christ exhorted to take upon them his name.

TITHING.

The history of ancient Israel, as given in the Old Testament, evidences that the law of tithing was in force from Abraham until their destruction as a nation. That it was a perpetual law of the Priesthood, and did not pertain, exclusively, to the Mosaic dispensation, is apparent, from the fact that Abram paid tithes to Melchisedek; *Gen.* 14. 20, and that Jacob covenanted to give a tenth to the Lord; 28. 22. They lived before Moses.

In the present dispensation the law of tithing was revived, and the keeping of that law is one of the first duties of the Latter-day Saints. About eighteen months after the organization of the church, September 11, 1831, the Lord, through Joseph the Seer, made this important declaration. Speaking after the manner of the Lord, he called "to-day," from the giving of the revelation until the coming of the Son of Man, and said, "Verily I say unto you, it is a day of sacrifice, and a day for the tithing of my people; for he that is tithed shall not be burned. For after to-day cometh the burning." That is, at the coming of the Son of Man; "For verily I say, to-morrow"—that is, at my coming—"all the proud and they that do wickedly shall be as stubble; and I will burn them up, for I am the Lord of Hosts;" *Doc. & Cov.* 64. 23, 24.

In this declaration we are assured that all who call themselves the Lord's people, and do not pay their tithing, will find their portion among the wicked at his coming, and will share their fate. In *sec.* 85. 3, the Lord reiterates the fact, that it is necessary his people should be tithed, "To prepare them against the day of vengeance and burning."

The names of those who do not keep this law of tithing shall not be enrolled with the people of God: "Neither is their genealogy to be kept, or to be had where it may be found on any of the records or history of the church; Their names shall not be found, neither the names of the fathers, nor the names of the children written in the book of the law of God, saith the Lord of Hosts;" 85. 4, 5. This revelation was also given soon after the organization of the Church; Nov. 27, 1832.

Like every principle connected with the latter-day work, tithing must needs commence with the leaders of the Dispensation. The following very interesting account of the first covenant and promise concerning this principle will be found in the History of Joseph Smith, under date of Nov. 29, 1834.

The occasion was one of rejoicing for the blessings received of the Lord. The narrative says: "After commencing and rejoicing before the Lord on this occasion, we agreed to enter into the following covenant with the Lord, viz.:—That if the Lord will prosper us in our business, and open the way before us, that we may obtain means to pay our debts, that we be not troubled nor brought into disrepute before the world, nor His people; after that, of all that He shall give us, we will give a tenth, to be bestowed upon the poor in His Church, or as He shall command; and that we will be faithful over that which He has entrusted to our care, that we may obtain much; and that our children after us, shall remember to observe *this sacred and holy covenant*; and that our children, and our children's children, may know of the same, we have subscribed our names with our own hands.

"JOSEPH SMITH, JUN.,
"OLIVER COWDERY."

After the above covenant the following is recorded: "And now, O Father, as thou didst prosper our father Jacob, and bless him with protection and prosperity wherever he went, from the time he made a like covenant before and with thee; as thou didst, even the same night, open the heavens unto him, and manifest great mercy and power, and give him promises, so wilt thou do with us his sons; and as his blessings prevailed above his progenitors unto the utmost bounds of the everlasting hills, even so may our blessings prevail like his."

Notwithstanding this principle began to be taught soon after the organization of the Church, it required some time to reach practical development, for no definite law concerning it was revealed, until July 8, 1838.

The custom of paying labor tithing, appears to have been commenced when building the Nauvoo Temple. Of a meeting of some of the leading authorities of the Church, in Lima, Illinois, the following is recorded, in His. of Joseph Smith, under date of October 23, 1841: "It was moved and seconded, That all those who are willing to consecrate one-tenth of their time and property to the building of the Temple at Nauvoo, under the superintendence of President Morley and Counselors, to signify it by uplifted hands; when the motion was carried unanimously."

The following is a "*Revelation given through Joseph, the Prophet, at Far West, Missouri, July 8th, 1838, in answer to the question, O Lord, show unto thy servants how much thou requirest of the properties of the people for a tithing?*

"Verily, thus saith the Lord, I require all their surplus property to be put into the hands of the bishop of my church of Zion, for the building of mine house, and for the laying of the foundation of Zion and for the Priesthood, and for the debts of the Presidency of my church.

"And this shall be the beginning of the tithing of my people; and after that, those who have thus been tithed, shall pay one-tenth of all their interest annually; and this shall be a standing law unto them for ever, for my holy Priesthood, saith the Lord.

"Verily I say unto you, it shall come to pass, that all those who gather unto the land of Zion shall be tithed of their surplus properties, and shall observe this law, or they shall not be found worthy to abide among you.

"And I say unto you, if my people observe not this law, to keep it holy, and by this law sanctify the land of Zion unto me, that my statutes and my judgments may be kept thereon, that it may be most holy, behold, verily I say unto you, it shall not be a land of Zion unto you; and this shall be an ensample unto all the

Stakes of Zion. Even so. Amen;" *Doc. & Cov. Sec.* 119.

The law of tithing, as embodied in the revelations referred to, is an immutable decree of Jehovah to his people, and admits of no evasion by those who would enjoy the blessings of the faithful on the land of Zion, or be classed among the righteous, and avoid the burning at the coming of our Lord.

Bible.

Lev. 27. 30 the tithe of the land shall be the Lord's.

32 the tenth of the herd and the flock shall be holy.

33 not to search whether it be good or bad, neither shall he change it.

Num. 18. 26-28 the Levites paid a tenth of their tithes to the priests.

Deut. 12. 17, 18 tithes to be eaten in the place the Lord should choose. *Chap.* 14. 23, 24.

28 the tithe of the third year to be laid up.

14. 22, 23 thou shalt surely tithe all he increase of thy seed.

26. 12 hast made an end of tithing all the tithes of thy increase.

2 *Chron.* 31. 5, 6 Israel brought the tithes of all things, abundantly.

Neh. 10. 37, 38 the tithes of Israel were brought to the Levites, and they paid a tenth to the house of the Lord.

13. 12 men appointed over the treasuries of the house of the Lord.

Amos 4. 4 bring your sacrifices every morning, and your tithes after three years.

Mal. 3. 8 wherein have we robbed thee? In tithes and offerings.

10 bring ye all the tithes into the storehouse.

Matt. 23. 23 Pharisees paid tithes, but omitted the weightier matters of the law.

Luke 11. 42 for ye tithe mint and rue, and pass over judgment and the love of God.

18. 12 I fast twice in a week, I give tithes of all I possess.

Heb. 7. 5 the sons of the Levites to take tithes of the people. 6, 8, 9.

See Sermon by B. Young, J. of D., Vol. 1, page 51.

See Sermon by G. Q. Cannon, J. of D., Vol. 15, page 147.

See Sermon by F. D. Richards, J. of D., Vol. 16, page 59.

See Sermon by B. Young, J. of D., Vol. 16, page 111.

APOSTACY OF THE PRIMITIVE CHURCH.

The Gospel dispensation inaugurated by our Savior, while on his earthly mission, was not a gathering one. Israel had already been widely scattered. That scattering was soon to result in the complete desolation of the land of Palestine.

Wherever the people received the Gospel through the preaching of the apostles, they were organized into churches. They not only had their old traditions and customs to contend with, but there was no relief from the general pagan influences under which they had been educated. Add to these things, the persecutions the early Saints were exposed to, and it could not well be otherwise than that many of them should be weak in the faith.

The epistles of the apostles inform us that they had often contended with false teachers and doctrines in the primitive churches. "Even now," said the apostle John, "are there many anti-Christs." 1 *John* 2. 18. The apostle Paul, in his second epistle to Timothy, informs us, that "In the last days perilous times shall come;" 2 *Tim.* 3. 1.

In the following three verses he enumerates all manner of wickedness which shall be prevalent in the latter times. He evidently means in the Christian churches, or among those who profess godliness, for in the fifth verse of the same chapter, he speaks of their having "A form of godliness, but denying the power thereof."

The apostle Paul exhorted the Colossians to "be not moved away from the hope of the Gospel, which ye have heard, and which was preached to every creature which is under heaven;" *Col.* 1. 23.

About fifty-seven years after the Savior had closed his earthly mission, if we are correctly informed in the second and third chapters of the Revelations of St. John, there were but seven churches in Asia whom the Lord considered worthy of notice. This, coupled with the assertion of Paul, that the Gospel had, in his day, been preached to every creature, proves that its light only faintly glimmered, in the otherwise universal darkness, which existed at the time John had his vision on the isle of Patmos.

John the Revelator saw Rome in all her glory, in his day, reigning over the kings of the earth, full of riches and all manner of abominations, and drunken with the blood of the Saints and of the martyrs of Jesus; *Rev.* 17. This great power, drenched in the blood of the martyrs, about 325 A.D., in the reign of Constantine, adopted what was then known as Christianity, as the religion of the empire.

It was not possible that such a wicked, corrupt element and the Gospel of Jesus could have any affinity. Rather, is it not evident that the antagonism of Christianity and paganism had measurably ceased? that they had assimilated? that they had both so nearly found the same level, that with a slight pressure of governmental policy they readily amalgamated?

Not only prophecy but general history, and especially the history of Christianity by its learned professors, furnish abundant evidence of its early departure from the pure principles of the Gospel.

The prophetic history of the preparatory work, for the coming of Christ to reign on the earth in the latter days, is predicated on the apostacy of the primitive Christian church, the general wickedness of the nations, and the gathering of the house of Israel.

Since the calling of Abraham, the authenticated personal manifestations of the Lord to man have been through him and his family. Christ came to his own chosen people. His earthly mission was commenced and consummated in the midst of Israel. The Gospel was first preached to the Jews. His apostles were chosen from his brethren of the seed of Abraham. The first church of Christ was established at Jerusalem. The apostles were commanded to remain there until endowed with power from on high. All the blessings of salvation are promised to mankind through the seed of Abraham.

When the Lord comes in glory and power, the prophets inform us that he will come to Zion and Jerusalem, the chief cities of gathered Israel. The apostle Paul informs us that "God hath set some in the church, first apostles, secondarily prophets, thirdly teachers, after that miracles, then gifts of healings, helps, governments, diversities of tongues;" 1 *Cor.* 12. 28.

From the above it is evident that, had the church of Christ been on the earth in the past centuries, it would have been organized like the primitive church, with apostles and prophets of the house of Israel at the head of it. More than that, it would have enjoyed all the spiritual gifts and blessings mentioned in the above chapter.

John the Revelator, in his visions of the latter times, says, "And I saw another angel fly in the midst of heaven, having the everlasting Gospel to preach unto them that dwell on the earth, and to every nation, and kindred, and tongue, and people;" *Rev.* 14. 6.

No one who has any faith in the Scriptures would assert that the Gospel preached by Jesus and his apostles was not the "Everlasting Gospel." If everlasting, it must of necessity be the same wherever found. If the same Gospel, it would always produce the same results. Its ordinances would be the same. Its followers would enjoy the same gifts and blessings. They would call themselves Saints. They would have an organization that would not vary from the church organized by Jesus and his apostles. They would have been led by apostles and prophets of the house of Israel.

Instead of this, the Christian churches and nations have for many centuries ground the House of Israel with the iron heel of oppression. They have robbed, driven and slain the covenant people of God, the chosen people of that same Jesus of Nazareth whose precepts and example they profess to follow.

The Shiloh came and the sceptre departed from Judah. A series of terrible oppressions commenced under Roman governors, which resulted in the destruction of Jerusalem, and of the Jews as a nation; that may be considered the beginning of the fulfilment of the prediction of our Savior, "Jerusalem shall be trodden down of the Gentiles, until the times of the Gentiles be fulfilled;" *Luke* 21. 24.

The reasonable construction of this passage is, that "The times of the Gentiles" means the period in which they will bear rule, oppress Israel, and hold possession of the heritage of the seed of Abraham.

When "The times of the Gentiles shall be fulfilled," when the angel, seen in vision by John the Revelator, shall have brought again to earth the "Everlasting Gospel," will also be "The times of restitution of all things, which God hath spoken by the mouth of all his holy prophets since the world began;" *Acts* 3. 21.

The first century of the Christian era was a very important one in the world's history. The covenant people of God ceased to exist as a nation. The civilized world, represented by the Roman empire, with Paganism as the prevailing religion, began to fill up the measure of its iniquity by shedding the blood of the apostles, and of the disciples of Jesus. Pagan philosophy counteracted Gospel influences. There was a constant tendency in Christianity and paganism to assimilate. This is evident from the writings of the apostles.

That, after Christianity became the leading element of the Roman empire, it ceased to be regenerative in its nature, is evidenced by the fact, that the empire was often scourged with destructive civil wars which prepared it for dissolution. It was finally crushed by barbarian hordes. They desolated whole provinces, leaving only remnants of corrupt peoples, to be measurably regenerated by an infusion of new blood from the plains of eastern Europe, and western Asia. Both sacred and profane history have failed to record an instance of a people who, living under the regenerating influences of the Gospel of Jesus, and enjoying the favor of God, were broken and destroyed by such terrible scourges as visited the Roman empire the first five centuries of the Christian era. Modern nations have risen from its ashes, have adopted its religion, its customs, its ethics, without inspiration from heaven, without any further Gospel dispensation, without apostles and prophets of the house of Israel, and without the guidance of the Holy Priesthood, after the order of the Son of God, which the Lord has decreed should only come through the seed of Abraham.

Bible.

Isa. 24. 2 as with the people, so with the priest.

5 the earth also is defiled under the inhabitants thereof.

17 fear and the pit are upon thee, O inhabitants of the earth.

Dan. 7. 25 he shall speak great words against the Most High, and shall wear out the Saints.

8. 10 it waxed great, even to the host of heaven.

11 by him the daily sacrifice was taken away.

12 it cast down the truth to the ground, and it practised and prospered.

23 the latter time of their kingdom, when the transgressors are come to the full.

25 through his policy he shall cause craft to prosper in his hand. 26.

Matt. 24. 10 many shall be offended, and shall betray and hate one another.

Acts 20. 29 after my departure shall grievous wolves enter in among you. 30.

1 *Tim.* 1. 6 some have turned aside to vain jangling. 7.

19 concerning faith have made shipwreck.

4. 1 in the latter times some shall depart from the faith.

2, 3 speaking lies in hypocrisy, forbidding to marry.

2 *Tim.* 2. 18 who concerning the truth have erred.

3. 1 know also, that in the last days perilous times shall come.

2-7 men shall be lovers of their own selves, without natural affection. Ever learning and never able to come to a knowledge of the truth.

12 all that will live Godly in Christ Jesus shall suffer persecution.

4. 16 at my first answer no man stood with me.

Titus 1. 10, 11 many unruly and vain talkers, deceivers, who subvert whole houses.

3. 9 avoid foolish questions, contentions, and strivings. 10.

2 *Peter* 2. 1 who, privily, shall bring in damnable heresies.

Rev. 16. 6 for they have shed the blood of the Saints and prophets.

17. 1, 2 the great whore that sitteth upon the waters. *Chap.* 18. 3, 9.

5 the mystery, Babylon, the mother of harlots.

6 the woman, drunken with the blood of the Saints, and the martyrs of Jesus.

15 the waters which thou sawest are peoples, multitudes and nations.

18 the woman is that great city which reigneth over the kings of the earth.

18. 2 Babylon is become the habitation of devils, the hold of every foul spirit.

24 in her was found the blood of the prophets.

19. 2 he hath judged the great whore which did corrupt the earth.

Book of Mormon.

1 *Nephi* 13. 5 the foundation of a church which is most abominable, which slayeth the Saints of God. *Chap.* 14. 3, 9, 10. *Chap.* 22. 14. 2 *Nephi* 28. 18.

9 for the praise of the world they destroy the Saints.

24-34 the Jewish record went forth in purity to the Gentiles, but the Gentiles took away the most precious parts, for which reason many stumble.

14. 11 she had dominion over all the earth, and sat upon many waters.

12 the Saints of God were scattered over the earth, and their dominions were small, because of the wickedness of the great whore.

13 mother of abominations gathered together multitudes to fight against the Lamb of God.

15 the wrath of God poured out on that abominable church. 16, 17.

15. 13 many generations after the Messiah shall be manifested in the body, the fulness of the Gospel shall come to the Gentiles.

22. 22, 23 the kingdom of the devil built up among the children of men.

2 *Nephi* 26. 19-22 refers to the time when the children of Lehi (the American Indians) shall be smitten and driven by the Gentiles, and gives an unmistakable description of the Christian world of the present day.

27. 1 in the latter days, all shall be drunken with iniquity.

28. 3 every one that hath built up churches, and not unto the Lord, shall say, I am the Lord's.

4 they and their priests shall contend one with another.

6 they shall say, in this day God is not a God of miracles.

29. 3 a Bible, we have got a Bible; there cannot be any more.

3 *Nephi* 16. 7 in the latter days shall the truth come unto the Gentiles. 1 *Nephi* 15. 13. *Rev.* 14. 6.

Doctrine & Covenants.

Sec. 1. 15 they have strayed from mine ordinances and broken mine everlasting covenant.

16 every man walketh in his own way, after the image of his own God.

17, 18 Joseph Smith, Jun., and others commanded to proclaim these things, that the sayings of the prophets might be fulfilled.

30 to bring forth the only true and living church, out of obscurity and darkness.

5. 6 you shall be ordained to deliver my words to the children of men.

29. 21 that great and abominable church shall be cast down.

35. 11 shall not anything be shown forth except desolations on Babylon?

38. 11 for all flesh is corrupted before me.

86. 1-7 an explanation of the parable of the wheat and tares. *Sec.* 88. 94.

133. 14 go ye out from among the nations, even from Babylon.

Pearl of Great Price.

Page 3. in a day when men would take many of the words from the book which Moses should write, the Lord promised to raise up another like him, when they should be had again among men. 2 *Nephi* 3. 9.

21. so will I come in the last days, in the days of wickedness and vengeance.

See O. Spencer's Letters to Rev. Wm. Crowel, No. 6.

"Universal Apostacy," a pamphlet by O. Pratt.

THE JERUSALEM OF THE EASTERN HEMISPHERE.

The earliest account we have of Jerusalem is in the fourteenth chapter of Genesis, under the date of 1913 B. C.

When Abram was returning from the slaughter of the five kings, Melchisedek, king of Salem, brought him refreshments. He was a righteous prince and a priest of the Most High God; and he blessed Abram.

Josephus, the Jewish historian, states that this city of Salem was afterwards called Jerusalem; *Ant. of the Jews, B. 1., Chapter* 10. It has been the scene of many great events connected with the ministry of the holy Priesthood on the earth.

Abram was commanded to offer his son Isaac, on one of the mountains in the land of Moriah; *Gen.* 22. 2. Josephus says, that the mountain on which Abram built an altar, to offer his son Isaac, was the same on which king David (Solomon) afterwards built a temple.

The Jebusites retained possession of the city of Jerusalem until 1048 B. C., when it was subdued by David. He first took the stronghold of Zion; "The same is the city of David." At that time, this was only a strong outwork or fortification for the defence of the city; 2 *Sam.* 5. 6-9.

In the days of Solomon, Jerusalem became a great and strong city, with a magnificent temple towering on Mount Moriah.

From its conquest by David, until the death of Solomon, it was the capital city of Israel, and afterwards of the kingdom of Judah. B. C. 585, Jerusalem was burned by the army of Nebuchadnezzar, and the better part of the inhabitants of the land were carried captive to Babylon; 3 *Kings, chapters* 24 and 25.

The city was re-established at the end of the seventy years' captivity. It afterwards played an important part in the history of that part of Asia.

Almost under the shadow of its walls, our Savior was born. It was the central place of the scenes of his earthly mission. In it he was scourged and condemned to death. Just outside of its walls, and in sight of its towers, and the glorious temple built to his name, the God of Israel died the death of a malefactor.

It was here, and near here, that he consummated his earthly mission, and ascended to his Father.

In A. C. 70, the land of Judea, and city of Jerusalem, were made a desolation by the Roman armies, and the Jews, as a nation, entirely rooted out of their heritage, and scattered among all nations.

For information on this subject, the student should read, carefully, Josephus' *"Wars of the Jews."*

Up to this time, in her history, many prophecies were fulfilled. In her future many more are to be fulfilled, for she is yet to take an important part in the great work of the latter days. Like the New Jerusalem of the American continent, this city will descend out of heaven, after the final change of the earth to its celestial condition; *Rev.* 21. 10-27.

It is often called Zion in the Old Testament, and will be the capital city of gathered Israel on the Eastern hemisphere, in the latter days.

There are many passages in the Scriptures relating to this important city. A few are appended to assist the student in further researches concerning it.

Bible.

Deut. 31. 29 evil will befall you in the latter days, because ye will do evil.

1 *Kings* 11. 11-13 Lord declared he would rend the kingdom from Solomon.

14. 15 Lord shall root up Israel, and scatter them beyond the river.

2 *Kings* 20. 17, 18 treasures laid up by the fathers, to be carried to Babylon.

23. 27 I will remove Judah out of my sight, as I have removed Israel.

2 *Chron.* 36. 21 the land shall enjoy her Sabbaths seventy years. *Jer.* 29. 10.

Isa. 4. this chapter evidently refers to the latter days, and to the Zion of the Western Hemisphere, and to the city of Jerusalem, on the Eastern.

25. 6-12 in this mountain shall the Lord make a feast of fat things. He will destroy the face of the covering cast over all people, He will swallow up death in victory.

32. 9-18 land of Israel to be desolate, until the Spirit is poured out from on high.

52. 9, 10 sing together, ye waste places of Jerusalem.

51. 17 stand up, O Jerusalem, which has drunk of the cup of his fury.

Jer. 25. 11 these nations shall serve the king of Babylon seventy years.

18 to make Jerusalem and her kings a desolation, and a curse.

26. 18 Micah prophesied that Zion should be plowed like a field.

50. 4 in those days Israel and Judah, together, shall come, going and weeping.

51. 19-23 Israel the rod of the Lord's inheritance, with which he will break in pieces their enemies.

Ezek. 38 and 39. these chapters are a prophecy of the gathering of the nations against Jerusalem in the latter days.

Zeph. 1. this chapter is, evidently, a prophecy of the desolation of Jerusalem.

Haggai 2. 9 the glory of this latter house, shall be greater than that of the former.

Zech. 12. the restoration of Judah.

Chap. 14. in the latter days the Lord will deliver Jerusalem from the nations that will go up to battle against it.

Matt. 24. Destruction of Jerusalem foretold. *P. of G. P., page* 38.

Luke 19. 41-44 Christ foretells the destruction of Jerusalem. *Chap.* 23. 28-30.

See Article, by C. W. Penrose, Mil. Star, Vol. 30, page 353.

"New Jerusalem," a pamphlet by O. Pratt.

NEW JERUSALEM.

The Jaredite prophet, Ether, predicted, 600 B. C., that a city which should be called a holy city, should be built on the land of North America, and that it should be built up unto the remnant of the seed of Joseph. He further informs us, that it should be called the New Jerusalem, to distinguish it from Jerusalem which should be built on the eastern hemisphere; *Ether* 13. 3-8.

Ether also saw that this New Jerusalem was the one that John the Revelator saw, in vision, coming down out of heaven. "Until the end come, when the earth shall pass away, and there shall be a new heaven and a new earth; and they shall be like unto the old, save the old have passed away, and all things have become new. And then cometh the New Jerusalem;" *verses* 8-10. *Rev.* 21. 2.

Our Savior, in his personal ministration among the Nephites, six hundred years after the predictions of Ether, renews the promise that a New Jerusalem should be built upon this land.

Speaking to the Nephites, he says: "This people will I establish in this land, unto the fulfilling of the covenant which I made with your father Jacob; and it shall be a New Jerusalem;" 3 *Nephi* 20. 22.

The Savior again says, speaking to the Gentiles, that those who shall come into the covenant, shall "be numbered among this the remnant of Jacob." "And they shall assist my people, the remnant of Jacob, and also, as many of the house of Israel as shall come, that they may build a city, which shall be called the New Jerusalem; and then shall they assist my people that they may be gathered in, who are scattered upon all the face of the land in unto the New Jerusalem;" 21. 22-24.

We learn from the Book of Doctrine and Covenants, that this New Jerusalem is to be the city of Zion, of the latter days. "And it shall be called the New Jerusalem, a land of peace, a city of refuge, a place of safety for the Saints of the most High God; And the glory of the Lord shall be there, and the terror of the Lord also shall be there, insomuch that the wicked will not come unto it, and it shall be called Zion;" *Doc. & Cov.* 45. 66, 67.

This is, also, the Zion spoken of by the ancient Jewish prophets, as separate and distinct from the Zion, or Mount Zion, that was in Jerusalem, in the land of Palestine.

In the following passages, evidently, two distinct places are intended. "Zion is a wilderness, Jerusalem a desolation;" *Isa.* 64. 10. "For the law shall go forth of Zion, and the word of the Lord from Jerusalem;" *Micah* 4. 2.

There are three Zions spoken of in the sacred writings—the Zion on the American continent, the Zion at Jerusalem, and the Zion of Enoch. For some account of the Zion of Enoch, *see Pearl of Great Price, pages* 18-22. On the 22d page we learn, that, when Christ shall come, the Zion of the western hemisphere and the Zion of Enoch shall be united in one. There the Lord will reside, and it will be the gathered Zion "which shall come forth out of all the creations which I have made."

Bible.

Psalm 14. 7 oh that the salvation of Israel were come out of Zion!

48. 2 beautiful for situation is Mount Zion, on the sides of the north. 11-14.

Isa. 1. 27 Zion shall be redeemed with judgment.

2. 3 out of Zion shall go forth the law, and the word of the Lord from Jerusalem.

40. 9 O Zion that bringest good tidings, get thee up into the high mountain.

49. 19-26 the land of thy destruction shall be too narrow. I will lift up mine hand to the Gentiles. Kings shall be thy nursing fathers. I will feed them that oppress thee with their own flesh.

51. 11 the redeemed of the Lord shall come to Zion.

52. 1 put on thy strength, O Zion.

59. 20 and the Redeemer shall come to Zion.

64. 10 Zion is a wilderness, Jerusalem a desolation.

Jer. 3. 14 will take you one of a city and two of a family, and bring you to Zion.

31. 6-14 arise, let us go up to Zion. Behold, I will bring them from the north country. They shall come with weeping. They shall come and sing in the heights of Zion. The virgin shall rejoice in the dance.

50. 4, 5 the children of Israel shall come, they and the children of Judah together. They shall ask the way to Zion, with their faces thitherward.

Joel 2. 32 for in Mount Zion, and in Jerusalem, shall be deliverance.

3. 16 the Lord shall roar out of Zion, and utter his voice from Jerusalem.

Obad. 21. Saviors shall come up on Mount Zion.

Zeph. 3. 14 sing, O daughter of Zion, rejoice, O daughter of Jerusalem.

16 said to Jerusalem, fear not; and to Zion, let not thine hands

be slack.

Zech. 1. 17 the Lord shall yet comfort Zion, and choose Jerusalem.

2. 10, 11 the Lord will dwell in the midst of Zion, and many nations shall be joined to him.

Rom. 11. 26 there shall come out of Zion the Deliverer.

Rev. 14. 1 a Lamb stood on Mount Zion.

Doctrine & Covenants.

Sec. 28. 9 no man knoweth where the city shall be built.

35. 24 Zion shall rejoice upon the hills and flourish. 39. 13. *Sec.* 49. 25.

38. 4 have taken the Zion of Enoch into my own bosom.

42. 9 shall be revealed when the New Jerusalem shall be prepared. 35, 62, 67.

48. 4, 5 the place for the city to be revealed to certain men.

57. 2 Missouri the place for the city of Zion. 3, 14.

58. 7 bearing record of the land on which the Zion of God shall stand.

59. 3 blessed are they whose feet stand upon the land of Zion.

63. 24 should assemble themselves together on the land of Zion.

29-31 land of Zion to be obtained by purchase, or by blood. 36.

64. 34 the obedient shall eat the good of the land of Zion.

68. 25 inasmuch as parents have children in Zion.

29 the inhabitants of Zion shall keep the Sabbath day holy. 30-32.

72. 15 every man that cometh to Zion must lay all things before the bishop.

76. 66 there are they who are come unto Mount Zion.

82. 13 Kirtland consecrated for a stake of Zion. 14. *Sec.* 94. 1. *Sec.* 96. 1.

85. 1 duty of the Lord's clerk to record what transpires in Zion.

89. 1 a word of wisdom for the church and Saints in Zion.

90. 8 that they might be perfected in their ministry, for the salvation of Zion.

93. 53 obtain a knowledge of history, countries, lands, etc., for the salvation of Zion.

97. 10 my will that an house be built in Zion, like the pattern given.

21 this is Zion, the pure in heart. 25.

100. 13 Zion shall be redeemed, although she is chastened for a little season.

101. 18 the pure in heart shall return to build up Zion. 19-21, 41.

70-75 land around the land of Zion to be bought with money. 103. 22-24.

103. 15-20 the redemption of Zion must needs come by power.

29-35 concerning the redemption of Zion, by gathering together the strength of Israel.

105. 5 Zion must be built according to the law of the celestial kingdom.

124. 2 Nauvoo planted as a corner stone of Zion. 6. 60.

136. 18 Zion shall be redeemed in mine own due time.

31 Saints to be tried, that they may receive the glory of Zion.

SPIRITUAL GIFTS.

In the churches established by our Savior and his apostles, the Holy Ghost manifested itself in the development of a variety of gifts. Of so great importance did the apostle Paul consider these gifts, to the well being and edification of the Saints in Rome, that he wrote, "For I long to see you, that I may impart unto you some spiritual gift, to the end ye may be established;" *Rom.* 1. 11.

The inspired writings do not indicate that these gifts were limited to any period of time, or to any one dispensation, but they are spoken of by the apostles, as ever characterizing the operations of the Holy Spirit.

In the twelfth chapter of the apostle Paul's first epistle to the Corinthians, we are assured that "there are diversities of gifts by the same spirit;" *verse* 4. "But the manifestation of the Spirit is given to every man to profit withal;" *verse* 7. From this we learn that the presence of the Spirit in a man is manifested by some gift. It is evident from the general tenor of this chapter, that these gifts will always be manifest in the church of Christ, for its members will ever have the Holy Ghost abiding in them, and, where that is, the gifts of the Spirit will be manifest.

The Book of Mormon speaks very plainly of the necessity of these gifts in the church. "Again I speak unto you, who deny the revelations of God, and say that they are done away, that there are no revelations, nor prophecies, nor gifts, nor healing, nor speaking with tongues, and the interpretation of tongues. Behold I say unto you, he that denieth these things, knoweth not the Gospel of Christ; yea, he has not read the scriptures; if so, he does not understand them;" *Mormon* 9, 7, 8.

In a revelation to Joseph, the prophet, given March 8, 1831, the Lord gives much instruction concerning spiritual gifts; "For all have not every gift given unto them; for there are many gifts, and to every man is given a gift by the Spirit of God;" *Doc. & Cov.* 46. 11. The Lord also adds, "That unto some it may be given to have all these gifts, that there may be a head;" *verse* 29.

Bible.

1 *Cor.* 1. 7 so that ye may come behind in no gift.

7. 7 every man hath his proper gift of God.

12. 8 to one is given the word of wisdom, to another the word of knowledge.

9 to another faith, to another the gift of healing by the same Spirit.

10 to another the working of miracles, to another prophecy.

11 but all worketh that one and the self-same Spirit.

31 covet earnestly the best gifts.

13. 2 though I have the gift of prophecy.

14. 1 desire spiritual gifts, but rather that ye may prophecy.

12 forasmuch as ye are zealous of spiritual gifts.

1 *Peter* 4. 10 as every man hath received the gift, so minister.

Book of Mormon.

Omni 1. 25 believe in the gift of speaking with tongues, and interpreting tongues.

Alma 9. 21 having the spirit of prophecy and revelation.

3 *Nephi* 29. 6 shall say the Lord no longer worketh by prophecy, nor gifts.

Moroni 10. 9-19 an enumeration of spiritual gifts.

Doctrine & Covenants.

Sec. 46. 10-26 an enumeration of spiritual gifts.

27 it is given to those ordained to watch over the church to discern all these gifts. 29.

See A Pamphlet by O. Pratt.

PRE-EXISTENCE OF SPIRITS.

In the first chapter of Genesis, we have an account of six days, or periods of time, which God occupied in the creation of this earth. According to the traditions of many centuries, it is considered by the Christian world a history of the creation of this earth, as it appears now, naturally to men who dwell upon it.

From the first and second chapters of Genesis, taken together, this view of the subject is evidently erroneous. In the first verse of the second chapter we read; "Thus the heavens and the earth were finished, and all the host of them." This creation is evidently in a very unfinished condition, for myriads of animal and vegetable life are coming upon it and going to decay.

The sacred writings not only testify that it is in a very imperfect condition, but that it must pass away and be changed into a more perfect earth.

In the second and third verses of the second chapter, we learn that there was a period of time called the seventh day, and that the Lord sanctified it as a day of rest. If there has ever been a period of time in which this earth, or its inhabitants, have had universal peace and rest, since the progenitors of the race partook of the forbidden fruit in the Garden of Eden, we have no account of it. "These are the generations of the heavens and of the earth when they were created, in the day that the Lord God made the earth and the heavens;" *verse* 4. This passage certainly states, that everything had been completed in the period of time stated in the previous account. Verse five very plainly states, in connection with the previous verse, that every plant of the field was created, "Before it was in the earth, and every herb of the field before it grew." During all this long period of time it had not rained upon the earth. What is still more singular, it says, "And there was not a man to till the ground."

This Mosaic history of the creation was written for men in their present temporal condition, and it is evident that these two verses give us to understand, that these things had not taken place naturally upon the earth, as they do now. As a sequence, when they did take place, they would indicate a great change in the condition of the earth. The first indication of this change is given in the sixth verse, "There went up a mist from the earth and watered the whole face of the ground."

Before the event mentioned in the seventh verse, the earth must have been fitted up for the abode of man, in this his natural or temporal condition. "And the Lord God formed man of the dust of the ground, and breathed into his nostrils the breath of life." That is, the ground furnished the elements for the growth of the body of this first temporal man; from its first conception, or germ, until it matured into perfect manhood by a universal law.

It should be noticed, that, in the first chapter, *verse* 27, it says, "God created man." That is he organized from the spiritual elements, the living, acting spiritual man. In the seventh verse of the second chapter, it only states that he formed man out of the ground. That is out of earthly elements he formed a tabernacle, a dwelling place for the man whom he had before created. The prophet Joseph Smith, in his translation of the Mosaic account of creation, fills up this gap, which is so evident in the Bible Genesis, between the seventh day of rest, and the formation of man from the dust of the ground.

"For I, the Lord God, created all things, of which I have spoken, spiritually, before they were naturally upon the face of the earth. For I, the Lord God, had not caused it to rain upon the face of the earth. And I, the Lord God, had created all the children of men; and not yet a man to till the ground; for in heaven created I them; and there was not yet flesh upon the earth; neither in the water, neither in the air; but I, the Lord God, spake, and there went up a mist from the earth, and watered the whole face of the ground. And I, the Lord God, formed man from the dust of the ground, and breathed into his nostrils the breath of life; and man became a living soul, the first flesh upon the earth, the first man also; nevertheless, all things were before created; but, spiritually, were they created and made according to my word;" *P. of G. P. page* 6.

This account of the creation, plainly sets forth the comprehensive fact, that all temporal organizations, pertaining to this earth, are animated by spiritual pre-existent organizations. The following is a very comprehensive passage on this subject: "When the Most High divided to the nations their inheritance, when he separated the sons of Adam, he set the bounds of the people according to the number of the children of Israel;" *Deut.* 32. 8. This passage certainly refers to a very early period, when the heritage of the nations was given in proportion to the numbers of Israel. It is difficult to conceive how their numbers were then known unless there was a spiritual Israel, of which the temporal is but the counterpart.

The sacred writings abound with evidences that Jesus Christ controlled the earth and ministered to man, as an organized spiritual intelligence before he came in the flesh in the meridian of time. The first chapter of John is very pointed on this subject: "In the beginning was the Word, and the Word was with God, and the Word was God;" *verse* 1. "And the Word was made flesh, and dwelt among us;" *verse* 14.

Bible.

Num. 16. 22 the God of the spirits of all flesh. *Chap.* 27. 16.

Job 12. 10 in whose hand is the soul of every living thing.

38. 3, 7 where wert thou when I laid the foundations of the earth? who hath laid the corner stone thereof when the morning stars sang together?

Eccl. 12. 7 the spirit shall return to God who gave it.

Jer. 1. 5 before I formed thee in the belly I knew thee.

John 6. 62 if ye shall see the Son of man ascend up where he was before.

9. 2 who did sin, this man or his parents, that he was born blind?

16. 27 and have believed that I came out from God.

28 I came forth from the Father. 30.

17. 5 glorify me with the glory I had with thee before the world was.

Heb. 1. 6 when he bringeth the First Begotten into the world.

12. 9 shall we not much rather be subject to the Father of our spirits?

Rev. 12. 7-12 the devil and his angels cast out of heaven.

Book of Mormon.

1 *Nephi* 13. 33-37 many sayings of the Lamb of God, concerning the future of Israel, repeated to Nephi by an angel—600 B. C.

17. 30 their Lord, their God, their Redeemer going before them.

19. 10 the God of our fathers yielded himself, as a man, into the hands of wicked men.

20. 17 thus saith the Lord thy Redeemer, the Holy One of Israel.

21. 26 all flesh shall know that I am the Lord thy Savior and Redeemer.

2 *Nephi* 6. 18 know that I, the Lord, am thy Savior and Redeemer.

9. 5 it behooveth the great Creator that he suffereth himself to become subject to man in the flesh, that all men might be subject to him.

11. 2 for he verily saw my Redeemer, as I have seen him. 3.

7 but there is a God, and he is Christ.

25. 12 Father of heaven and earth shall manifest himself to them in the flesh.

Mos. 3. 5 the Lord omnipotent shall come down from heaven among men.

8 he shall be called Jesus Christ, the Creator of all things from the beginning.

4. 2 Jesus Christ, who created heaven and earth and all things.

7. 27 because he said Christ was God, the Father of all things.

13. 33, 34 the prophets prophesied that God should come down among men.

15. 1 God, himself, shall come among men and redeem his people.

Hel. 14. 12 Jesus Christ the Father of heaven and earth. *Chap.* 16. 18.

3 *Nephi* 1. 12-14 this night shall the sign be given, and on the morrow come I into the world.

9. 15 I created the heavens and the earth and all things.

Ether 2. 12 if they will serve Christ, who is the God of the land.

3. 6-20 an account of a remarkable manifestation of Jesus Christ as God the Son, and the Father, but still a personage of spirit.

12. 22 the Lord hath commanded me, even Jesus Christ.

Doctrine & Covenants.

Sec. 10. 57 I came to my own and they received me not.

29. 36 the devil, who was before Adam, rebelled against Christ.

38. 1-3 Jesus Christ looked on the wide expanse of eternity, and the hosts of heaven before the worlds were made, and all things came by him. 4.

76. 13 Jesus Christ in the bosom of the Father from the beginning.

24 by him, of him, through him, the worlds were made.

86. 9 lawful heirs, and have been hid from the world, with Christ in God.

93. 23 ye were also in the beginning with the Father.

See Sermon by O. Pratt, J. of D., Vol. 14, page 233.

See Sermon by O. Pratt, J. of D., Vol. 15, page 241.

PLURALITY OF GODS.

The passages are numerous in the inspired writings which indicate a plurality of Gods. In the account of creation, in the Book of Abraham, the plural Gods is exclusively used; *P. of G. P. page* 33.

The Psalmist, speaking of God, says: "Thou lovest righteousness, and hatest wickedness: therefore God, thy God, hath anointed thee with the oil of gladness above thy fellows;" *Psalm* 45. 7. It is not possible that any other than the true God is here referred to, for the God that was anointed above his fellows had loved righteousness and hated iniquity. "God standeth in the congregation of the mighty; he judgeth among the Gods;" 82. 1. In this passage the number of Gods among whom God judgeth is indefinite, and the words, "congregation of the mighty," indicate that they might be quite numerous.

John, the Evangelist, opens his history of our Savior thus; "In the beginning was the Word, and the Word was with God, and the Word was God;" 1. 1. In this passage we have an account of two Gods, one of which dwelt with the other in the beginning. That the "Word," spoken of, is Jesus Christ is evident from *verse* 14: "And the Word was made flesh, and dwelt among us."

"Which in his times he shall shew, *who is* the blessed and only Potentate, the King of kings, and Lord of Lords;" 1 *Tim.* 6. 15. From the context of this passage we learn that the kings and lords here referred to were holy men. Of like significance is the following: "And hath made us kings and priests unto God and his Father;" *Rev.* 1. 6. That is to God and the Father of God.

"A Lamb stood on the Mount Sion, and with him an hundred forty *and* four thousand, having his Father's name written in their foreheads;" 14. 1. From the third verse we learn that these were redeemed from the earth. Whether this name of the Father of Jesus Christ was God, or some other title indicating his power and attributes, is not revealed to us, but, whatever it was, it evidently identified those who received it as Gods.

Bible.

Gen. 1. 26 and God said, let us make man in our image.

Exo. 15. 11 who is like unto thee, O Lord, among the gods.

Deut. 10. 17 Lord your God is God of gods, and Lord of lords.

Josh. 22. 22 the Lord God of gods. Israel he shall know.

1 *Chron.* 16. 25 great is the Lord, to be feared above all gods.

2 Chron. 2. 5 for great is our God, above all gods.

Psalm 86. 8 among the gods, there is none like unto thee, O Lord.

126. 2, 3 O give thanks to the God of gods.

138. 1 before the gods will I sing praise unto thee.

Dan. 2. 11 none can shew it before the king, except the gods.

47 your God is a God of gods, and a Lord of kings.

4. 8 in whom is the Spirit of the holy Gods.. *Chap.* 5. 14.

11. 36 and shall speak marvellous things against the God of gods.

Matt. 5. 48 be ye perfect, as your Father in heaven is perfect.

John 5. 19 the Son doeth nothing except what he seeth the Father do.

1 Cor. 8. 5 for though there be that are called gods.

Phil. 3. 21 that it may be fashioned like unto his glorious body.

1 Tim. 6. 15 who is the King of kings and Lord of lords.

1 John 3. 2 when he shall appear we shall be like him.

Rev. 3. 21 to him that overcometh, will I grant to sit on my throne.

14. 1 with him 144,000, having his Father's name in their foreheads.

17. 14 for he is Lord of lords, and King of kings.

20. 4 I saw thrones, and they that sat upon them.

21. 7 he that overcometh shall inherit all things.

Book of Mormon.

Alma 12. 31 becoming as Gods, knowing good and evil.

3 Nephi 27. 27 what manner of men ought ye to be? verily I say unto you, even as I am.

28. 10 ye shall be as I am, and I, even as the Father.

Doctrine & Covenants.

Sec. 35. 2 one in me, even as I am one in the Father.

39. 4 as many as received me, gave I power to become my sons.

76. 24 worlds were created, and the inhabitants begotten sons and daughters of God.

55-59 have received of his fulness and glory; they are Gods.

94, 95 know as they are known; and he makes them equal in power and dominion.

84. 35-39 receiveth me, receiveth my Father and his kingdom.

93. 20 be glorified in me, as I am in the Father.

121. 28 whether there be one God or many Gods, they shall be manifest.

32 in the midst of the council of the eternal God of all other Gods.

128. 23 proclaiming in our ears eternal life, kingdoms, principalities and powers.

132. 17 and from henceforth are not Gods. but angels of God, forever. 18.

19 shall pass by the angels and the Gods which are set there.

37 entered into their exaltation; sit upon thrones, and are not angels but Gods.

History of Joseph Smith, June 16, 1844.

*   *   *   *   *

GOD A PERSONAGE.
Bible.

Gen. 1. 25-27 man created in the image of God.

3. 9, 10 Adam heard the voice of the Lord.

4. 6 the Lord said unto Cain. 14.

5. 1, 2 Lord created man male and female, in his own likeness.

6. 6 it repented and grieved the Lord that he had made man.

13-21 God talked with Noah. *Chap.* 7. 1-4. *Chap.* 9. 8.

8. 1 God remembered Noah. 15, 21. *Chap.* 9, 16.

11. 5 the Lord came down to see the city and the tower. 7.

12. 7 the Lord appeared to Abraham. *Chap.* 17. 22.

Chap. 18. the Lord ate and talked with Abraham.

28. 13 the Lord stood above the ladder Jacob saw.

32. 30 Jacob saw God face to face. 35. 13.

Exo. 3. 6 Moses was afraid to look on God.

15. 3 the Lord is a man of war. 8, 16, 17.

24. 10, 11 they saw God and did eat and drink. 12.

31. 18 the tables of testimony, written with the finger of God.

33. 11 the Lord talked with Moses as one man speaks with a friend.

23 thou shalt see my back parts, but not my face.

Num. 12. 8 with him will I speak, mouth to mouth.

35. 34 for I, the Lord, dwell among the children of Israel.

Deut. 5. 15 the Lord's mighty hand and stretched out arm.

2 *Sam.* 22. 16 the breath of his nostrils. *Job* 1. 11. *Chap.* 89. 20.

2 *Chron.* 16. 9 the eyes of the Lord run to and fro.

Job 13. 8 will ye accept his person?

Psalm 13. 1 how long wilt thou hide thy face?

34. 15 the eyes of the Lord are upon the righteous. 16.

45. 3 gird thy sword upon thy thigh.

89. 13 thou hast a mighty arm and strong is thy hand.

139. 16 thine eyes did see my substance. *Prov.* 15. 3.

Isa. 30. 27 his lips are full of indignation, his tongue as a devouring fire.

40. 11 he shall gather his lambs with his arm.

48. 13 mine hand hath laid the foundations of the earth.

Ezek. 1. 27 from the appearance of his loins upward.

38. 18 my fury shall come up in my face.

43. 7 the place of the soles of my feet.

Zech. 14. 4 and his feet shall stand upon the Mount of Olives.

Heb. 1. 10 the heavens are the work of thine hands. 2. 7.

Rev. 1. 14 his head and his hair like wool, and his eyes like fire.

See Sermon by O. Pratt, J. of D., Vol. 18, page 286.

Gibson and Woodman's Discussion, second night.

THE TRUE AND LIVING GOD.

"There are two personages who constitute the great, matchless, governing, and supreme, power over all things, by whom all things were created and made, that are created and made, whether visible or invisible, whether in heaven, on earth, or in the earth, under the earth, or throughout the immensity of space.

"They are the Father and the Son—the Father being a personage of spirit, glory, and power, possessing all perfection and fulness, the Son, who was in the bosom of the Father, a personage of tabernacle, made or fashioned like unto man, or being in the form and likeness of man, or rather man was formed after his likeness and in his image; he is also the express image and likeness of the personage of the Father, possessing all the fulness of the Father, or the same fulness with the Father; being begotten of him, and ordained from before the foundation of the world to be a propitiation for the sins of all those who should believe on his name, and is called the Son because of the flesh, and descended in suffering below that which man can suffer; or, in other words, suffered greater sufferings, and was exposed to more powerful contradictions than any man can be.

"But, notwithstanding all this, he kept the law of God, and remained without sin, showing thereby that it is in the power of man to keep the law and remain also without sin; and also, that by him a righteous judgment might come upon all flesh, and that all who walk not in the law of God may justly be condemned by the law, and have no excuse for their sins.

"And he being the Only Begotten of the Father, full of grace and truth, and having overcome, received a fulness of the glory of the Father, possessing the same mind with the Father, which mind is the Holy Spirit, that bears record of the Father and the Son, and these three are one; or, in other words, these three constitute the great, matchless, governing and supreme, power over all things; by whom all things were created and made that were created and made, and these three constitute the Godhead, and are one; the Father and Son possessing the same mind, the same wisdom, glory, power, and fulness—filling all in all; the Son being filled with the fulness of the mind, glory, and power; or, in other words, the Spirit, glory and power, of the Father, possessing all knowledge and glory, and the same kingdom, sitting at the right hand of power, in the express image and likeness of the Father, mediator for man, being filled with the fulness of the mind of the Father; or, in other words, the Spirit of the Father, which Spirit is shed forth upon all who believe on his name and keep his commandments; and all those who keep his commandments shall grow up from grace to grace, and become heirs of the heavenly kingdom, and joint heirs with Jesus Christ; possessing the same mind, being transformed into the same image or likeness, even the express image of him who fills all in all; being filled with the fulness of his glory, and become one in him, even as the Father, Son and Holy Spirit are one.

"From the foregoing account of the Godhead, which is given in his revelations, the saints have a sure foundation laid for the exercise of faith unto life and salvation, through the atonement and mediation of Jesus Christ; by whose blood they have a forgiveness of sins, and also a sure reward laid up for them in heaven, even that of partaking of the fulness of the Father and the Son through the Spirit. As the Son partakes of the fulness of the Father through the Spirit, so the saints are, by the same Spirit, to be partakers of the same fulness, to enjoy the same glory; for as the Father and the Son are one, so, in like manner, the saints are to be one in them. Through the love of the Father, the mediation of Jesus Christ, and the gift of the Holy Spirit, they are to be heirs of God, and joint heirs with Jesus Christ;" *Doc. & Cov., Fifth Lecture on Faith.*

"And now Abinadi said unto them, I would that ye should understand that God himself shall come down among the children of men, and shall redeem his people; and because he dwelleth in flesh, he shall be called the Son of God: and having subjected the flesh to the will of the Father, being the Father and the Son; the Father, because he was conceived by the power of God; and the Son, because of the flesh; thus becoming the Father and Son; and they are one God, yea, the very eternal Father of heaven and earth;" *Mos.* 15. 1-4.

"And shall be brought and be arraigned before the bar of Christ the Son, and God the Father, and the Holy Spirit, which is one eternal God, to be judged according to their works;" *Alma* 11. 44.

"Behold, I am Jesus Christ the Son of God. I created the heavens and the earth, and all things that in them are. I was with the Father from the beginning. I am in the Father, and the Father in me; and in me hath the Father glorified his name;" 3 *Nephi* 9. 15.

"And after this manner shall ye baptize in my name, for behold, verily I say unto you, that the Father, and the Son, and the Holy Ghost are one; and I am in the Father, and the Father in me, and the Father and I are one;" 3 *Nephi* 11. 27.

"I bear record of the Father, and the Father beareth record of me, and the Holy Ghost beareth record of the Father and me. * * And whoso believeth in me, and is baptized, the same shall be saved; and they are they who shall inherit the kingdom of God.

"And whoso believeth not in me, and is not baptized, shall be damned. Verily, verily, I say unto you, that this is my doctrine, and I bear record of it from the Father; and whoso believeth in me, believeth in the Father also, and unto him will the Father bear record of me; for he will visit him with fire, and with the Holy Ghost.

"And thus will the Father bear record of me, and the Holy Ghost will bear record unto him of the Father and me; for the Father, and I, and the Holy Ghost are one;" *verses* 32-36.

"God himself was once as we are now, and is an exalted Man, and sits enthroned in yonder heavens! That is the great secret. If the vail was rent to-day, and the Great God who holds this world in its orbit, and who upholds all worlds and all things by his power, was to make himself visible,—I say, if you were to see him to-day, you would see him like a man in form—like yourselves in all the person, image, and very form as a man; for Adam was created in the very fashion, image, and likeness of God, and received instruction from, and walked, talked, and conversed with him, as one man talks and communes with another;" *His. J. Smith, April 7, 1844.*

Bible.

Matt. 11. 25 I thank thee, O Father, Lord of heaven and earth 26, 27.

26. 39 take away this cup from me, nevertheless, not as I will, but as thou wilt.

Luke 10. 22 no man knoweth who the Son is but the Father, and who the Father is but the Son.

23. 34 Father, forgive them, for they know not what they do. 46.

John 1. 14 the glory as of the Only Begotten of the Father. 18.

4. 23 shall worship the Father in spirit and in truth, for the Father seeketh such to worship him.

5. 19 the Son can do nothing of himself, but what he seeth the Father do. 20, 21.

22 the Father judgeth no man, but hath committed all judgment unto the Son. 23.

26 as the Father hath life in himself, so hath he given to the Son.

27 hath given authority to execute judgment, because he is the Son of Man. 30.

45 think not that I will accuse you unto the Father.

6. 27 for him hath God the Father sealed.

37 all that the Father giveth me shall come to me. 44-46.

8. 16 I am not alone, but I and the Father that sent me. 18.

10. 15 as the Father knoweth me, even so know I the Father.

12. 27 Father save me from this hour, but for this cause came I unto this hour.

13. 1 Jesus knew that he should depart out of this world to the Father.

14. 6 no man cometh to the Father but by me. 8.

9 he that hath seen me hath seen the Father. 11, 13, 16.

26 but the Comforter whom the Father will send.

15. 26 when the Comforter is come, whom I will send unto you from the Father.

16. 15 all things that the Father hath are mine. 16, 25-28.

17. 1 Father, the hour is come, glorify thy Son.

3 eternal life is to know the only true God, and Jesus Christ whom he has sent. 5, 11, 24, 25.

10 all mine are thine, and thine are mine.

21 that they may be one, as thou, Father, art in me and I in thee.

22 the glory which thou gavest me I have given them, that they may be one, even as we are one.

23 I in them, and thou in me, that they may be made perfect in one.

24 Father, I will that they also, whom thou hast given me, be with me where I am.

Acts 2. 33 received of the Father the promise of the Holy Ghost.

Rom. 1. 20 being understood by the things that are made, even his eternal power and Godhead.

8. 16 the Spirit itself beareth witness with our spirit.

9. 5 Christ came who is over all, God blessed forever.

11. 36 of him, through him, and to him are all things, to whom be glory forever.

16. 27 to God only wise, be glory through Jesus Christ forever.

1 *Cor.* 2. 4 in demonstration of the Spirit and of power.

8. 6 but to us there is but one God, the Father.

15. 24 when he shall have delivered up the kingdom to God, even the Father.

Gal. 4. 4 when the fulness of time was come, God sent forth his Son made of a woman.

Eph. 3. 11 to the eternal purpose which he purposed in Christ Jesus.

4. 6 one God and Father of all, who is above all.

Col. 1. 19 for it pleased the Father that in him should all fulness dwell.

2. 9 in him dwelleth all the fulness of the Godhead, bodily.

Heb. 1. 8 to the Son he saith, thy throne, O God, is forever.

5. 9 being made perfect he became the author of eternal salvation.

7. 28 maketh the Son who is consecrated forevermore.

9. 14 who, through the eternal Spirit, offered himself without spot to God.

12. 9 be in subjection unto the Father of spirits and live.

13. 8 Jesus Christ, the same yesterday, to-day and forever.

2 *Peter* 1. 17 for he received from God the Father, honor and glory.

1 *John* 2. 1 we have an advocate with the Father, Jesus Christ the righteous. 23, 24.

5. 7 there are three that bear record in heaven, the Father, Son and Holy Ghost.

Rev. 1. 18 he that liveth and was dead, and am alive forever more.

2. 7 hear what the Spirit saith to the churches.

5. 13 unto him that sitteth on the throne, and to the Lamb for ever.

10. 6 sware by him that liveth forever, that time shall be no longer.

11. 15 and he shall reign for ever and ever.

15. 7 full of the wrath of God who liveth forever.

Book of Mormon.

1 *Nephi* 10. 18 for he is the same yesterday, to-day and forever.

19 wherefore the course of God is one eternal round.

11. 21 behold the Lamb of God, the Son of the eternal Father. *Chap.* 13. 40.

32 the Son of the everlasting God was judged of the world.

2 *Nephi* 2. 4 for the Spirit is the same yesterday, to-day and for ever.

9. 16 it is his eternal word which cannot pass away.

10. 14 I will be a light to them forever, that hear my words.

27. 23 that I am the same yesterday, to-day and forever. 29. 9.

Mos. 3. 5 is from all eternity to all eternity.

15. 4 yea, the very eternal Father of heaven and earth.

16. 9 the light and life of the world, yea, a light that is endless.

Alma 7. 16 he shall have eternal life, according to the testimony of the Holy Spirit.

11. 39 he is the very eternal Father of heaven and earth. 40.

44 Christ, the Father and the Holy Spirit, one eternal God.

13. 9 Only Begotten of the Father, without beginning of days or end of years.

34. 14 the great, last, infinite and eternal sacrifice will be the Son of God.

3 *Nephi* 9. 18 Alpha and Omega, the beginning and the end.

Mormon 6. 22 the Father, yea, the eternal Father of heaven and earth.

Moroni 7. 22 God knowing all things, being from everlasting to everlasting. 28.

8. 18 he is unchangeable from all eternity to all eternity.

10. 4 exhort you that you would ask God, the eternal Father. 28.

Doctrine & Covenants.

Sec. 14. 9 Jesus Christ created the heavens and the earth.

19. 1 I am Alpha and Omega, the beginning and the end.

20. 17 we know there is a God, infinite and eternal, from everlasting to everlasting. 28.

29. 34 neither Adam, your father, whom I created.

41 the Lord God cast Adam out of the Garden of Eden.

35. 1, 2 Alpha and Omega, the beginning and the end.

39. 1 the voice of him who is from all eternity to all eternity.

45. 1 by whom all things live, and move, and have a being. 7.

49. 12 believe on the Lord Jesus, the beginning and the end.

56. 11 though heaven and earth pass away, these words shall not pass away.

68. 6 Son of the living God. That I was, that I am, and that I am to come.

88. 13 who is in the bosom of eternity, in the midst of all things.

41 all things are by him and of him, even God for ever and ever.

121. 32 according to that which was ordained, in the council of the eternal God.

132. 20 then shall they be gods, because they have no end. 22. 24 this is eternal life, to know the only wise and true God.

See Sermon by B. Young, J. of D., Vol. 1, page 46.
See Sermon by B. Young, J. of D., Vol. 4, page 215.
Article Mil. Star, Vol. 15, page 301.

ORDINANCES, COVENANTS, ETC., ETERNAL.

Bible.

Gen. 21. 33 Abraham called on the name of the everlasting God. *Isa.* 40. 28. *Rom.* 16. 26.

Exo. 3. 15 this is my name forever and my memorial to all generations.

12. 14 Israel to keep the feast of Passover by an ordinance forever. 24.

27. 21 it shall be a statute forever to Israel.

31. 16, 17 the Sabbath a perpetual covenant and sign between the Lord and Israel forever.

Num. 10. 8 an ordinance forever throughout your generations.

1 *Sam.* 3. 14 the iniquity of Eli's house shall not be purged for ever.

2 *Sam.* 7. 24 hast confirmed Israel to be a people to thee for ever.

1 *Chron.* 17. 14 David's throne established for evermore.

23. 13 Aaron and his sons sanctified forever.

2 *Chron.* 33. 4 in Jerusalem shall my name be forever.

Psalm 19. 9 the fear of the Lord is clean, enduring forever.

24. 7 lift up, ye everlasting doors, and the King of glory shall come in.

33. 11 the counsel of the Lord standeth forever.

45. 6 thy throne, O God, is forever and ever. 17.

72. 19 blessed be his glorious name forever, let the earth be filled with his glory.

100. 5 his mercy is everlasting and his truth endureth.

119. 89 forever, O Lord, thy word is settled in heaven.

145. 13 thy kingdom is an everlasting kingdom.

Eccl. 3. 14 what God doeth it shall be forever; nothing can be put to it or taken taken from it.

15 that which hath been is now; that which is hath already been.

Isa. 9. 6 a child is born, he shall be called the everlasting Father.

32. 17 and the effect of his righteousness quietness and assurance forever.

33. 14 who among us shall dwell in everlasting burnings.

Ezek. 37. 26 make a covenant of peace with them it shall be an everlasting covenant.

Dan. 7. 14 his dominion is an everlasting dominion.

18 the Saints shall take and possess the kingdom forever.

12. 3 they that turn many to righteousness shall shine as the stars forever.

Matt. 19. 16 Master, what good thing shall I do that I may inherit eternal life.

Luke 16. 9 make friends with the mammon of unrighteousness, that when you fail they may receive you into everlasting habitations.

18. 30 manifold more in this present time, and in the world to come life everlasting.

John 3. 15 that whosoever believeth in him should not perish, but have eternal life.

4. 14 the water I give him shall be in him a well of water springing up into everlasting life. 36.

5. 24 he that believeth on him that sent me, hath everlasting life.

39 search the scriptures, for in them ye think ye have eternal life.

6. 68 to whom shall we go? Thou hast the words of eternal life.

10. 28 I give unto them eternal life and they shall never perish.

12. 25 he that hateth his life in this world shall keep it unto life eternal.

17. 2 that he should give eternal life to as many as thou hast given him.

3 life eternal to know thee, the only true God, and Jesus Christ whom thou hast sent.

Acts 13. 48 as many as were ordained to eternal life believed.

Rom. 1. 20 being understood by the things that are made, even his eternal power and Godhead.

2. 7 by patient continuance in well doing seek for immortality and eternal life.

5. 21 might grace reign through righteousness unto eternal life.

6. 23 the wages of sin are death; but the gift of God is eternal life.

11. 36 for of him, and through him, and to him, are all things.

2 *Cor.* 4. 17 our light affliction worketh for us a far more exceeding and eternal weight of glory.

5. 1 a house not made with hands, eternal in the heavens.

Gal. 1. 5 to whom be glory for ever and ever.

6. 8 he that soweth to the Spirit, shall of the Spirit reap life everlasting.

Eph. 3. 11 according to the eternal purpose which he purposed in Christ Jesus.

2 *Thess.* 1. 9 who shall be punished with everlasting destruction.

1 *Tim.* 6. 12 fight the good fight of faith, lay hold on eternal life.

Titus 1. 2 in hope of eternal life, which God promised before the world began.

Heb. 5. 9 being made perfect he became the author of eternal salvation, unto all them that obey him.

9. 14 who, through the eternal Spirit, offered himself without spot to God.

1 *Peter* 1. 23 born again by the word of God, which abideth forever.

5. 10 who hath called us unto his eternal glory by Christ Jesus.

2 *Peter* 2. 17 to whom the mist of darkness is reserved forever.

1 *John* 1. 2 shew unto you that eternal life which was with the Father.

2. 25 this is the promise he hath promised us, even eternal life.

3. 15 no murderer hath eternal life abiding in him.

5. 11 this is the record that God hath given to us eternal life, and this life is in his Son. 13, 20.

2 *John* 2. for the truth's sake, which dwelleth in us, and shall

be with us forever.

Jude 21. looking for the mercy of our Lord Jesus Christ unto eternal life.

Rev. 7. 12 honor, power and might be unto our God forever.

10. 6 sware by him that liveth forever that time shall be no longer.

22. 5 for the Lord God giveth them light, and they shall reign forever.

Book of Mormon.

1 *Nephi* 10. 19 wherefore the course of God is one eternal round.

11. 21 the Lamb of God even the Son of the eternal Father.

32 the Son of the everlasting God was judged of the world.

2 *Nephi* 1. 19 his ways are righteousness for ever.

2. 4 for the Spirit is the same yesterday, to-day and forever.

12 must needs destroy the wisdom and eternal purposes of God.

9. 13 all men became incorruptible, immortal, living souls.

16 it is his eternal word and cannot pass away.

39 to be spiritual minded is life eternal.

11. 5 the great and eternal plan of deliverance from death.

Jacob 2. 21 created them to keep his commandments and glorify him forever.

Mos. 5. 15 ye may have everlasting salvation and eternal life.

16. 11 if good to the resurrection of endless life; if evil to the resurrection of endless damnation.

Alma. 34. 14 the great, last, infinite and eternal sacrifice will be the Son of God.

Mormon 5. 14 may bring about his great and eternal purposes.

Doctrine & Covenants.

Sec. 1. 15 have broken mine everlasting covenant.

6. 7 he that hath eternal life is rich. 11. 7.

14. 7 eternal life the greatest of all the gifts of God.

20. 28 which Father, Son and Holy Ghost are one God, infinite and eternal.

22. 1 this is a new and everlasting covenant, which was from

the beginning.

39. 1 the voice of him who is from all eternity to all eternity.

45. 8 to them that believed on my name gave I power to obtain eternal life.

56. 11 though heaven and earth pass away, these words shall not pass away.

76. 4 from eternity to eternity he is the same.

59 all things are theirs, whether life or death, things present or to come.

62 shall dwell in the presence of God and his Christ forever.

109. 77 the earth in its sanctified, immortal and eternal state.

85. 7 whose mouth shall utter words, eternal words.

88. 13 who is in the bosom of eternity in the midst of all things.

20 that bodies of the celestial kingdom may possess it forever.

41 all things are by him and of him, even God, forever.

101. 22 and worship me according to mine everlasting Gospel.

77 an infinity of fulness from everlasting to everlasting.

121. 2 behold from the eternal heavens the wrongs of thy people.

32 according to that which was ordained in the council of the eternal God.

128. 23 let the eternal creations declare his name forever.

132. 19 there shall be a continuation of the seeds for ever.

20 then shall they be gods, because they have no end.

24 this is eternal lives to know the only wise and true God.

46 whosesoever sins ye remit shall be remitted eternally.

Pearl of Great Price.

Page 1. Endless is my name. My works and words are without end. 3.

9. repent and call upon God in the name of the Son forevermore.

16. and enjoy the words of eternal life in this world and eternal life in the world to come.

17. the record of the Father and the Son from henceforth and forever.

19. seeing thou art holy from all eternity to all eternity, end-

less and eternal is my name also.

20. Enoch wept and stretched forth his arms, and his heart swelled as wide as eternity.

29. the blessings of the Gospel of salvation, even of life eternal.

32. they shall have no end for they are gnolaum, or eternal.

49. the angel said the fulness of the everlasting Gospel was contained in the records of the Book of Mormon.

PASSOVER OR SACRAMENT.

"This word (passover) comes from the Hebrew verb, pasach, which signifies to pass, to leap, or skip over. They gave the name of Passover to the feast which was established in commemoration of the coming forth out of Egypt, because the night before their departure, the destroying angel, who slew the first-born of the Egyptians, passed over the Israelites, because they were marked with the blood of the lamb which was killed the evening before; and which for this reason was called the Paschal Lamb;" *Cruden's Con.*

We have an account of the institution of the Passover in the twelfth chapter of Exodus. The Lord commanded Israel, saying, "And the day shall be unto you for a memorial; and ye shall keep it a feast to the Lord throughout your generations; ye shall keep it a feast by an ordinance for ever:" *verse* 14. This command rather implies that there might be a change in the manner and time of keeping this passover, by the house of Israel. The essential part of it is that it shall be kept by a feast forever.

That the passover, as instituted the evening before the departure of Israel out of Egypt, was typical of the sacrifice of the Lamb of God, appears to be the generally received opinion of all who have faith in the Bible and its institutions. It is evident that the apostle Paul entertained this view of the subject when he made the following assertion, "For even Christ our passover is sacrificed for us;" 1 *Cor.* 5. 7.

That our Savior considered the ordinance of the passover a part of the Mosaic law which was to be done away in his sufferings and death, is evident from the wish, which he expressed to his disciples, while keeping the passover with them the evening before his death, "With desire I have desired to eat this passover with you before I suffer;" *Luke* 22. 15. The type was no longer needed and the ordinance was changed to commemorate the great sacrifice he was about to make. Hence, he commanded his disciples to partake of the bread and wine in remembrance of him.

We cannot do better than to insert here, *verbatim*, the account of the first administration of the sacrament among the Nephites, by our Savior. "And it came to pass that Jesus commanded his disciples that they should bring forth some bread and wine unto him. And while they were gone for bread and wine, he commanded the multitude that they should sit themselves down upon the earth."

"And when the disciples had come with bread and wine, he took of the bread, and brake and blessed it; and he gave unto the disciples, and commanded that they should eat. And when they had eat, and were filled, he commanded that they should give unto the multitude. And when the multitude had eaten and were filled, he said unto the disciples, behold there shall one be ordained among you, and to him will I give power that he shall break bread, and bless it, and give it unto the people of my church, unto all those who shall believe and be baptized in my name.

"And this shall ye always observe to do, even as I have done, even as I have broken bread, and blessed it, and gave it unto you. And this shall ye do in remembrance of my body, which I have shewn unto you. And it shall be a testimony unto the Father, that ye do always remember me. And if ye do always remember me, ye shall have my Spirit to be with you.

"And it came to pass that when he said these words, he commanded his disciples that they should take of the wine of the cup, and drink of it, and that they should also give unto the multitude, that they might drink of it. And it came to pass that they did so, and did drink of it, and were filled; and they gave unto the multitude, and they did drink, and they were filled. And when the disciples had done this Jesus said unto them, Blessed are ye for this thing which ye have done, for this is fulfilling my commandment, and this doth witness unto the Father that ye are willing to do that which I have commanded you. And this shall ye always do to those who repent and are baptized in my name; and ye shall do it in remembrance of my blood, which I have shed for you, that ye may witness unto the Father that ye do always remember me. And if ye do always remember me, ye shall have my Spirit to be with you. And I give unto you a commandment that ye shall do these things. And if ye shall always do these things, blessed are ye, for ye are built upon my rock;" 3 *Nephi* 18. 1-12.

Bible.

Lev. 23. 5 the fourteenth day of the first month is the Lord's passover.

Num. 9. 5 they kept the passover at even. *Josh.* 5. 10.

33. 3 on the morrow after the passover Israel went out of Egypt.

Deut. 16. 2 place the Lord should choose, Israel was to sacrifice the passover. 5.

2 *Kings* 23. 22 not holden such a passover from the days of the Judges.

2 *Chron.* 35. 1-19 a description of the solemn passover of Josiah.

Ezra 6. 19, 20 the children of the captivity kept the passover.

Ezek. 45. 21 ye shall have the passover, a feast of seven days.

Matt. 26. 17-29 Christ kept the passover, with his disciples, the evening before his death. *Mark* 14. 12-25. *Luke* 22. 8-38.

Luke 24. 30, 31 Christ made himself known to his disciples by the breaking of bread.

John 2. 13 and the Jews' passover was at hand.

6. 53-58 he that eateth the flesh and drinketh the blood of Christ hath eternal life.

11. 55 many went to Jerusalem, before the passover, to purify themselves.

18. 39 have a custom that I should release one unto you, at the passover.

19. 14 and it was the preparation of the passover.

Acts 2. 46 they continued daily in breaking bread. 20. 7.

1 *Cor.* 11. 23-30 the same night in which he was betrayed took bread.

Heb. 11. 28 through faith he kept the passover.

Book of Mormon.

3 *Nephi* 18. 27-30 none to eat and drink unworthily.

20. 1-9 Jesus administered the sacrament, the second time, among the Nephites.

Moroni 4. 5 the manner of administering the sacrament.

6. 6 did meet together oft to partake of bread and wine.

Doctrine & Covenants.

Sec. 20. 75 expedient that the church meet together oft, to partake of bread and wine.

77-79 the form of administering the sacrament.

27. 2 it matters not what we eat and drink in the sacrament.

46. 4 those who have trespassed to make reconciliation.

See Sermon by Jos. F. Smith, J. of D., Vol. 15, page 324.

Article by J. G. B., Mil. Star, Vol. 34, page 520.

MILLENNIAL REIGN.

The inspired writings teach us that, at the second coming of Christ, his reign of a thousand years, on the earth, will commence. A veritable kingdom of the house of Israel will have been prepared to receive him.

"The Son of man shall come down in heaven, clothed in the brightness of his glory, to meet the kingdom of God which is set up on the earth;" *Doc. & Cov.* 65. 5. The kingdom of God in heaven and on the earth will then unite and constitute but one kingdom. "The kingdoms of this world are become *the* kingdoms of our Lord, and of his Christ; and he shall reign for ever and ever;" *Rev.* 11. 15.

Those that have part in the first resurrection, "Shall be priests of God and of Christ, and shall reign with him a thousand years;" 20. 6.

The earth will go through a purifying process to fit it for the residence of its millennial inhabitants. "Behold, I create new heavens and a new earth: and the former shall not be remembered;" *Isa.* 65. 17. That this passage refers to the preparation for the millennium is evident by the twentieth verse: "There shall be no more thence an infant of days, nor an old man that hath not filled his days: for the child shall die a hundred years old; but the sinner *being* a hundred years old shall be accursed."

This view of the subject is also presented to us in a revelation to Joseph, the Seer: "Old things shall pass away, and all things become new. * * * And he that liveth when the Lord shall come, and has kept the faith, blessed is he; nevertheless it is appointed to him to die at the age of man; wherefore children shall grow up until they become old, old men shall die;" *Doc. & Cov.* 63. 49-51.

There are three conditions of the earth spoken of in the inspired writings—the present, in which everything pertaining to it must go through a change which we call death; the millennial condition in which it will be sanctified for the residence of purer intelligences, some mortal and some immortal, and the celestial condition spoken of in the twenty-first and twenty-second chapters of Revelation, which will be one of immortality and eternal life.

When Christ's reign is fully established on the earth, there will be two capitals to his immense empire—Jerusalem on the eastern hemisphere and Zion on the western. "When the Lord of hosts shall reign in Mount Zion, and in Jerusalem;" *Isa.* 24. 23. "For out of Zion shall go forth the law, and the word of the Lord from Jerusalem;" 2. 3.

In this, "The fulness of times when Christ shall have subdued all enemies under his feet, and shall have perfected his work, when he shall deliver up the kingdom, and present it to the Father spotless, then shall he be crowned with the crown of his glory, to sit on the throne of his power to reign forever and ever;" *Doc. & Cov.,* 76. 106-108.

The prophet Daniel speaks of this great event:

"I saw in the night visions, and, behold, one like the Son of Man came with the clouds of heaven, and came to the Ancient of days, and they brought him near before him. And there was given him dominion, and glory, and a kingdom, that all people, nations, and languages, should serve him: his dominion is an everlasting dominion, which shall not pass away, and his kingdom *that* which shall not be destroyed;" 7. 13, 14. This passage evidences that Christ's reign on the earth will be real and tangible; and that his kingdom will embrace a great variety of nations and peoples, and that he is also subservient to his Father.

The following passage, with its context, is a beautiful description of the final coming of our Lord, and of his reign on the earth:

"That my people may gird up their loins, and be looking forth for the time of my coming; for there shall be my Tabernacle, and it shall be called ZION, a New Jerusalem. And the Lord said unto Enoch, Then shalt thou and all thy city meet them there and we will receive them into our bosom, and they shall see us; and we will fall upon their necks, and they shall fall upon our necks, and we will kiss each other; and there shall be mine abode, and it shall be Zion, which shall come forth out of all the creations which I have made; and for the space of a thousand years shall the earth rest.

"And it came to pass that Enoch saw the day of the coming of the Son of Man, in the last days, to dwell on the earth in righteousness for the space of a thousand years;" *P. of G. P., page* 22.

Bible.

Isa. 52. 7 that saith unto Zion, thy God reigneth.

Jer. 23. 5 a king shall reign and shall execute justice and judgment. 6.

Mic. 4. 7 the Lord shall reign over them in Zion forever.

Luke 1. 33 and he shall reign over the house of Israel forever.

Rom. 15. 12 he that shall rise to reign over the Gentiles.

1 *Cor.* 15. 25 till he hath put all enemies under his feet.

2 *Tim.* 2. 12 if we suffer, we shall also reign with him.

Rev. 5. 10 made us kings and priests, and we shall reign on the earth.

20. 4 they lived and reigned with Christ a thousand years.

21. 22, 27 description of the celestial earth.

Doctrine & Covenants.

Sec. 1. 36 the Lord shall reign in the midst of his Saints.

29. 11 and dwell in righteousness with me on the earth a thousand years.

43. 30 for the great Millennium of which I have spoken shall come.

45. 59 the Lord shall be their king and lawgiver.

56. 18 shall see the kingdom of God come in power and great glory.

58. 22 until he reigns whose right it is to rule.

133. 25 the Savior shall reign over all flesh.

See Sermon by B. Young, J. of D., Vol. 1, page 198.

See Sermon by O. Pratt, J. of D., Vol. 16, page 312.

See Sermon by O. Pratt, J. of D., Vol. 18, page 314.

See Sermon by O. Pratt, J. of D., Vol. 18, page 335.

Article Mil. Star, Vol. 1, pages 4 and 73.

Article by. O. Pratt, Mil. Star, Vol. 28, page 561.

DESTRUCTION OF THE WICKED.

Passages are numerous in the inspired writings which assert that the wicked shall be destroyed. The prophet Isaiah, speaking of the latter times, says, "Zion shall be redeemed with judgment, and her converts with righteousness. And the destruction of the transgressors and of the sinners shall be together, and they that forsake the Lord shall be consumed;" 1. 27, 28.

The Lord further declared through the same prophet, that, because the inhabitants of the earth had defiled it, the curse had devoured it; "And they that dwell therein are desolate;" 24. 5, 6. "For, behold, the Lord cometh out of his place to punish the inhabitants of the earth for their iniquity;" 26. 21.

Many of the sayings concerning the destruction of the wicked are general in their application, to all times in which wickedness is prevalent. But there are many passages in the inspired writings which point to the latter times for a general destruction of the ungodly, and the cleansing of the earth from wickedness.

The following from Isaiah are of this character. "For the indignation of the Lord is upon all nations, and his fury upon all their armies. * * For it is the day of the Lord's vengeance, and the year of recompense for the controversy of Zion;" 34. 2-8.

"For by fire and by his sword will the Lord plead with all flesh: and the slain of the Lord shall be many;" 66. 16.

The Book of *Doc. & Cov.* being a record of revelations concerning the dispensation of the fulness of times, it says much concerning the destruction of the wicked, and the redemption of man, and of the earth.

It is evident that the visions of the prophet Joseph were vivid and well defined on this subject, for the Lord said through him, "The hour is nigh, and the day soon at hand when the earth is ripe: and all the proud, and they that do wickedly, shall be as stubble, and I will burn them up, saith the Lord of hosts, that wickedness shall not be upon the earth;" 29. 9, 14-21. *Sec.* 64. 24.

The records of the times are a daily testimony of the fulfilment of the following: "And in that day shall be heard of wars and rumors of wars, and the whole earth shall be in commotion, and men's hearts shall fail them;" *sec.* 45. 26. And men shall be standing in that generation in which these things shall appear, "That shall not pass, until they shall see an overflowing scourge; for a desolating sickness shall cover the land;" *verse* 31.

"Among the wicked, men shall lift up their voices, and curse God and die. And there shall be earthquakes also in divers places, and many desolations; yet men will harden their hearts against me, and they will take up the sword, one against another, and they will kill one another;" *verses* 32, 34.

The testimony of the elders is the great preparatory work for the destruction of the wicked in this dispensation. Their labors are "To bind up the law and seal up the testimony, and to prepare the saints for the hour of judgment which is to come;" *sec.* 88. 84. And, after their testimony, "cometh wrath and indignation upon the people;" *verse* 88.

The testimonies that will follow the testimony of the elders are fearful to contemplate: "For after your testimony cometh the testimony of earthquakes, that shall cause groanings in the midst of her (the earth), and men shall fall to the ground, and shall not be able to stand. And also cometh the testimony of the voice of thunderings, and the voice of lightnings, and the voice of tempests, and the voice of the waves of the sea, heaving themselves beyond their bounds. And all things shall be in commotion; and surely men's hearts shall fail them; for fear shall come upon all people;" *sec.* 88. 89-91.

These testimonies are becoming historical facts. The words of the ancient prophets are being fulfilled. That Joseph Smith, Jun., saw and predicted their fulfilment, evidences the divinity of his mission.

Bible.

Job 4. 8 they that sow wickedness reap the same.

18. 5-21 curses on the wicked. *Chap.* 20. 4-29.

Psalm 1. 4, 5 nor sinners in the congregation of the righteous.

2. 4, 5 the Lord shall have them in derision.

7. 11-16 God is angry with the wicked every day.

9. 17 the wicked shall be turned into hell.

37. 28 the seed of the wicked shall be cut off.

35, 36 I have seen the wicked in great power, and he passed away.

Isa. 2. 19 they shall go into holes of the rocks and caves of the earth.

18. 6 the carcasses of the wicked shall be left to the beasts of the earth.

24 1-12 the earth is made empty, because both priests and people have gone astray.

28. 22 a consumption determined upon the whole earth.

29. 20 for the terrible one is brought to nought.

21 that make a man an offender for a word.

63. 1-6 the wicked kingdoms shall be broken. *Jer.* 25. 30-38. *Dan.* 2. 44.

Jer. 23. 19, 20 a whirlwind shall fall on the head of the wicked.

Mal. 4. 1 the day cometh that shall burn them up, saith the Lord of hosts.

Matt. 13. 49 the angels shall sever the wicked from the just.

Luke 21. 25, 26 signs in the sun and moon and stars. Men's hearts failing them.

1 *Peter* 4. 17 judgment must first begin at the house of God.

Rev. 2. 23 I will kill her children with death.

8. 7 the plagues of hail, fire and blood, 8.

Chap. 9. the plagues of the last days.

Chap. 16. the seven vials of wrath poured out.

Chap. 17. the great mystery, Babylon.

18. 1-24 the fall of Babylon.

19. 20, 21 the destruction of the beast and the false prophet.

Book of Mormon.

1 *Nephi* 11. 36 all nations to be destroyed that fight against the apostles of the Lamb.

14. 3 the great and abominable church destroyed.

6 wo to the Gentiles! if they harden their hearts against the Lamb of God.

17 the wrath of God poured out upon the mother of harlots.

22. 13 that great and abominable church shall be drunken with her own blood.

14 those that fight against Israel shall be turned one against another.

23 all churches not built up in righteousness to be consumed as stubble.

2 *Nephi* 6. 15 those who do not believe in Christ shall be destroyed.

9. 16 the filthy shall go into everlasting fire.

27 wo unto him that has the commandments of God, and transgresseth them.

26. 3-6 terrible destruction of the wicked at the crucifixion of Christ. 3 *Nephi, Chapters* 8. 9. 10.

27. 1, 2 in the last days all nations shall be drunken with iniquity, and be visited with terrible destruction.

Mos. 15. 26 those who have known the commandments of

God, and not kept them, shall have no part in the first resurrection.

16. 1, 2 when all shall see that the judgments of God are just, the wicked shall be cast out.

Alma 5. 57 the names of the wicked shall be blotted out.

9. 28 those who have been evil shall reap the damnation of their souls.

11. 41 the wicked remain as though there had been no redemption made.

12. 16 he that dieth in his sins, shall die as to things pertaining to righteousness. 17, 18.

40. 13 those who choose evil to be cast into outer darkness 14, 26.

41. 4 those who work evil shall have evil restored to them. 5.

Hel. 14. 18 those who do not repent are hewn down and cast into the fire.

3 *Nephi* 20. 23 every soul that will not hear that prophet shall be cut off. *Deut.* 18. 15. *Acts* 3. 22, 23.

Mormon, Chapters 2-6. great destruction of the Nephites for their wickedness.

Ether 11. 7 great destruction of the Jaredites for their wickedness.

Doctrine & Covenants.

Sec. 35. 11 without faith nothing shall be shown except desolation on Babylon.

56. 1 in the day of visitation and of wrath on the nations.

63. 6 the day of wrath shall come upon them as a whirlwind. 32, 33.

Sec. 87. concerning the wars that shall come to pass, beginning at South Carolina.

88. 79 the wars and perplexities of nations.

97. 21-24 the Lord's scourge shall pass over by night and by day.

101. 14 mine indignation is soon to be poured out upon all nations. 89.

103. 2 on whom I will pour out my wrath without measure.

112. 24 vengeance cometh speedily on the inhabitants of the earth. 25, 26.

130. 12 the beginning of the wars of the latter times to be in South Carolina.

133. 2 the Lord shall come down with a curse to judgment.

136. 35 now cometh the day of their calamity.

Pearl of Great Price.

Page 20. the blood of the righteous to be shed in the meridian of time, in the days of wickedness and vengeance.

21. the Lord to come in the last days, in the days of wickedness and vengeance. The earth shall rest; but before that day there shall be great tribulations among men.

22. Enoch saw the coming of the Son of man in the last days, but, before that day, he saw great tribulation among the wicked. He saw that the sea was troubled, and men's hearts failed them with fear for the judgment of Almighty God.

38. the abomination of desolation spoken of by Daniel the prophet, before the destruction of Jerusalem.

39. before the coming of the Son of Man in the last days, nation shall rise against nation, and kingdom against kingdom; there shall be famine, and pestilences, and earthquakes, in divers places. The Gospel of the kingdom shall be preached to all nations, for a witness, and again shall the abomination of desolation spoken of by Daniel the prophet be fulfilled.

See History of Joseph Smith, July 2, 1839.

See History of Joseph Smith, May 18, 1843.

O. Spencer's Letters to Rev. Wm. Crowel, No. 11.

P. P. Pratt's Voice of Warning.

MIRACLES.

To mortal man the creation of the earth was a mysterious, miraculous work. "God said let there be light and there was light." To the uninspired the production of that light remains a supernatural manifestation of power. From that time to this the Creator has been the same wonder working God.

The Mosaic dispensation opened up with mighty miracles in the land of Egypt. To Israel, for fifteen hundred years, the Lord God was a God of miracles.

Nicodemus, a ruler of the Jews, well understood the power of the Priesthood as manifested in the history of his fathers, when he said to Jesus, "No man can do these miracles that thou doest, except God be with him;" *John* 3. 2.

The Jews had faith in miracles as a witness that a man was sent of God. "Many of the people believed on him, and said, when Christ cometh, will he do more miracles than these which this *man* hath done?" 7. 31. The Gospel dispensation, like the Mosaic, which preceded it, was one of miraculous manifestations. When Jesus sent out his disciples to preach the Gospel he said to them, "Heal the sick, cleanse the lepers, raise the dead, cast out devils; freely ye have received, freely give;" *Matt.* 10. 8.

The Book of Mormon evidences that the Mosaic dispensation, among the Nephites, was also one of miraculous manifestations. The Gospel dispensation, among them, was preceded and ushered in, by miraculous wonders which involved the destruction of the wicked, and increased the knowledge and faith of those who had the testimony of Jesus.

We have the testimony of the writings of Moses, of the prophets, of ancient Israel on both continents, of both Gospel dispensations as recorded in the New Testament and Book of Mormon, that the God of Israel, and of former day saints, was a God of miracles, of signs, and wonders. We have the testimony of many thousands of Latter-day Saints, that God manifests himself to them as he did to his people anciently.

The Revelation of St. John assures us, that there will be many miraculous manifestations of the power of God in the last days. The sacred records everywhere evidence, that God is a God of miracles. No people can claim to be saints of the Most High without the testimony of miracles.

At the same time there may be miraculous manifestations that are not of God, for in the latter times one of the beasts which John saw, will have power to do great wonders and deceive them that dwell on the earth; *Rev.* 13. 13, 14.

John also saw the spirits of devils working miracles; 16. 14. The magicians worked miracles in common with Moses and Aaron, but Aaron's rod swallowed up their rod. Thus it will ever be. The devil may have great power over the elements, and over the hearts of men, but the Lord will come off conqueror. The elect will never be deceived for they will discern the difference between the two powers. Whoever is sent of God will work miracles in the name of Jesus, and no man can work miracles in the name of Jesus, "Save he were cleansed every whit from his iniquity;" 3 *Nephi* 8. 1-3.

There are two classes of miracles. One, manifesting the power of God in the destruction of the wicked, the other a means of preserving, blessing, and confirming the saints in the faith. If there be no faith God can do no miracles; *Ether* 12. 12. The apostle Paul declared that the power to work miracles was one of the gifts of the Holy Spirit; 1 *Cor.* 12. 10. Hence we may conclude that this gift will be ever manifest where the Holy Ghost is conferred by the authority of the Holy Priesthood.

Bible.

Gen. 15. 17 a smoking furnace and a burning lamp passed between the pieces.

19. 11 the men of Sodom smitten with blindness.

24, 25 the Lord destroyed the cities of the plain.

26 Lot's wife turned into a pillar of salt.

Exo. 3. 2 the angel appeared to Moses in a burning bush.

4. 3 Moses' rod transformed into a serpent.

6 Moses' hand became leprous.

Chapters 7-12 a history of the wonders which the Lord wrought, in the deliverance of Israel out of Egypt.

13. 21, 22 the Lord went before Israel in a pillar of a cloud by day.

14. 19, 20 the pillar of a cloud covered the Egyptians with darkness.

21-30 Israel passed through the Red Sea, but the Egyptians were destroyed.

15. 25 the waters of Marah sweetened.

16. 10 the glory of the Lord appeared in a cloud.

13-15 Israel fed on quails and manna.

23, 24 a double quantity of manna sent for the Sabbath.

17. 6 water brought forth from the rock in Horeb.

19. 16 thunderings and lightnings and a thick cloud on the mount.

18 Mount Sinai was altogether on a smoke.

24. 15, 16 a cloud covered the mount six days.

17 the sight of the glory of the Lord was like devouring fire.

18 Moses was in the mount forty days and forty nights.

34. 28 Moses was in the mount forty days without food. *Deut.* 9. 18.

40. 34 a cloud covered the tent of the congregation.

38 the cloud of the Lord was on the tabernacle by day, and fire by night.

Lev. 10. 1, 2 Nadab and Abihu destroyed. *Num.* 3. 4.

Num. 11. 1-3 the fire of the Lord burnt among Israel.

31-33 quails sent into the camp of Israel and a great plague.

12. 10 Miriam struck with leprosy. 14, 15 healed of leprosy.

14. 37 the spies who brought an evil report died of a plague.

16. 16-35 Korah and company destroyed. *Chap.* 26. 10.

46-50 the Lord sent a plague among the congregation.

17. 8 the rod for the tribe of Levi budded.

20. 11 Moses smote the rock and the water came out.

21. 6-9 the plague of fiery serpents.

22. 28 the Lord opened the mouth of Baalam's ass. 2 *Peter* 2. 16.

25. 9 24,000 of Israel destroyed by a plague.

Deut. 29. 5 the clothes of Israel did not grow old.

31. 15 the Lord appeared in the tabernacle in a pillar of a cloud.

Josh. 3. 14-17 the waters of Jordan divided and Israel passed through.

6. 20 the walls of Jericho fell down.

7. 14-21 the theft of Achan discovered.

10. 11 the enemies of Israel destroyed by hailstones.

12-14 the sun stood still and the moon stayed.

Judges 6. 21 fire consumed the flesh and unleavened bread of Gideon.

36-40 the sign given by a fleece of wool.

7. 6, 7 three hundred of Gideon's men lapped water.

14. 5, 6 Samson slew a lion. 19.

15. 14 the cords on the arms of Samson became as flax burnt with fire.

15 Samson slew a thousand Philistines with the jaw bone of an ass.

19 water came out of the jaw-bone for Samson.

16. 29, 30 Samson slew many Philistines at the time of his death.

1 *Sam.* 5. 4 Dagon falls and is broken before the ark of God.

6, 7 the men of Ashdod smitten on account of the ark.

9-12 the cities of Gath and Ekron smitten on account of the ark.

28. 11-14 the witch of Endor brought up Samuel.

2 *Sam.* 6. 7 the Lord smote Uzziah for taking hold of the ark.

24. 12-25 the Lord sent a pestilence on Israel, which destroyed seventy thousand men. 1 *Chron.* 21. 14.

1 *Kings* 8. 11 the glory of the Lord had filled the house. 2 *Chron.* 5. 13, 14.

13. 4-6 Jeroboam's hand dried up and restored again.

24 a prophet slain by a lion, for disobedience.

17. 6 Elijah fed by ravens,

14-16 the widow's barrel of meal and cruise of oil that did not fail by using.

21, 22 the widow's child brought to life.

18. 38 the fire of the Lord consumed Elijah's offering.

41-46 rain came in answer to the prayer of Elijah.

19. 6-8 Elijah fed by an angel, after which he fasted forty days.

20. 35, 36 a man slain by a lion for not obeying a prophet.

22. 20-23 the Lord put a lying spirit into the prophets of Ahab.

2 *Kings.* 1. 9-14 two companies, of fifty men each, destroyed by fire.

2. 8 the waters of Jordan divided, and Elijah passed through.

11 Elijah went up in a chariot with horses of fire.

14 Elisha smote the waters of Jordan with the mantle of Elijah.

20-22 the waters of Jericho healed by Elisha.

23, 24 forty-two children torn by bears, because they mocked Elisha.

3. 16-20 the armies of Israel and Edom supplied with water.

4. 1-7 the widow's pot of oil increased, so as to pay the debts of her husband.

32-37 the son of the Shumanite brought to life.

38-41 the poison removed from the pot of pottage.

42-44 one hundred men miraculously fed.

5. 14 Naaman healed of leprosy by washing in Jordan.

27 the servant of Elisha cursed with the leprosy of Naaman.

6. 5-7 an axe floats in the water.

17 the servant of Elisha saw horses and chariots of fire.

18 the Syrians smitten with blindness.

13. 21 a dead man raised by coming in contact with the bones of Elisha.

19. 35 an angel of the Lord smote the Assyrians. 2 *Chron.* 32. 21.

20. 11 the shadow went back ten degrees on the dial of Ahaz.

2 *Chron.* 7. 1 fire came down from heaven and consumed the sacrifice.

20. 23, 24 the Lord destroyed a great army in defence of Judah.

21. 14-19 Jehoram smitten with disease of the bowels.

26. 19 king of Judah struck with leprosy for burning incense.

Job 1. 16 the fire of God hath burned up the sheep and servants.

Dan. 3. 13-27 the three Israelites delivered from the fiery furnace.

6. 16-24 Daniel delivered from the den of lions.

Matt. 8. 2, 3 leper healed. 13 centurion's servant healed.

14, 15 Jesus healed Peter's wife's mother.

26 Jesus rebuked the winds and the sea.

28-34 devils entered into the herd of swine.

9. 2-8 a man sick with palsy, healed.

20-22 a woman healed of an issue of blood.

23-25 the ruler's daughter raised from the dead.

27-31 blind man healed. 32-34 devil cast out.

12. 13 withered hand restored. 15 the multitudes healed.

22 blind and dumb lunatic healed.

14. 14 Jesus healed the sick of the multitude.

17-21 the multitude fed on five loaves and two fishes.

25-27 Jesus walked on the water.

36 as many as touched the hem of Jesus' garment were healed.

15. 28 the Canaanitish woman's daughter healed.

30, 31 Jesus healed some blind and dumb of the multitude.

35-38 the multitude fed on seven loaves and a few fishes.

17. 14-18 Jesus cures a lunatic.

27 tribute money taken from a fish.

20. 30-34 two blind men restored to sight.

21. 14 Jesus healed the blind and lame in the temple.

19 the fig tree cursed.

27. 45 three hours of darkness at the crucifixion.

51 vail of the temple rent. 28. 2 a great earthquake.

Mark 1. 23-26 unclean spirit rebuked.

4. 39 Jesus rebuked the wind and the sea.

7. 32-35 the deaf man healed and his speech restored.

8. 22-25 blind man received his sight.

Luke 1. 20-22 Zacharias struck dumb.

2. 9 the glory of the Lord shone round about them.

7. 10 centurion's servant healed.

14, 15 widow's son raised from the dead.

21 many cured of their infirmities and plagues.

13. 11-13 the woman healed of a spirit of infirmity.

14. 2-4 man healed of the dropsy.

17. 12-14 ten lepers healed.

John 2. 6-10 water turned into wine.

4. 49-53 nobleman's son healed.

5. 8, 9 the impotent man healed.

9. 6, 7 the blind man healed by washing in the pool of Siloam.

11. 43, 44 Lazarus raised from the dead.

Acts 3. 6-8 a lame man healed.

5. 3, 10 Ananias and wife killed for lying.

15, 16 the sick of the multitude healed.

18, 19 an angel delivered the apostles from prison.

8. 7 unclean spirits cast out, and many healed.

9. 1-8 miraculous conversion of Saul.

17, 18 Saul receives his sight. *Chap.* 22. 13.

34 Eneas healed of the palsy.

40, 41 Dorcas raised from the dead.

12. 7-10 Peter delivered from prison by an angel.

21-23 Herod smitten by an angel.

14. 8-10 impotent man healed by Paul.

16. 16-18 Paul cast the spirit of divination out of a damsel.

26-30 Paul and Silas delivered from prison.

19. 11, 12 many miracles wrought by Paul.

20. 10-12 the young man restored who fell from an upper window.

28. 3-5 Paul received no injury from a viper on his hand.

8 Paul heals the father of Publius. 9.

Book of Mormon.

1 *Nephi* 1. 6 a pillar of fire appeared before Lehi.

16. 10 the Lord prepared a director to guide Lehi in his travels.

17. 45 the Lord spake to the brothers of Nephi and the earth shook.

52-55 the brothers of Nephi dare not touch him for many days.

18. 12 after Nephi was bound the compass ceased to work.

21 compass worked in the hands of Nephi. Through prayer the storm ceased.

Mos. 27. 11 the angel of the Lord spake to Alma and the earth shook. *Alma* 36. 7.

19 Alma became dumb. *Alma* 36. 10.

Alma 8. 31 Alma and Amulek could not be slain.

14. 26-29 Alma and Amulek delivered from prison.

15. 6-11 Zeezrom healed through the ministration of Alma.

17. 36-39 through a miraculous manifestation of strength, Ammon saved the flocks of Lamoni.

18. 42 King Lamoni overcome by the power of God.

19. 1-12 miraculous conversion of Lamoni.

13-32 account of the conversion of the servants and wife of

Lamoni.

22. 17-25 miraculous conversion of the king of the land of Nephi.

Hel. 5. 20-52 Nephi and Lehi delivered from prison.

Chap. 9. miraculous manifestations connected with the murder of the chief judge.

16. 6, 7 miraculous preservation of the prophet Samuel.

3 *Nephi, Chapters* 8, 9 and 10. an account of the destruction of the wicked on the American continent, at the death of Christ.

19. 25 the countenance and garments of Jesus exceeding white.

20. 3-7 miraculous furnishing of bread and wine for sacrament.

26. 14-16 tongues of the Nephite children loosed.

18 many saw and heard remarkable things.

Chap. 28. account of the three Nephite disciples who were to remain on the earth.

4 *Nephi* 1. 30 the disciples delivered from prison.

Ether 3. 1-6 the Lord prepared stones to give light in the Jaredite vessels.

8-16 the brother of Jared saw the Lord.

RECORDS OF THE JAREDITES.

The book of Ether, now forming a part of the Book of Mormon, is an abridgment of the original book of Ether, the last historian of the Jaredites. It was written by Moroni, during the period of thirty-six years, between the destruction of his people at the great battle of Cumorah, A. C. 384, and the time of closing up the Nephite records, about A. C. 421.

At the time of writing it, approximately one thousand years had passed away since the people, of whom it gives a short account, were destroyed by a civil war which was carried to the extreme of extermination.

The account occupies about thirty-eight pages of the present edition of the Book of Mormon. It can only be considered an outline sketch of a people who occupied North America, probably a little over sixteen hundred years.

The Lord told the brother of Jared, the leader of this early American colony, that "There shall be none greater than the nation which I will raise up unto me of thy seed, upon all the face of the earth;" *Ether* 1. 43.

We cannot doubt but what this prophetic blessing of the Lord upon them, when they were about to commence their long and tedious journey from the tower of Babel, was amply fulfilled.

Their history informs us that they, in time, occupied the continent from the Isthmus of Darien to the great lake on the north, and that the states of their vast empire occupied the shores of both the eastern and western oceans.

Moroni says, "I take mine account from the twenty and four plates which were found by the people of Limhi, which is called the Book of Ether;" *Ether* 1. 2. Some account of the finding of these plates may be found in *Mos.* 8. 8-11. *Chap.* 21. 25, 27.

The fact that these plates were called the Book of Ether, after the last prophet and historian of the Jaredites, indicates that they were an abridgment from the general records of the Jaredites. The Book of Ether bears the same relation to the general Jaredite records, that the Book of Mormon does to those of the Nephites.

Moroni states that he gives only a part of the account of the Jaredites from the tower down to their destruction; *Ether* 1. 5. At the completion of this record he says, "And the hundredth part I have not written;" 15. 33. From these statements it is evident that the Book of Ether, written by Moroni, is a very limited abridgment of the record of Ether contained on the twenty-four plates.

From the genealogy of Ether, given in the first chapter of the book, we learn that he was the last of the royal line of the Jaredites, as well as their last historian.

In the days of the first Nephite king, called Mosiah, who reigned in the land of Zarahemla, there was a stone brought to the city of Zarahemla, on which was engraved a short account of the Jaredites; *Omni* 1. 20-22.

The twenty-four plates, and this stone, are the only original records of the Jaredites of which we have any information. Moroni does not appear to have made any use of this stone record in writing his abridgment.

We are informed, in the Book of Ether, that the twenty-four plates contained the visions of the brother of Jared; 4. 4-7. Therefore we may conclude, that they are in the sealed portion of the plates from which the Book of Mormon was translated, by Joseph Smith, the Seer.

There was, evidently, an original record from which Ether wrote his account of the creation, and the history of the world down to the tower. Probably this record is the one referred to by the daughter of king Jared, when she asked her father if he had not read the record which their fathers had brought across the great deep 8. 9.

To the student who desires to dig deep, to learn the inspired history of the earth and its inhabitants, this short account of a great people, who occupied North America from about one hundred and twenty-five years after the flood, until some 600 B. C., greatly increases the desire for further information concerning them.

RECORDS

MENTIONED IN THE BIBLE, BUT NOT IN IT.

Gen. 5. 1 the book of the generations of Adam.

Exo. 24. 7 the book of the covenant.

32. 15-19 tables of testimony written on both sides.

32 and 33 the book which the Lord had written.

Num. 21. 14 book of the wars of the Lord.

Josh. 10. 13 written in the book of Jasher. 2 *Sam*. 1, 18.

1 *Sam*. 10. 25 the book in which the manner of the kingdom was written.

1 *Kings* 4. 32, 33 books containing three thousand proverbs, a thousand and five songs, a treatise on natural history and botany, written by Solomon.

11. 41 book of the Acts of Solomon.

14. 19 book of the Chronicles of the kings of Israel.

1 *Chron*. 29. 29 the book of Samuel the Seer, of Nathan the prophet, and of Gad the Seer.

2 *Chron*. 9. 29 book of Nathan the prophet, the prophecy of Ahijah, the Shilonite, and in the visions of Iddo the Seer.

12. 15 book of Shemaiah the prophet and of Iddo the Seer concerning genealogies.

13. 22 the story of the prophet Iddo.

20. 34 the book of Jehu the son of Hanani.

24. 27 the story of the book of the kings.

26. 22 the Acts of Uzziah, written by Isaiah, son of Amoz.

28. 26 book of the kings of Judah and Israel. 35. 27. *Chap*. 36. 8.

33. 18, 19 life of Manasseh, the words of the Seers that spake to him, in the book of the kings of Israel.

Jer. 36. 2 the words which Jeremiah wrote against Israel and Judah, and all the nations, in the roll of a book.

13 the roll in which Baruch, the scribe, wrote.

Dan. 22. 4 the book that was sealed to the time of the end.

Hab. 2. 2 the vision that was made plain on tables.

Mal. 3. 16 the book of remembrance that was written for those that feared the Lord.

Luke. 1. 1 many wrote concerning the faith of the early Saints.

1 *Cor.* 5. 9 a third epistle to the Corinthians; we have only two.

Philip 4. 3 the book of life. *Rev.* 13. 8. *Chap.* 20. 12.

Col. 4. 16 read the epistle from Laodicea.

2 *Tim.* 4. 13 books and parchments left at Troas.

Jude 3 a second epistle of Jude; we have but one.

14 the prophecy of Enoch.

Rev. 1. 11 the book sent to the seven churches of Asia.

5. 1 a book sealed with seven seals.

10. 2 little book which a mighty angel had in his hand.

20. 12 the books out of which the dead will be judged.

RECORDS OF THE NEPHITES.

The record of first importance to the Nephites was that of the plates of brass, which was taken from the treasury of Laban by Nephi. It contained the five books of Moses, the history of the Jews down to the reign of Zedekiah, and a genealogy of the family of Lehi.

This record was invaluable to the Jewish-American colony as a means of perpetuating the religion, customs and civilization of their fathers. Lehi prophesied, in his first camp in the wilderness, "That these plates of brass should go forth unto all nations, kindreds, tongues, and people who were of his seed;" 1 *Nephi* 5. 18. He further said "That these plates of brass should never perish; neither should they be dimmed any more by time;" *verse* 19.

Nearly two thousand five hundred years have passed away since this prophecy of Lehi's was recorded, and we are assured that these plates of brass are well preserved, and are yet to come forth to all the tribes and peoples of the aboriginal American race, and to all the race of Lehi who may be scattered on the islands of the sea. This record, on brass plates, was written in the Egyptian language; *Mos.* 1. 4. It appears to have borne the same relationship to the Nephites, that the Bible has to Christian nations, and to have been not only their guide in religion, but also the foundation of their ethics and jurisprudence.

From the first, Nephi was strongly impressed with the importance of keeping a faithful record of his people. He says in the beginning of his first book, "I make a record in the language of my father, which consists of the learning of the Jews, and the language of the Egyptians;" 1. 2. The Egyptian language must have had about the same relation to the Jews, that the Latin has to modern Christian nations.

The purpose of the Lord, in inspiring Nephi to make ample preparations for keeping a record of his people, was gradually developed to him, for he says in 9. 5, of his first book, "The Lord hath commanded me to make these plates for a wise purpose in him; which purpose I know not."

The importance of the future record of his people was afterwards shown him in vision: "For behold, saith the Lamb, I will manifest myself unto thy seed, that they shall write many things which I shall minister unto them, which shall be plain and precious; and after thy seed shall be destroyed, and dwindle in unbelief, and also the seed of thy brethren; behold, these things shall be hid up, to come forth unto the Gentiles, by the gift and power of the Lamb;" 13. 35. The remainder of this chapter further explains this subject.

By reading the third chapter of 2 *Nephi*, we learn that this subject had become well developed in the mind of Lehi before his death. Joseph, who was sold into Egypt, had left on record a remarkable prophecy—which was probably engraven on the plates of brass—that the writing of the fruit of his loins (the Book of Mormon), and the writing of the fruit of the loins of Judah (the Bible), should not only be joined together in the latter days, but that a great Seer should be raised up who should write the writing of the fruit of his loins for the benefit of his brethren. Such a plain description is given of things connected with this Seer, that we are perfectly safe in concluding that he and Joseph Smith, Jun., are identical.

From this time, during the existence of the Nephites, the coming forth of their record to the Lamanites, and to their own posterity in the latter times, was ever associated in the minds of the faithful, with the Seer whom the Lord should raise up to bring them forth. Both were the subject of their earnest prayers, and called forth the exercise of a living faith; *Mormon*, 8. 25.

The history of the Nephite-American colony commences with their leaving Jerusalem, 600 B. C.; 1 *Nephi* 10. 4, and closed when Moroni finished the record, from which the Book of Mormon was translated, and hid it up in the hill Cumorah, A. C. 421; a period of one thousand and twenty-one years.

When Lehi and his colony left Jerusalem, the renowned city of Babylon was in the height of its glory, and the city of Rome had been founded only one hundred and fifty years.

The importance of the Book of Mormon, as a history, will be recognized by the fact that it is the only history of the western hemisphere, known to the world, for the long period of thirty-eight hundred years between Noah's flood, and the discovery of America by Christopher Columbus, in 1492.

Book of Mormon.

1 *Nephi* 3. 3 the record of Laban. 4, 13, 19, 26. *Chap.* 4. 10-27.

5. 11-13 the record contained the five books of Moses, and a history of Jews. 16.

21, 22 the records on the plates of brass very desirable. *Chap.* 6. 1-6.

9. 2-4 one set of plates for sacred things, the other historical *Chap.* 19. 1-6.

13. 23 the record that proceedeth out of the mouth of a Jew. 25, 38, 40, 41.

14. 18-30 concerning the writings of the apostle John, and of Nephi.

2 *Nephi* 3. 12 the writings of Judah and Joseph to grow together.

5. 12 Nephi took with him, into the wilderness, the record on the plates of brass. 30-33.

25. 18 the Lord will bring forth his word to the Jews. 18-23.

26. 17 the things done among them shall be written and sealed up.

27. 7 in the book shall be a revelation from God, from the beginning. 10-29.

29. 2 my words shall hiss forth to the ends of the earth. 8, 10-14.

30. 3 the book written to be carried forth to the seed of Nephi. *Chap*. 31. 1, 2. *Jacob* 4. 1-3.

Enos 1. 13 Enos prayed that a record might be preserved to come forth to the Lamanites. 14, 16-18.

Jarom 1. 2 the small plates written for the benefit of the Lamanites.

Omni 1. 17 the people of Zarahemla had no records. 18.

Words of Mormon 1. 1, 2 many years after the coming of Christ, Mormon delivered the records to Moroni, and wrote these "Words."

Mos. 2. 34 the people of Mosiah taught concerning the records on the plates of brass.

8. 5 Limhi caused the records of his people to be brought to Ammon.

9 the people of Limhi discovered the records of the Jaredites. 10-19. *Chap.* 21. 27.

12. 8 leave a record which I will preserve for other nations. *Chap.* 22. 14.

25. 5, 6 the record of Zeniff and of Alma. 28. 10-20.

Alma 22. 12, 13 Alma expounded the scriptures from the creation. 23. 5. *Chap.* 33. 12-15.

37. 1-6 Alma prophesied that the records, containing holy writ, should retain their brightness. 7-27. *Chap.* 45. 2.

Hel. 3. 13-16 many particular and large records kept by the Nephites.

3 *Nephi* 5. 8-18 Mormon explains concerning the abridgment of the records of his people.

26. 7 the plates of Nephi contain the more part of what Christ taught. 11.

27. 23-27 things not forbidden to be written. All things written by the Father.

4 *Nephi* 1. 19, 20 Amos kept the records eighty-four years. 21.

48. 49 Ammaron hid up the sacred records in the earth.

Mormon 1. 1 Mormon makes a record and calls it the Book of Mormon. 2-5. *Chap.* 2. 17, 18.

7. 8 the Jewish records to go from the Gentiles to the remnants. *Chap.* 8. 5, 12, 14, 15.

8. 25 their prayers were in behalf of him who should bring these things forth.

9. 32, 33 record written in the reformed Egyptian. 34.

Ether 1. 3 the record of Ether speaks of the creation.

4-6 Moroni gives only a partial account of the Jaredites.

3. 21-24 the brother of Jared commanded to write what he had seen and heard.

4. 1 the things written by the brother of Jared not to be revealed until Christ should come. 3-7, 16.

5. 1 touch not the things sealed up.

3, 4 these things shall be established by the mouth of three witnesses.

15. 33 Ether hid the record so that the people of Limhi found it.

Moroni 1. 1-4 Moroni only wrote an abridgment of Jaredite history. 9. 24. *Chap.* 10. 2.

Doctrine & Covenants.

Sec. 1. 29 after having received the records of the Nephites. 3. 19. *Sec.* 5. 1, 3, 4, 11, 26, 30.

6. 26 records kept back because of the wickedness of the people.

8. 1 shall receive a knowledge concerning ancient records. 9. 1.

10. 1 because you have given up those records you had power to translate. 38-42.

44-49 the prayers of the ancient Saints answered, in the bringing forth of the Book of Mormon. *Sec.* 11. 22. *Sec.* 17. 1-3.

20. 35 these things are true and according to the revelations of John.

21. 1 Joseph Smith, Jun., to be called a Seer, a translator.

24. 1 Joseph Smith, Jun., called and chosen to write the Book of Mormon. *Sec.* 28. 7.

42. 12 Bible and Book of Mormon contain the fulness of the Gospel. 15.

93. 6 the fulness of John's record hereafter to be revealed.

107. 57 written in the book of Enoch.

Sec. 128. the dead to be judged from the books. Things that have never been revealed shall be revealed in the dispensation of the fulness of times.

20 Moroni declaring the fulfilment of the prophets—the book to be revealed.

135. 3 the books brought forth by Joseph Smith, Jun.

See Sermon by O. Pratt, J. of D., Vol. 16, page 47.

See Sermon by Prest. B. Young, Farmington, June 17, 1877, J. of D., Vol. 19. page 36.

VISIONS AND DREAMS.

"Surely the Lord God will do nothing, but he revealeth his secret unto his servants the prophets;" *Amos* 3. 7. "Where there is no vision the people perish;" *Prov*. 29. 18.

By visions and dreams the Lord has made known his will to his people, in every dispensation of the Priesthood. This method of communicating information, in its operations, is beyond the comprehension of our natural powers, and, for this reason, ranks among the supernatural.

In the past, the Lord has made known to his prophets many of the important events that were to become history, down through the centuries of coming time.

In the writings of Moses, as revealed to Joseph, the Seer, we have an account of wonderful things, made known in this way, to the prophet Enoch, who lived several hundred years before Noah's flood. He says: "As I was journeying, and stood in the place Mahujah, and cried unto the Lord, there came a voice out of heaven, saying, Turn ye, and get ye upon the mount Simeon.

"And it came to pass that I turned and went up on the mount; and as I stood upon the mount, I beheld the heavens open, and I was clothed upon with glory, and I saw the Lord; and he stood before my face, and he talked with me, even as a man talketh one with another, face to face; and he said unto me, Look, and I will show unto thee the world for the space of many generations." When we reflect that this great prophet lived nearly five thousand years ago, and that the Lord revealed to him the great events that were to take place on the earth until the coming of Christ in the latter-days, it will give us some little comprehension of the wonderful and great things revealed to him. The account of this is in *P. of G. P., pages* 17-22.

The Book of Mormon gives us a short account of another prophet, the brother of Jared, who lived about one hundred years after the flood. The Lord "Shewed unto the brother of Jared all the inhabitants of the earth which had been, and also all that would be; and he withheld them not from his sight, even unto the ends of the earth; For he had said unto him in times before, That if he would believe in him, that he could shew unto him all things—it should be shewn unto him; therefore the Lord could not withhold anything from him, for he knew that the Lord could shew him all things."

We have no account of any greater vision than this which the brother of Jared had. "And the Lord said unto him, Write these things and seal them up, and I will shew them in mine own due time unto the children of men;" *Ether* 3. 2-27. Thus we learn from the twenty-seventh verse, that all the great things which pertain to the history of man, from the beginning unto the end of the earth, are yet to be revealed, through the record of the brother of Jared, to all who are prepared to receive them.

Lehi, the head of the first Jewish colony to America, was commanded by the Lord, in a dream, to leave Jerusalem, take his family and go into the wilderness, preparatory to going to a strange land; 1 *Nephi* 2. 2; *verse* 4 proves his supreme faith in this dream: "And it came to pass that he departed into the wilderness. And he left his house, and the land of his inheritance, and his gold, and his silver, and his precious things, and took nothing with him, save it were his family, and provisions, and tents, and departed into the wilderness."

This great patriarch, on other occasions, showed his faith in dreams and visions. In these ways the Lord revealed many great things to him and his son Nephi.

The Mosaic dispensation opened by an angel of the Lord appearing unto Moses in a flame of fire "Out of the midst of a bush;" *Exo.* 3. 2.

The Old Testament gives an account of many visions and dreams, but perhaps the most important of the latter is the dream of Nebuchadnezzar, which was interpreted by the prophet Daniel; *Dan.* 2. It is now over twenty-four hundred years since the king of Babylon had that dream, and its fulfilment can be traced in the history of the world down through all these centuries.

The last great event, shown in this dream, was, that in the latter times the God of heaven would set up a kingdom which would break down other kingdoms and stand forever. This is the kingdom that it was the mission of Joseph Smith, Jun., to establish, and which the Latter-day Saints are laboring to build up.

Dreams characterized the opening up of the New Testament dispensation. After the birth of our Savior the wise men, who came from the east to see him, were warned to disobey the command of the wicked king Herod, who sought the life of the young child. The reputed father of the child, Joseph, was warned in a dream to take the child and its mother and flee into Egypt for the same reason. When Herod was dead, Joseph was warned in a dream to take the child and its mother and return into the land of Israel.

This great latter-day dispensation was opened up by a vision. When Joseph Smith, Jun., was a lad, in his fifteenth year, he retired to a secret place to ask the Lord to direct him and give him wisdom. When he kneeled down to offer up the desires of his heart to God, he was nearly overcome by the powers of darkness.

He says, in the narrative of his life written by himself, "Just at this moment of great alarm, I saw a pillar of light exactly over my head, above the brightness of the sun, which descended gradually until it fell upon me. It no sooner appeared than I found myself delivered from the enemy which held me bound. When the light rested upon me, I saw two personages, whose brightness and glory defy all description, standing above me in the air. One of them spake unto me, calling me by name, and said (pointing to the other), THIS IS MY BELOVED SON, HEAR HIM." *P. of G. P., page* 47.

An account of one of the most remarkable visions of this dispensation, is recorded in *Doc. & Cov., sec.* 76. The narrative commences as follows: "We, Joseph

Smith, Jun., and Sidney Rigdon, being in the Spirit on the sixteenth of February, in the year of our Lord, one thousand eight hundred and thirty-two, by the power of the Spirit our eyes were opened and our understandings were enlightened, so as to see and understand the things of God—even those things which were from the beginning before the world was, which were ordained of the Father, through his Only Begotten Son, who was in the bosom of the Father, even from the beginning, of whom we bear record, and the record which we bear is the fulness of the Gospel of Jesus Christ, who is the Son, whom we saw and with whom we conversed in the heavenly vision;" *verses* 11-14. In Joseph Smith's first vision, God the Father bore testimony of Jesus Christ his Son. In this last vision, the Son appeared to Joseph Smith and Sidney Rigdon, and revealed to them many great and glorious truths concerning the resurrection, and the final reward of all men according to their works. The account of the vision will repay much careful study.

The Lord said, through his prophet Joel, speaking of the times when Israel should be gathered in the latter days, "I will pour out my Spirit upon all flesh; and your sons and your daughters shall prophesy, your old men shall dream dreams, your young men shall see visions;" 2. 28. Thousands of Latter-day Saints can testify that this prophecy is being fulfilled, and that dreams and visions characterize this as they have all former dispensations of the Priesthood.

Bible.

Gen. 15. 12 a horror of great darkness fell on Abraham.

20. 3 God came to Abimelech in a dream by night. 6.

28. 12-15 Jacob's dream in Bethel.

31. 10-12 Jacob's dream of the speckled cattle.

24 God appeared to Laban.

37. 5-8 Joseph's dream of the sheaves.

9. 10 Joseph's dream of the sun, moon and stars.

40. 5-19 the dreams of Pharaoh's chief butler and chief baker.

41. 1-32 Pharaoh's dreams and Joseph's interpretation.

46. 2 God spake to Jacob in the visions of the night.

2 *Sam.* 7. 17 according to all this vision did Nathan speak to David.

1 *Kings* 3. 5-14 Solomon's dream in which he asks the Lord for wisdom.

9. 2 the Lord appeared to Solomon in a dream, as he had appeared unto him at Gibeon.

22. 19-22 Micah's vision of the lying spirit.

Job 4. 12, 13 was secretly brought to me from the visions of the night.

Jer. 1. 11-16 visions of a rod, and of a seething pot.

Ezek. 1. vision of four living creatures.

2. 9, 10 the visions of the roll of a book.

3. 22, 23 a vision of the glory of the Lord.

Chap. 8. vision of the glory of the Lord and of the rebelliousness of Judah.

Chap. 9. vision of the destruction of the wicked and of the preservation of the righteous in Jerusalem.

Chap. 10. vision of the coals of fire scattered over Jerusalem and of living creatures which Ezekiel had before seen by the river Chebar.

11. 22 vision of the Cherubim.

23 vision of the glory of the Lord departing from Jerusalem.

24, 25 Ezekiel in vision was carried by the Spirit into Chaldea.

37. 1-10 vision of dry bones, their coming together and being covered with flesh and filled with life.

Chap. 40. and remainder of Ezekiel is probably a vision of Jerusalem during the Millennium.

Dan. 4. Nebuchadnezzar's dream of a great tree.

Chap. 5. the handwriting on the wall of the palace of Belshazzar.

Chap. 7. Daniel's vision of the four beasts, and of the sitting of the Ancient of days.

Chap. 8. Daniel's vision of the ram and the goat.

Hab. 2. 2, 3 write the vision and make it plain upon tables.

Zech. 1. 8-11 the vision of the horses among the myrtle trees.

18-21 visions of the horns and carpenters.

2. 1, 2 vision of the measuring line.

Chap. 4. vision of the golden candlestick.

Chap. 5. vision of the flying roll. 6. 1-8 of the four chariots.

Matt. 1. 20 an angel appeared to Joseph in a dream.

Luke 1. 5-19 Gabriel promised Zacharias that his wife Elizabeth should have a son named John.

Acts 9. 12 Saul's vision of Ananias.

10. 10-16 Peter's vision of all manner of beasts. 11. 5-10.

30-32 Cornelius' vision of a man in bright clothing.

16. 9 Paul's vision of a man from Macedonia wanting help.

18. 9, 10 the Lord appeared to Paul in a vision.

22. 17-21 Paul had a trance in the temple.

Rev. 1. 12-18 vision of the seven golden candlesticks.

Chap. 4. vision of the throne of God, of twenty-four elders and of four beasts.

Chap. 5. the book sealed with seven seals.

Chap. 6. the opening of the seven seals.

Chap. 7. 144,000 of the tribes of Israel sealed in their foreheads, an innumerable multitude stood before the throne.

Chap. 8. the opening of the seventh seal and the plagues that follow.

Chap. 9. opening of the bottomless pit, the plague of locusts; other woes follow.

Chap. 10. the book which John is commanded to eat.

Chap. 11. vision of two witnesses who shall be slain and rise after three days. The seventh trumpet sounds.

Chap. 12. vision of the woman with child, and of the great red dragon.

Chap. 13. the beast with seven heads and ten horns.

Chap. 14. the Lamb standing on Mount Zion; the Gospel preached; the fall of Babylon.

Chap. 15. the seven angels with the seven last plagues; the seven vials full of wrath.

Chap. 16. the angels pour out their vials full of wrath; the coming of Christ.

Chap. 17. great Babylon represented by a woman.

Chap. 18. the fall of Babylon; the gathering of the Saints.

Chap. 19. the blood of the Saints avenged; the marriage of the Lamb; the fowls called to the great slaughter.

Chap. 20. Satan bound for a thousand years; he is let loose again; Gog and Magog; the last resurrection.

Chap. 21. a new heaven and a new earth; the heavenly Jerusalem.

Chap. 22. the river and tree of life.

Book of Mormon.

1 *Nephi* 1. 6 there came a pillar of fire and dwelt upon a rock before Lehi.

8 Lehi was overcome by the Spirit and carried away in a vision, in which he saw many things.

3. 2, 3 Lehi commanded, in a dream, to send his sons to Jerusalem for the record of the Jews.

Chap. 8. Lehi's vision of the tree with the white fruit, the river and the rod of iron, and of a great and spacious building.

Chap. 11. Nephi's vision of the Son of Man, his ministry, sufferings and death.

Chap. 12. Nephi's vision of his own seed, the seed of his brethren, and of the promised land.

Chap. 13. Nephi's vision of the Gentile nations across the "many waters," of the discovery of America by Christopher Columbus, and of many other great events that were to take place in the future.

18. 2 Nephi built the ship after the manner the Lord had shown him.

2 *Nephi* 1. 4 Lehi had a vision in which he knew that Jerusalem was destroyed.

Mos. 27. 11-13 an angel of God descended in a cloud and appeared to Alma.

SIGNS AND TOKENS.

Signs may or may not be miraculous manifestations. They may indicate something that has taken place, and also be a token of a continuance of some certain blessing. For instance, the Lord covenanted with Noah, and with every living creature, that he would not again destroy all flesh from the earth with a flood.

As a token of this covenant the Lord said to Noah, "I do set my bow in the cloud, and it shall be for a token of a covenant between me and the earth. And it shall come to pass, when I bring a cloud over the earth, that the bow shall be seen in the cloud." The Lord further assured Noah, "And the bow shall be in the cloud; and I will look upon it, that I may remember the everlasting covenant between God and every living creature of all flesh that is upon the earth;" *Gen.* 9. 9-17.

They may also indicate that certain things shall take place periodically, as "God said, Let there be lights in the firmament of the heaven to divide the day from the night; and let them be for signs, and for seasons, and for days, and for years;" 1. 14.

The prophets have foretold signs that should precede great events that were to take place on the earth. Speaking of the birth of our Savior, the prophet Isaiah says, "The Lord himself shall give you a sign; Behold, a virgin shall conceive, and bear a Son;" 7. 14.

The Lamanite prophet, Samuel, foretold to the Nephites in the city of Zarahemla, that for two days and one night preceding the birth of Christ there should be no darkness, and that a new star should arise, such an one as the Nephites had never before beheld; *Hel.* 14. 3, 5. These signs appeared as Samuel predicted; 3 *Nephi* 1. 13-21.

He also predicted terrible judgments that should destroy the wicked among the Nephites and Lamanites when the Savior should die. Simultaneously with that event there should be thunderings, lightnings, tempests and earthquakes. These should continue for many hours, and darkness should cover the land for three days; *Hel.* 14. 21-27. *Chapters* 8, 9, and 10, of 3 *Nephi*, give us a very vivid description of these judgments that were predicted by Samuel.

In the sacred writings, many signs are predicted that should precede the coming of the Son of Man, in the latter days. The Jewish apostles of our Savior manifested great interest in this matter. On a certain occasion when Jesus sat upon the Mount of Olives, they asked concerning the destruction of Jerusalem; after which they especially inquired, "What is the sign of thy coming and of the end of the world?" *P. of G. P., page* 38.

Jesus first answered them concerning the destruction of the Temple and the Jews. He told his disciples that they should be afflicted and killed, and be hated of all nations for his name's sake. "Then shall many be offended, and shall betray one another; and many false prophets shall arise, and shall deceive many; and because iniquity shall abound, the love of many shall wax cold; but he that remaineth steadfast and is not overcome, the same shall be saved."

"When you, therefore, shall see the abomination of desolation, spoken of by Daniel the prophet, concerning the destruction of Jerusalem (*Dan.* 12. 11), then you shall stand in the holy place." In this paragraph, continuing on to *page* 39, Christ says, "In those days, shall be great tribulation on the Jews, and upon the inhabitants of Jerusalem, such as was not before sent upon Israel of God, since the beginning of their kingdom until this time; no, nor ever shall be sent again upon Israel."

After these judgments should come upon Jerusalem and the Jews, then false Christs and prophets should arise, and shew great signs and wonders, insomuch that they would deceive the Elect according to the covenant, if it were possible.

Then he assures his disciples that they shall hear of wars and rumors of wars, but he assures them that will not be the end. For afterwards there will be those who will predict the coming of the Son of Man. He tells his disciples that they need not be deceived with regard to this great event, "For as the light of the morning cometh out of the east, and shineth even unto the west, and covereth the whole earth, so shall also the coming of the Son of Man be." That is, the indications of his coming will be so unmistakable that they need not be deceived.

One very significant sign of his coming, he stated would be, that his Elect should be gathered from the four quarters of the earth. Through the instrumentality of Joseph Smith and the Holy Priesthood, this great work is now going on: "And they," that is those who are being gathered, "shall hear of wars, and rumors of wars, * * for nation shall rise against nation, and kingdom against kingdom; there shall be famine, and pestilences, and earthquakes, in divers places; and again, (for the second time) because iniquity shall abound, the love of many shall wax cold." Again Jesus gave the assurance that he who was not overcome should be saved: "And again"—that is when the Elect are being gathered and judgments were being poured out upon the nations for the second time—"This Gospel of the kingdom shall be preached in all the world, for a witness unto all nations, and then shall the end come," or the destruction of the wicked; "and again"—that is for the second time—"shall the abomination of desolation, spoken of by Daniel the prophet, be fulfilled. And immediately after the tribulation of those days, the sun shall be darkened, and the moon shall not give her light, and the stars shall fall from heaven, and the powers of heaven shall be shaken; verily, I say unto you, this generation, in which these things shall be shewn forth, shall not pass away until all I have told you shall be fulfilled. * * * After the tribulation of those days, and the powers of the heavens shall be shaken; then shall appear the sign of the Son of Man in heaven, and then shall all the tribes of the earth mourn; and they shall see the Son of Man coming in the clouds of heaven, with power and great glory;" *P. of G. P., pages* 38-40.

This translation of the twenty-fourth chapter of Matthew, commencing with the last verse of the twenty-third chapter, by Joseph Smith, the Seer, is both very interesting and instructive to the student of theology. It contains much more than can be made to appear in a short sketch like this.

Every dispensation of the Priesthood has been characterized by miracles, by signs, and wonders, and none more than this, the dispensation of the fulness of times. It was to be opened up by an angel who should fly through the midst of heaven, having the everlasting Gospel to preach to the nations of the earth; *Rev.* 14. 6.

An angel, named Moroni, has come and brought forth to the world the Book of Mormon, which contains the fulness of the everlasting Gospel; *P. of G. P., pages* 49-53. It is the same Gospel that was preached by Jesus and his apostles. Thus, the saying of the Savior to his disciples upon the Mount of Olives is being fulfilled: "This Gospel of the kingdom shall be preached to all the world for a witness unto all nations; and then shall the end come;" *Matt.* 24. 14. Israel is being gathered from the four quarters of the earth in fulfilment of numerous predictions of the ancient prophets.

Jesus, also, told his disciples that they should hear of wars and rumors of wars. "For nation shall rise against nation, and kingdom against kingdom; and there shall be famines, and pestilences, and earthquakes, in divers places;" *verses* 6, 7. The world is witness that these sayings are being fulfilled.

These are only a few of the many signs and tokens that the coming of the Son of Man in power and great glory is near at hand. Signs and tokens will increase as manifestations that God is at work among the nations. Only those who have faith in God will comprehend their meaning. He has promised his saints that it should be given them to understand the signs of the times; *Doc & Cov.* 68. 11.

The wicked are ever seeking after signs, but they have no faith in the Giver, and therefore their motives are evil. Jesus said, "An evil and adulterous generation seeketh after a sign;" *Matt.* 12. 39. We are promised that signs shall follow the believer; *Mark* 16. 17-20. This promise is not limited to any specified time or place; but extends to all believers. They are nowhere promised to the unbeliever except for a testimony against them; for the Lord has said, "He that seeketh signs, shall see signs, but not unto salvation;" *Doc. & Cov.,* 63. 7.

Signs are a gift of God, and, to be beneficial to those who receive them, they must come by faith; "Signs come by faith, not by the will of men, nor as they please, but by the will of God;" *verse* 10. Hence, they are a blessing to the believer, but not to those who would treat with contempt a manifestation of the power and goodness of God.

Bible.

Exo. 4. 17 thou shalt take this rod in thine hand, wherewith thou shalt do signs.

12. 13 and the blood shall be for a token upon the houses.

Deut. 13. 1, 2 if a prophet or a dreamer of dreams give thee a sign or a wonder.

28. 46 they shall be upon thee and thy seed forever for a sign and for a wonder.

Dan. 4. 3 how great are his signs, and how mighty his wonders.

6. 27 he worketh signs and wonders in heaven and on earth.

Matt. 12. 38 Master, we would see a sign from thee.

16. 1 desired him that he would shew them a sign from heaven. 3.

Mark 8. 11, 12 seeking of him a sign from heaven.

13. 4 what shall be the sign when all these things shall be fulfilled? 22.

Luke 2. 34 for a sign that shall be spoken against.

21. 11 fearful sights and great signs shall there be from heaven. 25.

John 2. 18 what sign shewest thou unto us?

4. 48 except ye see signs and wonders ye will not believe.

6. 30 what sign shewest thou that we may see and believe thee?

Acts 2. 19 I will shew wonders in heaven above, and signs in the earth beneath. 43.

4. 30 that signs and wonders may be done by the name of Jesus. 5. 12. *Chap.* 14. 3.

Rom. 4. 11 received the sign of circumcision, a seal of righteousness.

1 *Cor.* 1. 22 for the Jews require a sign.

2 *Thess.* 2. 9 with all powers, and signs, and lying wonders.

Rev. 15. 1 I saw another sign in heaven, great and marvelous.

Book of Mormon.

1 *Nephi* 19. 10 Zenos spake of three days' darkness, a sign of the death of Christ.

11 after Messiah shall come there shall be signs given to all Israel.

Jacob 7. 3, 14 Sherem said, shew a sign by this power of the Holy Ghost.

Mos. 3. 15 many signs, wonders, types and shadows shewed

he unto them.

Alma 32. 17 many who say, shew us a sign from heaven and we shall believe.

37. 27 all these signs and wonders ye shall retain from this people.

Hel. 16. 13 in the nineteenth year of the judges were great signs and wonders.

3 *Nephi* 2. 1 the people began to forget the signs and wonders they had seen.

8 the Nephites began to reckon time from the appearing of the sign.

11. 2 the people conversed about Jesus Christ and the sign of his death.

21. 2 this is the thing I will give to you for a sign.

7 be a sign to them that the work of the Father hath commenced.

Ether 4. 18 and signs shall follow those that believe.

Doctrine & Covenants.

Sec. 39. 23 and they shall be looking forth for the signs of my coming.

45. 16 as ye have asked of me concerning the signs of my coming. 39, 40.

46. 9 not for a sign that he may consume it on his lusts.

58. 64 the Gospel must be preached to every creature, with signs following.

63. 9 faith cometh not by signs, but signs follow those that believe. 10, 12.

68. 10 he that believeth shall be blest with signs following.

11 to you it shall be given to know the signs of the times.

84. 65 these signs shall follow those that believe.

88. 93 immediately there shall appear a great sign in heaven, and all people shall see it together.

124. 98 these signs shall follow him.

ANGELS.

Angels have acted an important part in every dispensation of the Priesthood. An angel first preached the Gospel of faith on the Son of God to Adam; *P. of G. P., page* 9. An angel of the Lord called to Abraham; *Gen.* 22. 11. An angel first attracted the attention of Moses to the burning bush; *Ex.* 3. 2. Their ministrations are often mentioned in the Old Testament history of ancient Israel. They were a prominent feature in the opening history of the New Testament dispensation. An angel appeared to Zacharias, the father of John the Baptist, and foretold his birth; *Luke* 1. 11, 12.

The angel Gabriel appeared to the virgin Mary and foretold the birth of the Savior; *verse* 31. An angel appeared to the shepherds, bringing the joyful news of a Savior's birth; 2. 10, 11. One warned Joseph to flee into Egypt to save the life of the child Jesus, and to return again after the death of Herod; *Matt.* 2. 13-15. According to the writings of the apostles they continued their ministrations, at least until John wrote his Revelation, for he was commanded to write to the angel of each of the seven churches of Asia; *Chapters* 2. 3.

According to prophecy, angels were to act an important part in the dispensation of the fulness of times. The dispensation was to be opened by one, for John the Revelator says, "And I saw another angel fly in the midst of heaven, having the everlasting Gospel to preach unto them that dwell on the earth;" *Rev.* 14. 6.

There is abundant evidence that an angel, calling himself Moroni, came to Joseph Smith, Jun., and taught him the principle and power of revelation from God, made known to him the real condition of the world, and when he had properly instructed him, delivered to him the record from which the Book of Mormon was translated by the power of God, containing the fulness of the everlasting Gospel; *P. of G. P., pages* 49-54.

The angel, John the Baptist, ordained Joseph Smith and O. Cowdery to the Priesthood of Aaron, "Which holds the keys of *the ministering of angels*, and of the Gospel of repentance, and of baptism by immersion for the remission of sins;" *Doc. & Cov.*, 13. From this second angel they received authority to preach the Gospel, revealed by the first angel, and to minister in its ordinances among all nations, thus fulfilling the prophetic vision of St. John.

Angels are to accompany Jesus Christ when he shall come in the glory of his Father; *Matt.* 16. 27. They are to gather the elect from the four quarters of the earth; 24. 31. The inspired writings, and especially the Revelation of St. John, assures us that they will act an important part in the great work of the latter days. There can be no truly Gospel church in which their ministrations are not recognized.

*   *   *   *   *

ANGEL OF THE LORD.

Bible.

Gen. 16. 7 an angel of the Lord found Hagar by a fountain.

28. 12 angels of God ascended and descended.

Exo. 14. 19 the angel of God, which went before the camp of Israel, removed and went behind them.

Judges 2. 4 when the angel of the Lord spake these words to the children of Israel.

6. 11 there came an angel of the Lord, and sat under an oak.

12 an angel of the Lord appeared to Gideon.

13. 3 an angel of the Lord appeared to the mother of Samson.

2 *Kings* 19. 35 the angel of the Lord smote and killed 185,000 of the Assyrians.

1 *Chron.* 22. 12 the angel of the Lord destroying throughout all the coasts of Israel.

30 David was afraid because of the sword of the angel of the Lord.

Psalm 34. 7 the angel of the Lord encampeth round about them that fear him.

Matt. 28. 2 the angel of the Lord rolled back the stone from the door.

Luke 2. 8, 9 the angel of the Lord came upon the shepherds.

Acts 5. 19 the angel of the Lord, by night, opened the prison doors.

8. 26 the angel of the Lord spake unto Phillip.

12. 23 the angel of the Lord smote Herod.

27. 23 there stood by me, this night, the angel of God.

Book of Mormon.

1 *Nephi* 3. 29 as they smote us with a rod, an angel of the Lord stood before them.

Mos. 27. 11-18 the angel of the Lord appeared to Alma and the sons of Mosiah.

Alma 9. 25 that ye may not be destroyed, the Lord hath sent his angel.

10. 7-11 an angel of the Lord appeared to me and said, Amulek!

24. 14 in his mercy he visits us by his angels.

Hel. 5. 11 he hath sent his angels to declare the conditions of repentance.

14. 26 angel said to me, there should be thunderings and lightnings for many hours. 28.

Doctrine & Covenants.

Sec. 63. 54 in that day will I send mine angels to pluck out the wicked.

103. 19, 20 I say not to you as I said to your fathers, mine angel shall go before you.

*   *   *   *   *

MINISTERING ANGELS.

Book of Mormon.

Jacob 7. 17 the power of the Holy Ghost and the ministering of angels.

Moroni 7. 25 by ministering of angels, men began to exercise faith in Christ. 29, 30.

Doctrine & Covenants.

Sec. 7. 6, 7 I will make him as a flaming fire and a ministering angel.

43. 25 called on you by my servants, and the ministering of angels.

67. 13 not able to abide the presence of God, neither the ministering of angels.

76. 88 the telestial receive it of the ministering of angels.

132. 16 but are appointed angels in heaven, which are ministering servants. 17-20.

136. 37 whom I did call upon by mine angels, my ministering servants.

Miscellaneous passages.

Gen. 19. 1 there came two angels to Sodom at even.

48. 16 the angel which redeemed me from all evil bless the lads.

Exo. 23. 20 I send an angel before thee, to keep thee in the way.

Num. 20. 16 sent an angel and brought us out of Egypt.

2 *Sam.* 24. 16 when the angel stretched out his hand upon Je-

rusalem to destroy it.

1 *Kings* 19. 5 an angel touched Elijah and said, arise and eat.

2 *Chron.* 32. 21 Lord sent an angel which cut off all the mighty men.

Psalm 8. 5 man made a little lower than the angels. *Heb.* 2. 7, 9.

68. 17 the chariots of God are twenty thousand, even thousands of angels.

78. 25 man did eat angels' food.

Dan. 9. 21 Gabriel touched Daniel about the time of the evening oblation. 10. 4-14, 20, 21.

Matt. 4. 11 angels came and ministered to Christ.

13. 39 the harvest is the end of the world: the reapers are the angels. 49.

18. 10 their angels do always behold the face of my Father.

24. 36 of that day knoweth no man, no, not the angels of heaven.

25. 31 Son of Man shall come, and all the holy angels with him.

26. 53 he shall presently give me more than twelve legions of angels.

Mark 8. 38 when he cometh in the glory of the Father, with the holy angels. *Luke* 9. 26.

12. 25 nor are given in marriage, but are as the angels.

Luke 1. 19 the angel said to Zacharias, I am Gabriel, that stand in the presence of God.

26 the angel Gabriel was sent from God to a city of Galilee.

16. 22 was carried by the angels into Abraham's bosom.

22. 43 there appeared an angel to Jesus, strengthening him.

Acts 7. 53 who received the law by dispensation of angels.

10. 22 was warned from God, by an holy angel, to send for thee.

Rom. 8. 38 I am persuaded that neither death, nor life, nor angels.

1 *Cor.* 6. 3 know ye not that we shall judge angels?

Gal. 1. 8 though we or an angel from heaven preach any other Gospel.

2 *Thess.* 1. 7 Lord Jesus shall be revealed from heaven with his mighty angels.

1 *Tim.* 5. 21 I charge thee before God and the elect angels.

Heb. 1. 4 being made so much better than the angels. 7.

2. 5 for unto the angels hath he not put in subjection the world to come? 16.

12. 22 the heavenly Jerusalem, and to an innumerable company of angels.

13. 2 not forgetful to entertain strangers, for thereby some have entertained angels unawares.

Rev. 5. 2 saw a strong angel proclaiming, who is worthy to open the book. 11. *Chap.* 7. 1. *Chap.* 8. 3. *Chap.* 10. 1, 5-10. *Chap.* 11. 15. *Chap.* 12. 7.

14. 6 I saw another angel fly in the midst of heaven, having the everlasting Gospel to preach to them that dwell on the earth. 8, 10, 15. *Chap.* 15. 6, 7. *Chap.* 17. 1. *Chap.* 18. 1. 21. *Chap.* 19. 17.

21. 12 had twelve gates, and at the gates twelve angels. 17.

Book of Mormon.

1 *Nephi* 13. 40 the angel said, these last records shall establish the truth of the first.

19. 8 he cometh according to the words of the angel, six hundred years from the time my father left Jerusalem. 10.

2 *Nephi* 6. 9 scourge and crucify him, according to the words of the angel. 11.

10. 3 the last night the angel said he should be called Christ. 25. 19.

32. 2, 3 angels speak by the power of the Holy Ghost.

Alma 9. 21 having been visited by the Spirit of God, having conversed with angels. 12. 29.

13. 22 the Lord, by the mouth of angels, doth declare it to all nations. 24-26.

29. 1 Oh, that 1 were an angel, that I might cry repentance to every people.

32. 23 now he imparteth his words, by angels, unto men, women and children.

Hel. 16. 14 angels appeared to wise men and declared unto them glad tidings of great joy.

3 *Nephi* 7. 18 so great was the faith of Nephi, that angels ministered unto him daily.

17. 24 they saw angels descending out of heaven and encir-

cling the little ones.

Doctrine & Covenants.

Sec. 38. 12 the angels are waiting the great command to reap down the earth.

88. 92 and angels shall fly through the midst of heaven sounding the trump of God. 96-107.

112 Michael, the seventh angel, shall gather together his armies.

128. 20 Moroni, an angel from heaven, declaring the fulfilment of the prophets.

129. 1 angels are resurrected personages, having bodies of flesh and bones. 5.

130. 4-7 no angels minister to this earth but those that belong to it.

Pearl of Great Price.

Page 9. after many days an angel of the Lord appeared to Adam.

12. the Gospel was preached from the beginning, being declared by angels.

27. the angel of the Lord's presence stood by Abraham.

29. thou didst send thine angel to deliver me from the gods of Elkanah.

38. who cometh in the clouds of heaven, and the holy angels with him.

40. he shall send his angels before him with the sound of a trumpet.

*   *   *   *   *

FALLEN ANGELS.

Bible.

Psalm 78. 49 he cast upon them the fierceness of his wrath, indignation and trouble, by sending evil angels among them.

Matt. 25. 41 depart from me, ye cursed, into everlasting fire, prepared for the devil and his angels.

2 *Cor.* 11. 14 for Satan, himself, is transformed into an angel of light.

2 *Peter* 2. 4 if God spared not the angels that sinned, but cast them down to hell.

Jude 6. angels which kept not their first estate he hath reserved in everlasting chains, under darkness, unto the judgment of the great day.

Rev. 9. 11 a king over them, which is the angel of the bottomless pit.

12. 9 the great dragon was cast out, and his angels with him.

Book of Mormon.

2 *Nephi* 2. 17 must needs suppose that an angel of God fell from heaven.

9. 8 our spirits must be subject to that angel who fell. 16.

Jacob 3. 11 that they may not become angels to the devil.

Mos. 26. 27 shall depart into everlasting fire prepared for the devil and his angels.

Alma 30. 53 hath deceived me, for he appeared in the form of an angel.

3 *Nephi* 9. 2 the devil laugheth, and his angels rejoice, because of the slain.

Moroni 7. 17 neither do the devil nor his angels persuade men to do good—no, not one.

Doctrine & Covenants.

Sec. 29. 28 depart from me, ye cursed, into everlasting fire prepared for the devil and his angels. 37.

76. 33 vessels of wrath, doomed to suffer with the devil and his angels. 44.

128. 20 Michael detecting the devil when he appeared as an angel of light. *Sec.* 129 8.

THE SABBATH DAY.

In the history of creation, as given in the Bible Genesis, we find that the Lord commenced and ended the labor of creating the world in six days or periods of time. That also, he ceased his labors on the seventh day and devoted it to rest.

As we have shown in the article on pre-existence, in this work, these seven periods of creative time were occupied in the creation and perfection of spiritual organizations. These have since given life to the organizations formed out of the crude elements, from which all animal and vegetable life is formed.

When Adam was formed out of these elements, and the Lord made every tree that is pleasant to the sight, and good for food, to grow out of the ground, another series of creative days, or periods of time, commenced. The six days of labor, which, according to present reckoning, is supposed to be about six thousand years, has nearly passed away.

The Christian world anticipate the time when antagonisms will cease, and there will be a time of universal peace, called the Millennium. While the Christian sects may entertain various theories as to how this millennium will be brought about, and what will be its practical results, to the Latter-day Saints it assumes a well defined outline, as delineated in the sacred books.

Typical of these great, creative sabbaths, the Lord has commanded man to rest every seventh day, according to his reckoning, as measured by one revolution of the earth on its axis. The sabbath was instituted for man's especial benefit, for the Savior, when on the earth, declared that "The sabbath was made for man, and not man for the sabbath;" *Mark* 2. 27.

There is nothing to indicate that the sabbath was a new institution at the time Israel came out of Egypt, but, being the beginning of a new dispensation, the institution was strengthened by direct commandment. In about one month after their deliverance from Egypt, when the Lord had commenced to feed them on manna, they were commanded to gather on the sixth day enough for the seventh day also. This obviated the necessity of gathering food on the sabbath, for the Lord said, "To-morrow is the rest of the holy sabbath unto the Lord;" *Exo.* 16. 23.

In the third month after Israel came out of Egypt, amidst a wonderful display of his glory and power upon Mount Sinai, the Lord gave to Israel ten commandments, one of which was, "Remember the sabbath day, to keep it holy. Six days shalt thou labor, and do all thy work: but the seventh is the sabbath of the Lord thy God: in it thou shalt not do any work, thou, nor thy son, nor thy daughter, thy manservant, nor thy maidservant, nor thy cattle, nor thy stranger that is within thy gates: for in six days the Lord made heaven and earth, the sea, and all that in them is, and rested the seventh day: wherefore the Lord blessed the sabbath day, and hallowed it;" 20. 8-11. This commandment is very sweeping and comprehensive, and the Lord makes it typical of the creative, sabbatic period of time.

In the Pentateuch the passages are quite numerous in which the children of Israel are reminded of the importance of keeping this commandment. The importance of keeping the sabbath day holy is urged upon Israel in the following passage, if possible, with still more force than in the Decalogue: "And the Lord spake unto Moses, saying, Speak thou also unto the children of Israel, saying, Verily my sabbaths ye shall keep: for it is a SIGN between me and you throughout your generations; that ye may know that I am the Lord that doth sanctify you;" 31. 12-18.

A very important feature of this subject is expressed in the last verse. The keeping of the sabbath day was to be a *sign* throughout the generations of Israel, that the people continually remembered that it was the Lord that sanctified them through keeping his commandments.

In *verse* 14, the Lord says, "Ye shall keep the sabbath therefore; for it is holy unto you. Every one that defileth it shall surely be put to death: for whosoever doeth any work therein, that soul shall be cut off from among his people." The command is repeated in a little different form in *verse* 15.

The sabbath was to be a perpetual covenant between the Lord and the children of Israel. "Wherefore the children of Israel shall keep the sabbath, to observe the sabbath throughout their generations, for a perpetual covenant;" *verse* 16. In *verse* 17 they are commanded to observe it as a sign that they remember that the Lord made heaven and earth, and rested on the seventh day.

In these quotations from *Exo.* 31, and in the Decalogue the most positive and weighty reasons are given by the Lord to the fathers of the house of Israel, for keeping the sabbath day. The obligation is evidently as binding upon the Latter-day Saints as it was upon their fathers, and they in like manner will reap the reward of obedience.

Israel was also required to give the land rest. "Six years thou shalt sow thy field, and six years thou shalt prune thy vineyard, and gather in the fruit thereof; but in the seventh year shall be a sabbath of rest unto the land, a sabbath for the Lord: thou shalt neither sow thy field, nor prune thy vineyard;" *Lev.* 25. 3, 4. After seven sabbaths of years had been numbered, making forty-nine years, then the fiftieth year was to be a year of Jubilee. This was a year of general release from all bondage. "And ye shall hallow the fiftieth year, and proclaim liberty throughout all the land unto all the inhabitants thereof: it shall be a jubilee unto you; and ye shall return every man unto his possession, and ye shall return every man unto his family;" *verse* 10. Both the forty-ninth and fiftieth were years of rest for the land. This chapter should be well studied for information with regard to the sabbatic year.

The Lord, in his revelations through his prophet Joseph, has commanded the saints to keep the sabbath day holy. "For verily this is a day appointed unto you to rest from your labors, and to pay thy devotions unto the Most High. * * * And on this day thou shalt do none other thing, only let thy food be prepared with singleness of heart that thy fasting may be perfect, or, in other words, that thy joy may be full;" *Doc. & Cov.*, 59. 10, 13. In *verse* 15-17, great blessings are promised as the result of keeping this commandment. To keep the sabbath holy is again positively enjoined upon the saints "And the inhabitants of Zion shall, also, observe the Sabbath day to keep it holy;" *Sec.* 68. 29.

Bible.

Lev. 19. 3 shall fear every man his father and mother, and keep my sabbaths. 30.

26. 34 then shall the land enjoy her sabbaths as long as it is desolate.

Num. 15. 32-36 a young man stoned for breaking the sabbath.

Neh. 10. 31 the people covenanted not to buy victuals on the sabbath.

13. 15-22 Nehemiah sharply reproved the people for laboring on the sabbath.

Isa. 56. 2 blessed is the man that keepeth the sabbath.

3-7 the eunuch and the stranger that keep the sabbath shall be blessed.

58. 13, 14 great blessings promised to those who keep the sabbath. *Jer.* 17. 21-27.

Sam. 2. 6 caused the solemn feasts and sabbaths to be forgotten in Zion.

Ezek. 20. 12 I gave my sabbaths to be a sign between me and them.

22. 26 have hid their eyes from my sabbaths.

Matt. 12. 8 for the Son of man is Lord even of the sabbath.

10-12 lawful to do good on the sabbath day.

ISRAEL A CHOSEN PEOPLE.

The name, Israel, is used to designate the descendants of Abraham through Isaac his son, and Jacob his grandson. The Lord gave the name to Jacob the father of twelve sons, the heads of the tribes of Israel. "And God appeared unto Jacob again, when he came out of Padan-aram, and blessed him. And God said unto him, thy name is Jacob: thy name shall not be called any more Jacob, but Israel shall be thy name; and he called his name Israel;" *Gen.* 35. 9, 10.

Abraham was a direct descendant of Shem, the son of Noah, and his native land was Ur of the Chaldees; *chap.* 11. "Now the Lord said unto Abram, Get thee out of thy country, and from thy kindred, and from thy father's house, unto a land that I will shew thee: and I will make of thee a great nation, and I will bless thee, and make thy name great; and thou shalt be a blessing: and I will bless them that bless thee, and curse him that curseth thee: and in thee shall all families of the earth be blessed;" 12. 1-3.

The promise to Abram, that he should become a great nation, has been fulfilled in his chosen seed occupying the land of Palestine, as such, for fifteen hundred years. It will again be fulfilled when they become a nation on that land forever.

The history of the eastern hemisphere for the two thousand years which intervened between the calling of Abraham and the destruction of Jerusalem by the Romans, witnesses that every nation that fought against Israel, or in any way oppressed them, passed away. Time will show the same general result, from the destruction of Jerusalem to the millennium.

The prophet Isaiah, speaking of the time when the Lord should favor Israel, said, "All they that were incensed against thee shall be ashamed and confounded: they shall be as nothing; and they that strive with thee shall perish;" 41. 11. "I will feed them that oppress thee with their own flesh; and they shall be drunken with their own blood;" 49. 26. "I have taken out of thine hand the cup of trembling, even the dregs of the cup of my fury; thou shalt no more drink it again: but I will put it into the hand of them that afflict thee; which have said to thy soul, Bow down, that we may go over;" 51. 22, 23.

The first Nephi saw the final result, as between Israel and their enemies, some six hundred years before the birth of our Savior. Speaking of the time when they should be brought out of captivity, and gathered to the lands of their inheritance, he says, "And the blood of that great and abominable church, which is the whore of all the earth, shall turn upon their own heads; for they shall war among themselves, and the sword of their own hands shall fall upon their own heads, and they shall be drunken with their own blood. And every nation which shall war against thee, O house of Israel, shall be turned one against another, and they shall fall into the pit which they digged to ensnare the people of the Lord;" 1 *Nephi* 22. 13, 14.

The sacred and profane history of the world evidences that all people, outside of the covenant seed of Abraham, when brought into association with that seed, have exhibited an instinctive antagonism to them. As a result, there are few nations that have not oppressed them, when there has been opportunity.

The quotations made on this subject, and many more not noticed, show that Israel will rule over all these in the future. As a result the future princes of the earth will be of that lineage. Then will be fulfilled another very important promise which the Lord made to Abraham: "Thy seed shall possess the gate of his enemies;" *Gen.* 22. 17.

The promise in the following, *verse* 18, which is also repeated in a number of places in the sacred writings, is a very important one: "In thy seed shall all the nations of the earth be blessed." It was through the lineage of Abraham that Jesus came in the flesh to redeem the world. It was only to the seed of Abraham that he personally ministered while in the flesh.

He was born in Bethlehem of Judea, almost under the walls of Jerusalem; *Luke, chap.* 2. He grew up in Nazareth, a city of Galilee; *verse* 39. He was baptized in Jordan, the chief river of the land of promise; *Matt.* 3. 13. His chosen twelve disciples were of the house of Israel. They were sent first to preach the Gospel to the house of Israel: "These twelve Jesus sent forth, and commanded them, saying, Go not into the way of Gentiles, and into any city of the Samaritans enter ye not: but go rather to the lost sheep of the house of Israel;" *Matt.* 10. 5, 6.

All the labors of Christ's earthly mission were in the midst of Israel. Among them he was slain for the sins of the world; his body was laid in a tomb cut in the rock of the promised land; in the midst of those with whose fathers he had covenanted he ascended up to his Father.

After his resurrection he told his disciples that Christ must needs suffer and rise from the dead, "That repentance and remission of sins should be preached in his name among all nations, beginning at Jerusalem;" *Luke* 24. 47.

So necessary did Jesus consider it, that the blessings and power of the Gospel should go forth to the world from the house of Israel, that just before his ascension he commanded his disciples, "Tarry ye in the city of Jerusalem, until ye be endued with power from on high;" *verse* 49.

Jesus once said to his Jewish disciples, "Other sheep I have, which are not of this fold: them also I must bring, and they shall hear my voice; and there shall be one fold, and one shepherd;" *John* 10. 16. While ministering among the Nephites, after his resurrection, he told them what he had said to his disciples at Jerusalem, and also that they were the other sheep which he referred to.

He further said to the Nephites, "And they (that is his disciples at Jerusalem) understood me not, for they supposed it had been the Gentiles; for they understand not that the Gentiles should be converted through their preaching; * * and they understand me not that the Gentiles should not at any time hear my voice;

that I should not manifest my self unto them, save it were by the Holy Ghost. But behold, ye have both heard my voice, and seen me;" 3 *Nephi* 15. 22-24.

In another place the Lord told the Nephites how the promise to Abraham, "In thy seed shall all the kindreds of the earth be blessed," would be fulfilled. "And after that ye were blessed, then fulfilleth the Father the covenant which he made with Abraham, saying, in thy seed shall all the kindreds of the earth be blessed, unto the pouring out of the Holy Ghost through me upon the Gentiles;" 20. 27.

Thus we are assured that Jesus never has ministered in person to the Gentiles, and there are no promises for the future to them which involve such administration. In this dispensation, all the blessings of the everlasting Gospel have been restored to the earth, through the agency of the house of Israel. Of them a people will be prepared, and through them a kingdom will be established, over which the Savior will reign on the earth. Then Israel will be the head of nations, and the promise made to Abraham, "Thy seed shall possess the gate of his enemies," will fully be realized.

For further information on this subject see the following subjects in this work: *Gathering of Israel, Apostacy of the Primitive Church*, and *Millennial Reign*.

Bible.

Exo. 3. 6 I am the God of thy fathers Abraham, Isaac and Jacob.

15 this is my name forever, and my memorial unto all generations.

6. 7 will take you to me for a people, and will be to you a God.

19. 5 ye shall be a peculiar treasure unto me above all people.

6 ye shall be to me a kingdom of priests and an holy nation.

23. 22 I will be an enemy unto thine enemies, and an adversary unto thine adversaries.

29. 45 I will dwell among the children of Israel, and be their God.

Num. 6. 27 they shall put my name upon Israel, and I will bless them.

24. 9 blessed is he that blesseth thee, and cursed is he that curseth thee.

Deut. 7. 15 I will lay them on all them that hate thee.

26. 18, 19 to make thee high above all nations, and an holy people.

27. 9 this day thou art become the people of the Lord thy God.

2 *Chron.* 9. 8 because the Lord loved Israel, to establish them forever.

Psalm 105. 6 ye seed of Abraham, his servant, ye children of

Jacob, his chosen.

135. 4 Lord hath chosen Jacob for himself, and Israel for his peculiar treasure.

137. 8, 9 O Babylon, happy shall he be that rewardeth thee as thou hast served us.

Isa. 10. 5-19 Assyria to be taken and destroyed.

14. 2 they shall take them captives whose captives they were.

29. 7, 8 all the nations that fight against Ariel shall be as a dream.

41. 8 Jacob, whom I have chosen, the seed of Abraham, my friend. 9.

43. 10 my witnesses, saith the Lord, and my servant whom I have chosen. 20.

45. 4 Israel, mine elect. I have even called thee by name.

49. 24, 25 even the captives of the mighty shall be taken away.

26 I will feed them that oppress thee on their own flesh.

54. 15 whosoever shall gather against thee shall fall. 17.

Jer. 2. 3 all that devour him shall offend; evil shall consume upon them.

10. 25 pour out thy fury on the heathen, for they have eaten up Jacob.

30. 11 though I make a full end of all nations whither I have scattered thee, I will not make a full end of thee. 16, 24.

Heb. 8. 10 I will be to them a God, and they shall be to me a people.

SPIRITS IN PRISON.

The writings of every dispensation of the Priesthood evidence that the Creator provided a place of confinement or retention, where intelligences await future events concerning themselves.

Several hundred years before the flood, the Lord, speaking to Enoch concerning the wicked, said: "Behold, these which thine eyes are upon shall perish in the floods; and behold, I will shut them up; a prison have I prepared for them;" *P. of G. P., page* 20.

The idea of a pit or prison for man, appears to have been quite definite in the mind of Job; speaking of God's dealings with man, he says, "He keepeth back his soul from the pit, and his life from perishing by the sword;" 33. 18.

The Psalmist David called this place hell or place of departed spirits, for he said of the Lord, "Thou wilt not leave my soul in hell;" *Psalm* 16. 10. The latter part of the passage evidences that he was looking forward to the resurrection of Christ, to open the way for his release, "Neither wilt thou suffer thine Holy One to see corruption."

Speaking of the latter times, the Lord said, through the prophet Isaiah, "Fear, and the pit, and the snare, are upon thee, O inhabitant of the earth. * * * And it shall come to pass in that day, that the LORD shall punish the host of the high ones that are on high, and the kings of the the earth upon the earth. And they shall be gathered together, as prisoners are gathered in the pit, and shall be shut up in the prison, and after many days shall they be visited;" 24. 17, 21, 22. This passage from Isaiah is very definite on this subject. The assertion, "After many days shall they be visited," certainly infers that a time would come when they might be released.

The Lord speaking of another person says, "I the *Lord* have called thee in righteousness, and will hold thine hand, and will keep thee, and will give thee for a covenant of the people, for a light of the Gentiles." The following verse shows that the Lord would call and keep this servant of his for a special work, and that was, "To open the blind eyes, to bring out the prisoners from the prison, and them that sit in darkness out of the prison house;" 42. 6, 7. This passage explains how those who would be gathered as prisoners into the pit, and be shut up in prison, were to be visited after many days. Of similar import is *Isa.* 49. 5-9.

The apostle Peter was evidently quite familiar with this subject: "For Christ also hath once suffered for sins, the just for the unjust, that he might bring us to God, being put to death in the flesh, but quickened by the Spirit: by which also he went and preached unto the spirits in prison; which sometime were disobedient, when once the long suffering of God waited in the days of Noah, while the ark was a preparing;" 1 *Pet.* 3. 18-20. The Nephite, as well as the Jewish prophets, speak of a place of confinement for spirits; "Wherefore, death and hell must deliver up their dead, and hell must deliver up its captive spirits, and the grave must deliver up its captive bodies, and the bodies and the spirits of men will be restored one to the other;" 2 *Nephi* 9. 12.

These spirits, which are delivered from hell, are not the spirits of the righteous, for, in the thirteenth verse of the same chapter, the prophet says, "For on the other hand, the paradise of God must deliver up the spirits of the righteous."

These passages show us that the spirits of the wicked go to a prison, or hell, and the spirits of the righteous to the paradise of God, a place of light and freedom. Doubtless it was the same paradise which Jesus referred to, when he said to the thief on the cross, "To-day shall thou be with me in paradise;" *Luke* 23. 43.

The Lord said, in a revelation to the prophet Joseph, "I am the same which have taken the Zion of Enoch into mine own bosom; and verily, I say, even as many as have believed in my name. * * * But behold, the residue of the wicked have I kept in chains of darkness until the judgment of the great day, which shall come at the end of the earth; and even so will I cause the wicked to be kept, that will not hear my voice but harden their hearts;" *Doc. & Cov.* 38. 4-6.

This subject is still more fully explained in another revelation, through Joseph, the Seer. After the Lord instructed him concerning the first resurrection he says, "And after this another angel shall sound, which is the second trump; and then cometh the redemption of those who are Christ's at his coming; who have received their part in that prison which is prepared for them, that they might receive the Gospel, and be judged according to men in the flesh;" 88. 99. This verse informs us that when Christ comes there will be a class of spirits who will be redeemed from prison, because they will have paid the penalty of transgression, and will have accepted the Gospel which will have been preached to them in prison.

After the spirits who are prepared for redemption shall be brought out of prison by the resurrection, then "Another trump shall sound, which is the third trump; and then cometh the spirits of men who are to be judged, and are found under condemnation. And these are the rest of the dead, and they live not again until the thousand years are ended, neither again, until the end of the earth;" *verses* 100 and 101. That is, all the dead that remain after the redemption of those prepared, are those who are under condemnation, and they will not come forth through the resurrection until after the Millennium of a thousand years, and not until after the "little season" in which Satan will be loosed; or the end of the earth. It is mournful to think, that, even after so long a period of probation, or trial, there will be then of these spirits those who will still have to remain in the prison house, for *verse* 102 says, "There are found among those who are to remain, until that great and last day, even the end, who shall remain filthy still."

In another revelation we are informed, that a part of those who inherit a terrestrial glory, will be "The spirits of men kept in prison, whom the Son visited, and preached the Gospel unto them, that they might be judged according to men in the flesh, Who received not the testimony of Jesus in the flesh, but afterwards received it;" *sec.* 76. 73, 74.

Bible.

Job 17. 16 they shall go down to the bars of the pit.

33. 24 deliver him from going down to the pit: I have found a ransom. 28, 30.

Psalm 9. 17 the wicked shall be turned into hell.

28. 1 lest, if thou be silent to me, I become like them that go down to the pit.

30. 3 thou hast kept me alive, that I should not go down to the pit.

69. 15 let not the pit shut her mouth on me.

142. 7 bring my soul out of prison, that I may praise thy name.

143. 7 hide not thy face from me, lest I be like unto those that go down to the pit.

Isa. 14. 15 yet thou shalt be brought down to hell, to the sides of the pit.

42. 16 I will bring the blind by a way that they knew not.

61. 1 to proclaim liberty to the captives, to open the prison to those that are bound.

Ezek. 26. 20 bring thee down with them that descend into the pit, and shall set thee in the low parts of the earth.

31. 14-18 for they are all delivered unto death, to the nether parts of the earth. Thou shalt lie in the midst of the uncircumcised. This is Pharaoh and all his multitude.

32. 18-32 several nations enumerated who were slain by the sword, and whose multitudes went down to the pit.

Zech. 9. 11 by the blood of thy covenant I have sent forth thy prisoners out of the pit.

Matt. 12. 32 whosoever speaketh against the Holy Ghost, it shall not be forgiven him in this world, nor the world to come.

Luke 12. 47, 48 some shall be beaten with few, some with many stripes.

Acts 2. 34 for David is not ascended into heaven.

Rev. 5. 13 every creature which is in heaven, on earth, and under the earth.

20. 7 when the thousand years are ended, Satan shall be loosed out of his prison.

Doctrine & Covenants.

Sec. 19. 6 it is not written that there shall be no end to this torment.

45. 17 as ye have looked upon the long absence of your spirits from your bodies to be a bondage, I will show you how the day of redemption will come. 45, 46.

54 and then shall the heathen nations be redeemed.

78. 12 be delivered over to the buffetings of Satan, until the day of redemption. *Sec*. 82. 21.

THE FIRST PRESIDENCY
AND TWELVE APOSTLES.

THE FIRST PRESIDENCY.

It is revealed unto us in *Doc. & Cov.*, 20. 2, 3, that Joseph Smith, Jun., was called of God and ordained an Apostle of the Lord Jesus Christ to be the first Elder of this church; and that Oliver Cowdery was also called of God, an Apostle of Jesus Christ, to be the second Elder of this church. In *sec.* 18. we are informed that Oliver Cowdery and David Whitmer were called with that same calling with which the apostle Paul was called; but of Joseph Smith. Jun., the Lord said, 8th *verse*, "Marvel not that I have called him unto mine own purpose, which purpose is known in me." In *sec.* 27. 12, the Savior says: "And also with Peter, and James, and John, whom I have sent unto you, by whom I have ordained you and confirmed you to be Apostles, and especial witnesses of my name, and bear the keys of your ministry, and of the same things which I revealed unto them."

Joseph, the first Apostle, continued as directed of the Lord from time to time to organize and develop the offices and ordinances of the church, for the saints were informed, in *sec.* 43. 3, "Ye shall know assuredly that there is none other appointed unto you to receive commandments and revelations until he be taken, if he abide in me."

In *sec.* 107, on Priesthood, instructions are given how to organize various councils and presidencies, in which is, *verse* 22, "Of the Melchisedek Priesthood, three presiding High Priests, chosen by the body, appointed and ordained to that office, and upheld by the confidence, faith and prayer of the church." *Verse* 9, "The Presidency of the High Priesthood, after the order of Melchisedek, have a right to officiate in all the offices in the church;" and, as in *verses* 18, 19, to hold the keys of all the spiritual blessings of the church" — to have the privilege of receiving the mysteries of the kingdom of heaven — to have the heavens opened unto them, to commune with the general assembly and church of the firstborn, and to enjoy the communion and presence of God the Father, and Jesus the Mediator of the new covenant.

In *verses* 91-2, "The duty of the President of the office of the High Priesthood is to preside over the whole church, and to be like unto Moses. Yea, to be a Seer, a revelator, a translator and a prophet, having all the gifts of God which he bestows upon the head of the church." In this light and sense does the church uphold, by their vote, their faith and their prayers, the First Presidency of the church, or the Presiding High Priest over the High Priesthood of the church.

*　　　*　　　*　　　*　　　*

THE TWELVE APOSTLES.

The Twelve Apostles, or the twelve traveling counselors, are called to be the Twelve Apostles, or special witnesses of the name of Christ in all the world; and they form a quorum, equal in authority and power to the three Presidents previously mentioned—the decisions of each being unanimous. *Doc. & Cov., sec.* 107, *verses* 23, 24. In *verse* 33 they "are to officiate in the name of the Lord, under the direction of the Presidency of the church, agreeable to the institution of heaven: to build up the church and regulate the affairs of the same in all nations; first unto the Gentiles, and secondly unto the Jews."

The foregoing laconic description of their duties is so comprehensive that we will not detail further than to refer the student to *verses* 23, 24, 35, 38, 39, 58 for further description of the duties of the Twelve Apostles.

In *sec.* 112, *verses* 30-32, the Lord says to them: "For unto you, (the Twelve,) and those (the First Presidency) who are appointed with you to be your counselors and your leaders, is the power of this Priesthood given, for the last days and for the last time, in the which is the dispensation of the fulness of times, which power you hold in connection with all those who have received a dispensation at any time from the beginning of the creation."

At the dedication of the Temple in Kirtland, the Prophet Joseph "called upon the quorums and the congregation of Saints to acknowledge the Twelve Apostles, who were present, as Prophets, Seers and Revelators, and special witnesses to all the nations of the earth, holding the keys of the kingdom, to unlock it, or cause it to be done, among them, and uphold them with their prayers, which they assented to by rising:" *His. of Joseph Smith, March* 27, 1836.

The following is a list of the names, time of birth and date of membership of the First Presidency and of the Twelve Apostles of this Dispensation, given in the order in which they were set apart to those offices, so far as we have ascertained:

Lyman E. Johnson was born October 24, 1811, at Pomfret, Windsor County, Vermont; was ordained an apostle at the organization of the first Council of Apostles, at Kirtland, February 14, 1835, and was cut off from the Council and the church April 13, 1838, at Far West, Missouri.

Brigham Young was born June 1, 1801, at Whittingham, Windsor County, Vermont; was ordained an apostle February 14, 1835, at Kirtland. From the apostacy of Thomas B. Marsh in October, 1838, he was President of the Twelve, and from December 27, 1847, was sustained as First President of the church, with Heber C. Kimball and Willard Richards as his counselors. This position he occupied until his death, on the 29th of August, 1877.

Heber C. Kimball was born June 14, 1801, at Sheldon, Franklin County, Vermont; was ordained an apostle February 14, 1835, at Kirtland, and was first counselor to President Brigham Young, from December 27, 1847, until his death, on the 22d of June 1868.

Orson Hyde was born January 8, 1805, at Oxford, New Haven County, Connecticut; was ordained an apostle February 15, 1835, at Kirtland, and died at Spring City, Utah, November 28, 1878.

David W. Patten was born in the State of New York, about A. D. 1800; was ordained an apostle February 15, 1835, at Kirtland. He was fatally shot, by a mob, at Crooked River, Missouri, on the 25th of October, 1838, and died the same day, firm in the faith.

Luke S. Johnson was born November 3, 1807, at Pomfret, Windsor County, Vermont; was ordained an apostle February 15, 1835, at Kirtland. He was disfellowshipped September 3, 1837, at Kirtland, and was cut off at Far West, April 13, 1838.

William E. McLellin was born in Tennessee, supposed in 1806; was ordained an apostle February 15, 1835, at Kirtland. He was cut off May 11, 1838, at Far West.

John F. Boynton was born September 20, 1811, at Bradford, Essex County, Massachusetts; was ordained an apostle February 15, 1835, at Kirtland. He was cut off September 3, 1837, at Kirtland.

William Smith was born March 13, 1811, at Royalton, Windsor County, Vermont; was ordained an apostle February 15, 1835, at Kirtland. He was deprived of the apostleship October 7, 1845, in Nauvoo, and was excommunicated October 12, 1845.

Parley P. Pratt was born April 12, 1807, at Burlington, Otsege County, New York; was ordained an apostle February 21, 1835, at Kirtland, and was assassinated near Van Buren, in Arkansas, May 14, 1857.

Thomas B. Marsh was born November 1, 1799, at Acton, Massachusetts; was ordained an apostle April 25 or 26, 1835, at Kirtland. He was cut off for apostacy, at Quincy, Illinois, March 17, 1839.

Orson Pratt was born September 19, 1811, at Hartford, Washington County, New York; was ordained an apostle April 26, 1835, at Kirtland. He died at his residence in Salt Lake City, October 3, 1881.

John Taylor was born November 1, 1808, at Milnthorpe, Westmoreland, England; was ordained an apostle December 19, 1838, at Far West, Missouri. He was President of the Twelve from the death of Brigham Young, and has been sustained as First President of the church since October 10, 1880, with apostles George Q. Cannon and Joseph F. Smith as his counselors.

John E. Page was born February 25, 1799, at Trenton, Oneida County, New York; was ordained an apostle December 19, 1838, at Far West, Missouri. He was cut off June 27, 1846.

Wilford Woodruff was born March 1, 1807, at Avon, Hartford County, Connecticut; was ordained an apostle April 26, 1839, at Far West, Missouri. Since October 10, 1880, has been sustained as President of the Twelve Apostles.

George A. Smith was born June 26, 1817, at Potsdam, St. Lawrence County, New York; was ordained an apostle April 26, 1839, at Far West, Missouri. He was appointed and sustained first counselor to President Brigham Young, at the October Conference, 1868. He continued to hold this office until his death, September 1, 1875.

Willard Richards was born June 24, 1804, at Hopkinton, Middlesex County, Massachusetts; was ordained an apostle April 14, 1840, at Preston, Lancashire, England, by President Brigham Young and the Council of Apostles held there on that day. He was second counselor to President Young from December 27, 1847, until his death, March 11, 1854.

Lyman Wight was born May 9, 1796, at Fairfield, Herkimer County, New York; was ordained an apostle April 8, 1841, at Nauvoo. He was excommunicated February 12, 1849.

Amasa M. Lyman was born March 30, 1813, at Lyman, Grafton County, New Hampshire; was ordained an apostle August 20, 1842, at Nauvoo. He was deprived of his apostleship October 8, 1867, and excommunicated May 12, 1870.

Ezra T. Benson was born February 22, 1811, at Mendon, Worcester County, Massachusetts; was ordained an apostle July 16, 1846, at Council Bluffs, Iowa. He died at Ogden, September 3, 1869.

Charles C. Rich was born August 21, 1809, in Campbell County, Kentucky, and was ordained an apostle February 12, 1849, at Salt Lake City. He died at Paris, Idaho, November 17, 1883.

Lorenzo Snow was born April 3, 1814, at Mantua, Portage County, Ohio; was ordained an apostle February 12, 1849, at Salt Lake City.

Erastus Snow was born November 9, 1818, at St. Johnsbury, Vermont; was ordained an apostle February 12, 1849, at Salt Lake City.

Franklin D. Richards was born April 2, 1821, at Richmond, Berkshire County, Massachusetts; was ordained an apostle February 12, 1849, at Salt Lake City.

George Q. Cannon was born January 11, 1827, at Liverpool, Lancashire, England; was ordained an apostle August 26, 1860, at Salt Lake City; was sustained first counselor to President John Taylor October 10, 1880.

Brigham Young, Jun., was born December 18, 1836, at Kirtland, Geauga County, Ohio; was set apart as one of the Twelve Apostles October 9, 1868, in Salt Lake City.

Joseph F. Smith was born November 13, 1838, at Far West, Missouri; was received into the Council of Apostles October 6, 1867, at Salt Lake City. He was sustained as second counselor to President John Taylor October 10, 1880.

Albert Carrington was born January 8, 1813, at Royalton, Windsor County, Vermont; was ordained an apostle July 3, 1870, at Salt Lake City.

Moses Thatcher was born February 2, 1842, at Sangamon County, Illinois; was ordained an apostle April 7, 1879, at Salt Lake City.

Francis M. Lyman was born January 12, 1840, near McComb, in McDonough County, Illinois; was ordained an apostle October 27, 1880, at Salt Lake City.

John H. Smith was born September 18, 1848, at Carbunca, Pottowattomie County, Iowa; was ordained an Apostle October 27, 1880, at Salt Lake City.

George Teasdale was born on the 8th of December, 1831, at London, England, and ordained one of the Twelve Apostles on the 16th of October, 1882, by President John Taylor, assisted by George Q. Cannon and others of the apostles.

Heber J. Grant was born on the 22d of November, 1856, in Salt Lake City, Utah, and ordained one of the Twelve Apostles on the 16th of October, 1882, by President George Q. Cannon, assisted by President John Taylor and others of the apostles.

John W. Taylor was born on the 15th of May, 1858, at Provo City, Utah County, Utah, and ordained one of the Twelve Apostles on the 9th day of April, 1884, by President John Taylor, assisted by Counselors Geo. Q. Cannon, Jos. F. Smith and others of the apostles.

The first First Presidency and Twelve Apostles of the church, in Kirtland, were:

FIRST PRESIDENCY.

Joseph Smith, Jun.,   Sidney Rigdon,   Frederick G. Williams.

TWELVE APOSTLES.

1. Thomas B. Marsh,   2. David W. Patten,   3. Brigham Young,

4. Heber C. Kimball,	5. Orson Hyde,	6. William E. McLellin,
7. Parley P. Pratt,	8. Luke S. Johnson,	9. William Smith,
10. Orson Pratt,	11. John F. Boynton,	12. Lyman E. Johnson.

The persons composing the first Council of Twelve Apostles were chosen by the three witnesses of the Book of Mormon, viz.: Oliver Cowdery, David Whitmer and Martin Harris, on the 14th day of February, 1835. They were ordained Apostles by Joseph Smith, Jun., Oliver Cowdery and David Whitmer, as stated in the History of Joseph Smith, under date of May 28, 1843.

In a revelation given through Joseph, the Seer, at Far West, Missouri, July 8, 1838, the Lord said to him: "Let my servant John Taylor, and also my servant John E. Page, and also my servant Wilford Woodruff, and also my servant Willard Richards, be appointed to fill the places of those who have fallen, and be officially notified of their appointments."

When Frederick G. Williams was rejected from the First Presidency, on the 7th of November, 1837, at Far West, Hyrum Smith was appointed a counselor in his stead, which position he occupied until called to officiate as Patriarch to the church, after the death of his father, Joseph Smith, Sen., which occurred in Nauvoo, September 14, 1840, when William Law was appointed counselor to the Prophet Joseph in Hyrum's stead. This office Wm. Law occupied until the assassination of the Prophet and Patriarch, which occurred June 27, 1844, at Carthage, Illinois.

The First Presidency and Twelve Apostles as they stood in Nauvoo, after the apostacy of Luke S. Johnson, William E. McLellin, John F. Boynton, Lyman E. Johnson, Thomas B Marsh and Frederick G. Williams, and the ordination of Hyrum Smith to the office of Patriarch, were:

FIRST PRESIDENCY.

Joseph Smith, Jun.,	Sidney Rigdon,	William Law.

TWELVE APOSTLES.

1. Brigham Young,	2. Heber C. Kimball,	3. Parley P. Pratt,
4. Orson Pratt,	5. Orson Hyde,	6. William Smith,
7. John Taylor,	8. John E. Page,	9. Wilford Woodruff,
10. Willard Richards,	11. George A. Smith,	12. Lyman Wight.

At a General Conference, held on December 27, 1847, at Kanesville, (now Council Bluffs,) Iowa, the Saints acknowledged Brigham Young President of the Church of Jesus Christ of Latter-day Saints, and Heber C. Kimball and Willard Richards his Counselors. This action was confirmed at the General Conference, held in Salt Lake Valley, after the companies had arrived in the Fall of 1848.

In Salt Lake City, February, 1849, after the assassination of the Prophet Joseph, the apostacy of Sidney Rigdon, William Law, William Smith, John E. Page and Lyman Wight, the First Presidency and Twelve Apostles stood as follows:

FIRST PRESIDENCY.

Brigham Young,   Heber C. Kimball,   Willard Richards.

TWELVE APOSTLES.

1. Orson Hyde,   2. Parley P. Pratt,   3. Orson Pratt,
4. John Taylor,   5. Wilford Woodruff,   6. George A. Smith,
7. Amasa M. Lyman,   8. Ezra T. Benson,   9. Charles C. Rich,
10. Lorenzo Snow,   11. Erastus Snow,   12. Franklin D. Richards.

After the death of Counselor Willard Richards, March 11, 1854, President B. Young nominated, and the church sustained Jedediah M. Grant, at the General Conference April 6, 1854, as his second counselor. Elder Grant filled this office until his death, at Salt Lake City, December 1, 1856. He was born in Windsor, Broome County, New York, February 21, 1816.

John W. Young was born October 1st, 1844, at Nauvoo, Hancock County, Illinois; was ordained an apostle November 22d, 1855, by President Brigham Young, assisted by Heber C. Kimball and Jedediah M. Grant, at Salt Lake City; on the 4th of February, 1864, he was set apart to be assistant counselor to the First Presidency by his father, President Brigham Young, and on the 8th of October, 1876, was set apart as first counselor to President Brigham Young, by his father, assisted by Daniel H. Wells and Brigham Young, Jr, at Salt Lake City, which position he occupied until the death of President Young. Since then he has officiated as counselor to the Twelve Apostles.

Daniel H. Wells was born October 27, 1814, at Trenton, Oneida County, New York; was ordained an apostle and set apart to be second counselor in the First Presidency by President Brigham Young, January 4th, 1857. He held this office until the death of President Young; since then he has officiated as counselor to the Twelve Apostles.

Since the death of Presidents Brigham Young and George A. Smith, Elders Orson Hyde, Parley P. Pratt, Ezra T. Benson, Orson Pratt and Charles C. Rich, and the apostacy of Amasa M. Lyman, the First Presidency and Council of Apostles have been as follows, from April 9, 1884:

FIRST PRESIDENCY.

John Taylor,   George Q. Cannon,   Joseph F. Smith.

TWELVE APOSTLES.

1. Wilford Woodruff,   2. Lorenzo Snow,   3. Erastus Snow,
4. Franklin D. Richards,   5. Brigham Young,   6. Albert Carrington,
7. Moses Thatcher,   8. Francis M. Lyman,   9. John H. Smith,
10. George Teasdale,   11. Heber J. Grant,   12. John W. Taylor.

Francis M. Lyman and John H. Smith were appointed and sustained at the General Conference in October, 1880, but were not ordained, on account of the absence of Elder Lyman, until the 27th day of that month.

Bible.

Matt. 10. 2-4 the names of the Twelve Apostles are these.

28. 19, 20 go ye therefore and teach all nations.

Mark 3. 14 he ordained Twelve that they should be with him.

John 15. 16 ye have not chosen me, but I have chosen you.

Acts 1. 25 that ye may take part in this ministry and apostle-ship.

4. 35 laid them down at the apostles' feet.

16. 4 the decrees ordained of the apostles.

Rom. 1. 5 by whom we have received grace and apostleship.

11. 13 inasmuch as I am an apostle of the Gentiles.

1 *Cor.* 12. 28 God hath set some in the church, first apostles.

2 *Cor.* 12. 12 truly the signs of an apostle were wrought among you.

Eph. 2. 20 built upon the foundation of apostles and prophets.

3. 5 as it is now revealed to his holy apostles and prophets.

4. 11 and he gave some apostles and some prophets, etc.

Neh. 3. 1 the apostle and high priest of our profession.

Jude 17. words spoken before of the apostles of our Lord.

Rev. 18. 20 rejoice over her, ye holy apostles and prophets.

Book of Mormon.

3 *Nephi* 12. 1 give heed unto these Twelve whom I have cho-sen.

13. 25 ye are they I have chosen to minister to this people.

19. 4 Jesus chose twelve disciples among the Nephites.

Chap. 28. Jesus' ministry to his Twelve Disciples; three chosen to remain.

Mormon 1. 16 disciples taken out of the land on account of wickedness.

3. 19 Nephites to be judged by the Twelve whom Jesus chose.

Doctrine & Covenants.

Sec. 18. 9 called with the same calling as the apostle Paul.

27-47 calling of the Council of Twelve Apostles in this dispensation.

19. 8 for it is meet for you to know, even as mine apostles.

20. 2, 3 Joseph Smith, Jun., and O. Cowdery called and ordained apostles.

27. 12 with Peter, James and John, by whom I have ordained you apostles.

84. 63 you are mine apostles, even God's high priests. 64.

95. 4 prepare mine apostles to prune my vineyard for the last time.

See A Pamphlet, Succession in the Priesthood, by John Taylor.

Sermon by O. Pratt, J. of D., Vol. 19, page 111.

Sermon by Geo. Q. Cannon, J. of D. Vol. 10, page 230.

CONSECRATION—STEWARDSHIP—UNITED ORDER.

To the Elder or Saint who has studied the revelations of our Lord Jesus Christ, as given in the Doctrine and Covenants, by the light of the Holy Spirit, it is most abundantly manifest that the human family has departed, degenerated or apostatized from original methods in their secular or business concerns, as truly, and as extensively, as they have in their spiritual interests, or the matters of their religious faith.

Enoch instituted an order of things among his people, in their business and financial relations, which so revolutionized their temporalities, that they had no poor among them, and all rejoiced together in equal hope of the life and exaltation, offered to them in the Gospel of Jesus Christ, the Only Begotten of the Father.

This very peculiar condition of things has been revealed to us under the style of United Order of Enoch, and it would surprise many who have given little attention to it to know how much is said in explanation and support of this doctrine in the Revelations.

We have thought that our little work could not be considered complete without a studied article, explanatory of this subject, but have concluded to give some references and citations, and invite the earnest students and scholars in the Church to investigate these great principles of social reform which have long puzzled the scientists and moralists of our age, which are worthy the efforts of our best minds, enlightened by the inspiration of the Holy Ghost, and which God has promised to set in order in his Church, in his own time and in his own way.

Bible.

Psalm 50. 5 gather my Saints together, that have made a covenant with me by sacrifice.

Matt. 19. 16-21 go and sell that thou hast and give to the poor.

Acts 4. 31, 32 but they had all things common.

35 distribution was made unto every man according as he had need.

Book of Mormon.

4 *Nephi* 1. 2, 3 they had all things common among them, therefore they were not rich and poor, bond and free.

16 there could not be a happier people who had been created by the hand of God.

24, 25 from that time they had their goods and substance no more common among them.

Doctrine & Covenants.

Sec. 19. 26 Martin Harris was commanded to impart of his substance, for printing the Book of Mormon.

34, 35 Martin Harris commanded to impart all his substance except sufficient for the support of his family.

42. 30 properties to be consecrated for the support of the poor, by deed and Covenant.

32 every man to be made accountable to the Lord, as a steward over his own property.

33 properties in the hands of the Church, or individuals, more than is necessary for their support, shall be kept to administer to those who have not.

39 the riches of those who embrace the Gospel among the Gentiles, to be consecrated to the poor of the house of Israel.

37 he that is cast out of the Church shall not receive that which he has consecrated to the poor.

51. 1, 2 must needs be that they be organized according to my laws, or they will be cut off.

3 appoint unto this people their portion, every man equal according to their families.

4 a writing given unto every man to secure unto him his portion. 5-7.

58. 35-87 Martin Harris to be an example unto the Church, in laying his monies before the bishop. This is the law to every man who would receive an inheritance in Zion.

70. 9-11 no man exempt from the law of consecration who belongs to the church.

78. 4 the order for the establishment of the poor to be everlasting.

5, 6 all to be equal in heavenly and earthly things.

11, 12 the Saints to organize by an everlasting covenant. He who breaks it to be delivered over to the buffetings of Satan.

82. 11 certain men to be bound together by a covenant not to be broken. 12-18.

21 the soul that sins against this covenant and hardens his

heart against it, to be turned over to the buffetings of Satan.

85. 3-5 those who do not keep the law of consecration and tithing, shall not have their names enrolled with the people of God; their genealogy shall not be found in the records of the church, neither shall the names of the fathers or children be written in the book of the law of God.

104. 1 the united order to be an everlasting order for the salvation of men until Christ come.

4-10 the penalty of breaking the covenants of the united order.

11-13 every man's stewardship to be appointed unto him.

15, 16 the Lord will provide for his Saints in his own way.

54, 55 the properties of the Saints are the Lord's, or else is their faith vain.

105. 2 were it not for the transgressions of my people, they might have been redeemed even now.

4 are not united according to the law of the celestial kingdom.

5 Zion cannot be built up except by the law of the celestial kingdom.

9 elders to wait a little season for the redemption of Zion.

Pearl of Great Price.

Pages 18, 19, 20 an account of the city of Enoch.

See Sermon by B. Young, J. of D., Vol. 15, page 220.

See Sermon by B. Young, J. of D., Vol. 17, page 56.

See Sermon by J. Taylor, J. of D., Vol. 17, page 47.

See Sermon by G. A. Smith, J. of D., Vol. 17, page 58.

See Sermon by W. Woodruff, J. of D., Vol. 17, page 69.

See Sermon by E. Snow. J. of D., Vol. 17, page 74.

See Sermon by O. Pratt, J. of D., Vol. 17, page 103.

See Sermon by L. Snow, J. of D., Vol. 18, page 371.

See Sermon by E. Snow, J. of D., Vol. 19, page 179.

See Sermon by L. Snow, J. of D., Vol. 19, page 341.

See Sermon by J. Taylor, J. of D., Vol. 20, page 55.

See Sermon by L. Snow, J. of D., Vol. 20, page 361.

See Sermon by J. Taylor, J. of D., Vol. 21, page 53.

See Sermon by O. Pratt, J. of D., Vol. 21, page 146.

GEMS FROM THE HISTORY OF JOSEPH SMITH.

May, 25, 1835, in a Council of the Twelve, Brigham Young, one of the Twelve, Elders John P. Greene and Amos Orton were set apart to open the door of the Gospel to the remnants of Joseph.

PRESIDENCY OF THE TWELVE.—*January* 16, 1836, in a Council of the Twelve the Prophet Joseph made the following remark: "The Twelve are not subject to any other than the First Presidency, viz.: myself, Sidney Rigdon, and Frederick G. Williams, who are now my Counselors; (and where I am not, there is no First Presidency over the Twelve.)"

A VISION.—*January* 21, 1836, the Prophet Joseph says of this time; "The heavens were opened upon us, and I beheld the celestial kingdom of God, and the glory thereof, whether in the body or out I cannot tell. I saw the transcendent beauty of the gate through which the heirs of that kingdom will enter, which was like unto circling flames of fire; also the blazing throne of God, whereon was seated the Father and the Son. I saw the beautiful streets of that kingdom, which had the appearance of being paved with gold. I saw Fathers Adam and Abraham, and my father and mother, my brother Alvin, that has long since slept, and marvelled how it was that he had obtained an inheritance in that kingdom, seeing that he had departed this life before the Lord had set his hand to gather Israel the second time, and had not been baptized for the remission of sins. Thus came the voice of the Lord unto me, saying—All who have died without a knowledge of this Gospel, who would have received it if they had been permitted to tarry, shall be heirs of the celestial kingdom of God; also all that shall die henceforth without a knowledge of it, who would have received it with all their hearts, shall be heirs of that kingdom, for I, the Lord, will judge all men according to their works, according to the desire of their hearts. And I also beheld all children who die before they arrive at years of accountability, are saved in the celestial kingdom of heaven. * * *

"Many of my brethren who received the ordinance with me saw glorious visions also. Angels ministered unto them as well as myself, and the power of the Highest rested upon us, the house was filled with the glory of God, and we shouted Hosanna to God and the Lamb."

THE SPIRIT OF PROPHECY.—*On the evening of March* 27, 1836, President Joseph Smith met the Quorums of the Priesthood in the Temple, and instructed them respecting the ordinance of washing of feet, and in relation to the Spirit of prophecy, "And called upon the congregation to speak, and not to fear to prophesy good concerning the Saints, for if you prophesy the falling of these hills, and the rising of the valleys, the downfall of the enemies of Zion, and the rising of the kingdom of God, it shall come to pass. Do not quench the Spirit, for the first one that opens his mouth shall receive the spirit of prophecy. Brother G. A. Smith arose, and began to prophesy, when a noise was heard like the sound of a rushing mighty wind, which filled the Temple, and all the congregation simultaneously arose, being moved upon by an invisible power; many began to speak in tongues, and prophesy; others saw glorious visions; and I beheld the Temple was filled with angels, which fact I declared to the congregation. The people of the neighborhood came running together, (hearing an unusual sound within, and seeing a bright light like a pillar of fire resting upon the Temple,) and were astonished at what was transpiring."

WHAT THE ELDERS SHOULD PREACH. — *March* 30, 1836, the Elders met in the Kirtland Temple, to attend to the ordinance of washing of feet, under the direction of the Prophet Joseph. He made the following remarks:

"That the time that we were required to tarry in Kirtland to be endued, would be fulfilled in a few days, and then the Elders would go forth, and each must stand for himself, as it was not necessary for them to be sent out, two by two, as in former times, but to go in all meekness, in sobriety, and preach Jesus Christ and him crucified; not to contend with others on account of their faith, or systems of religion, but pursue a steady course. This I delivered by way of commandment; and all who observe it not, will pull down persecution upon their heads, while those who do, shall always be filled with the Holy Ghost; this I pronounced as a prophecy, and sealed with hosanna and Amen."

THE COMFORTER. — From instructions of the Prophet Joseph, given at a Conference of the Twelve, *June* 27, 1839.

"There are two Comforters spoken of. One is the Holy Ghost, the same as given on the day of Pentecost, and that all Saints receive after faith, repentance, and baptism. This first Comforter or Holy Ghost has no other effect than pure intelligence. It is more powerful in expanding the mind, enlightening the understanding, and storing the intellect with present knowledge, of a man who is of the literal seed of Abraham, than one that is a Gentile, though it may not have half as much visible effect upon the body; for as the Holy Ghost falls upon one of the literal seed of Abraham, it is calm and serene; and his whole soul and body are only exercised by the pure spirit of intelligence; while the effect of the Holy Ghost upon a Gentile, is to purge out the old blood, and make him actually of the seed of Abraham.

That man that has none of the blood of Abraham (naturally) must have a new creation by the Holy Ghost. In such a case, there may be more of a powerful effect upon the body, and visible to the eye, than upon an Israelite, while the Israelite at first might be far before the Gentile in pure intelligence.

THE OTHER COMFORTER spoken of is a subject of great interest, and perhaps understood by few of this generation. After a person hath faith in Christ, repents of his sins, and is baptized for the remission of his sins and receives the Holy Ghost, (by the laying on of hands,) which is the first Comforter, then let him continue to humble himself before God, hungering and thirsting after righteousness, and living by every word of God, and the Lord will soon say unto him, Son, thou shalt be exalted, etc. When the Lord has thoroughly proved him, and finds that the man is determined to serve him at all hazards, then the man will find his calling and his election made sure, then it will be his privilege to receive the *other Comforter*, which the Lord hath promised the Saints, as is recorded in the testimony of St. John, in the 14th chapter, from the 12th to the 27th verses. * *

Now, what is this *other Comforter*? It is no more or less than the LORD JESUS CHRIST himself; and this is the sum and substance of the whole matter; that when any man obtains this last Comforter, he will have the personage of Jesus Christ to attend him, or appear unto him from time to time, and even he will manifest the Father unto him, and they will take up their abode with him, and the visions of the heavens will be opened unto him, and the Lord will teach him face to face, and he may have a perfect knowledge of the mysteries of the kingdom of God; and this is the state and place the ancient Saints arrived at when they had such glorious visions—Isaiah, Ezekiel, John upon the Isle of Patmos, St. Paul in the three heavens, and all the Saints who held communion with the general assembly and *Church of the First Born*, etc.

"The Spirit of Revelation is in connection with these blessings. A person may profit by noticing the first intimations of the Spirit of Revelation; for instance, when you feel pure intelligence flowing unto you, it may give you sudden strokes of ideas, that by noticing it, you may find it fulfilled the same day or soon; (i. e.,) those things that were presented unto your mind by the Spirit of God, will come to pass; and thus by learning the Spirit of God and understanding it, you may grow into the principle of Revelation, until you become perfect in Christ Jesus."

Forgive One Another.—"Ever keep in exercise the principle of mercy, and be ready to forgive our brother on the first intimations of repentance, and asking forgiveness; and should we even forgive our brother, or even our enemy, before they repent or ask forgiveness, our Heavenly Father would be equally as merciful unto us."

Keys.—*July* 2, 1839, at a meeting of the Twelve and some of the Seventies, President Joseph Smith made the following remarks: "O ye Twelve! and all Saints! profit by this important KEY—that in all your trials, troubles, temptations, afflictions, bonds, imprisonments and death, see to it, that you do not betray heaven; that you do not betray *Jesus Christ*; that you do not betray the *brethren*; that you do not betray the *revelations* of God, whether in the Bible, Book of Mormon, or Doctrine and Covenants, or any other that ever was or ever will be given and revealed unto man in this world or that which is to come. Yea, in all your kicking and flounderings, see to it that you do not this thing, lest innocent blood be found in your skirts, and you go down to hell. All other sins are not to be compared to sinning against the Holy Ghost, and proving a traitor to thy brethren.

I will give unto you one of the *keys* of the mysteries of the kingdom. It is an eternal principle, that has existed with God from all eternity: That man who rises up to condemn others, finding fault with the Church, saying that they are out of the way, while he himself is righteous, then know assuredly, that that man is in the highroad to apostacy; and if he does not repent, will apostatize, as God lives.

The principle is as correct as the one Jesus put forth in saying, that he who seeketh a sign is an adulterous person; and that principle is eternal, undeviating, and firm as the pillars of heaven; for whenever you see a man seeking after a sign, you may set it down that he is an adulterous man.

Coming of the Son of Man.—On another occasion about this time the prophet Joseph made the following remarks: "Men profess to prophesy. I will prophesy that the signs of the coming of the Son of Man are already commenced. One pestilence will desolate after another. We shall soon have war and bloodshed. The moon will be turned into blood. I testify of these things, and that the coming of the Son of Man is nigh, even at your doors. If our souls and our bodies are not looking forth for the coming of the Son of Man; and after we are dead, if we are not looking forth, &c.; we shall be among those who are calling for the rocks to fall upon us, &c. * * * The time is soon coming when no man will have any peace but in Zion and her Stakes.

"I saw men hunting the lives of their own sons, and brother murdering brother, women killing their own daughters, and daughters seeking the lives of their mothers. I saw armies arrayed against armies. I saw blood, desolation, fires. &c.

"The Son of Man has said that the mother shall be against the daughter, and the daughter against the mother, &c. These things are at our doors. They will follow the Saints of God from city to city. Satan will rage, and the spirit of the devil is now enraged. I know not how soon these things will take place; and with a view of them, shall I cry peace? No! I will lift up my voice and testify of them. How long you will have good crops, and the famine be kept off, I do not know; when the fig tree leaves, know then that the summer is nigh at hand."

The Saints must Suffer.—*September* 29, 1839, "Explained concerning the coming of the Son of Man, &c.; also that it is a false idea that the Saints will escape all the judgments, whilst the wicked suffer; for all flesh is subject to suffer, and 'the righteous shall hardly escape;' still many of the Saints will escape, for the just shall live by faith; yet many of the righteous shall fall a prey to disease, to pestilence, etc., by reason of the weakness of the flesh, and yet be saved in the kingdom of God. So that it is an unhallowed principle to say that such and such have transgressed because they have been preyed upon by disease or death, for all flesh is subject to death; and the Savior said, 'Judge not, lest ye be judged.'"

Translation.—*October* 5, 1840. "Many may have supposed that the doctrine of translation was a doctrine whereby men were taken immediately into the presence of God, and into an eternal fulness, but this is a mistaken idea. Their place of habitation is that of the terrestrial order, and a place prepared for such characters, be held in reserve to be ministering angels unto many planets, and who as yet have not entered into so great a fulness as those who are resurrected from the dead. * * * This distinction is made between the doctrine of the actual resurrection and translation: translation obtains deliverance from the tortures and sufferings of the body, but their existence will prolong as to the labors and toils of the ministry, before they can enter into so great a rest and glory."

SACRIFICE TO BE RESTORED. — "It is generally supposed that sacrifice was entirely done away when the Great Sacrifice was offered up, and that there will be no necessity for the ordinance of sacrifice in future; but those who assert this are certainly not acquainted with the duties, privileges, and authority of the Priesthood, or with the Prophets. * *

"These sacrifices, as well as every ordinance belonging to the Priesthood, will, when the Temple of the Lord shall be built, and the sons of Levi be purified, be fully restored and attended to in all their powers, ramifications, and blessings. This ever did and will exist when the powers of the Melchizedec Priesthood are sufficiently manifest; else how can the restitution of all things spoken of by all the holy Prophets be brought to pass?"

BOOK OF MORMON. — *November* 28, 1841. In council with the Twelve Apostles, Joseph Smith said, "I told the brethren that the Book of Mormon was the most correct of any book on earth, and the keystone of our religion, and a man would get nearer to God by abiding by its precepts, than by any other book."

THE RESURRECTION. — *March* 20, 1842. From a sermon of Joseph Smith's: "As concerning the resurrection, I will merely say that all men will come from the grave as they lie down, whether old or young; there will not be 'added unto their stature one cubit,' neither taken from it; all will be raised by the power of God, having spirit in their bodies, and not blood."

SPIRIT AND MATTER. — *April* 1, 1842. The Prophet Joseph said, "In tracing the thing to the foundation, and looking at it philosophically, we shall find a very material difference between the body and the spirit: the body is supposed to be organized matter, and the spirit, by many, is thought to be immaterial, without substance. With this latter statement we should beg leave to differ, and state that spirit is a substance; that it is material, but that it is more pure, elastic, and refined matter than the body; that it existed before the body, can exist in the body, and will exist separate from the body, when the body will be mouldering in the dust; and will in the resurrection, be again united with it."

MUST BE LIKE GOD. — *April* 10, 1842. Joseph Smith said, "If you wish to go where God is, you must be like God, or possess the principles which God possesses, for if we are not drawing towards God in principle, we are going from Him and drawing towards the devil. * * * A man is saved no faster than he gets knowledge, for if he does not get knowledge, he will be brought into captivity by some evil power in the other world, as evil spirits will have more knowledge, and consequently more power than many men who are on the earth. Hence it needs revelation to assist us, and give us knowledge of the things of God.".

KEYS. — *May* 1, 1842. "The KEYS are certain signs and words by which false spirits and personages may be detected from true, which cannot be revealed to the Elders till the Temple is completed. The rich can only get them in the Temple, the poor may get them on the mountain top as Moses did."

CHARITY. — "The rich cannot be saved without charity, giving to feed the poor when and how God requires."

SIGNS.—"There are signs in heaven, earth, and hell; the Elders must know them all, to be endowed with power, to finish their work and prevent imposition. The devil knows many signs, but does not know the sign of the Son of Man, or Jesus. No one can truly say he knows God until he has handled something, and this can only be in the Holiest of Holies."

A PROPHECY.—*August* 6, 1842. "I prophesied that the Saints would continue to suffer much affliction and would be driven to the Rocky Mountains, many would apostatize, others would be put to death by our persecutors, or lose their lives in consequence of exposure or disease, and some of you will live to go and assist in making settlements and build cities and see the Saints become a mighty people in the midst of the Rocky Mountains."

THE MILLENNIUM.—*December* 30, 1842. "Christ and the resurrected Saints will reign over the earth during the thousand years. They will not probably dwell on the earth, but will visit it when they please, or when it is necessary to govern it. There will be wicked men on the earth during the thousand years. The heathen nations who will not come up to worship will be visited with the judgments of God, and must eventually be destroyed from the earth."

SIGN OF A DOVE.—*January* 29, 1843. "The sign of the dove was instituted before the creation of the world, a witness for the Holy Ghost, and the Devil cannot come in the sign of a dove."

COMING OF THE SON OF MAN.—*April* 6, 1843. "Judah must return, Jerusalem must be rebuilt, and the Temple, and water come out from under the Temple, and the waters of the Dead Sea be healed. It will take some time to build the walls of the city and the Temple, &c.; and all this must be done before the Son of Man will make his appearance. There will be wars and rumors of wars, signs in the heavens above and on the earth beneath, the sun turned into darkness and the moon to blood, earthquakes in divers places, the seas heaving beyond their bounds; then will appear one grand sign of the Son of Man in heaven. But what will the world do? They will say it is a planet, a comet, &c. But the Son of Man will come as the sign of the coming of the Son of Man, which will be as the light of the morning cometh out of the east."

SOME SEEK TO EXCEL.—*May* 14, 1843. "In this world, mankind are naturally selfish, ambitious, and striving to excel above one another. * * So in the other world there is a variety of spirits. Some seek to excel. And this was the case with Lucifer when he fell. He sought for things which were unlawful. Hence he was cast down, and it is said he drew away many with him; and the greatness of his punishment is, that he shall not have a tabernacle. This is his punishment."

THE MORE SURE WORD OF PROPHECY.—"Now for the secret and grand key. Though they might hear the voice of God and know that Jesus was the Son of God, this would be no evidence that their election and calling was made sure, that they had part with Christ, and were joint heirs with him. They then would want that more sure word of prophecy, that they were sealed in the heavens and had the promise of eternal life in the kingdom of God. Then, having this promise sealed unto them, it was an anchor to the soul, sure and steadfast."

Hɪᴅ ᴡɪᴛʜ Cʜʀɪsᴛ ɪɴ Gᴏᴅ.—*May* 16, 1843. "Your life is hid with Christ in God, and so are many others. Nothing but the unpardonable sin can prevent you from inheriting eternal glory, for you are sealed up by the power of the Priesthood unto eternal life, having taken the step necessary for the purpose. * * * The unpardonable sin is to shed innocent blood, or be accessory thereto. All other sins will be visited with judgment in the flesh, and the spirit being delivered to the buffetings of Satan until the day of the Lord Jesus."

Tʜʀᴇᴇ Dᴇɢʀᴇᴇs ɪɴ Cᴇʟᴇsᴛɪᴀʟ Gʟᴏʀʏ.—"In the celestial glory there are three heavens or degrees; and in order to obtain the highest, a man must enter into this order of the Priesthood; and if he does not, he cannot obtain it. He may enter into the other, but that is the end of his kingdom: he cannot have an increase."

Sᴀʟᴠᴀᴛɪᴏɴ.—*May* 17, 1843. "Salvation means a man's being placed beyond the power of all his enemies. The more sure word of prophecy means a man's knowing that he is sealed up unto eternal life by revelation and the spirit of prophecy, through the power of the holy Priesthood. It is impossible for a man to be saved in ignorance."

Eᴛᴇʀɴᴀʟ Dᴜʀᴀᴛɪᴏɴ ᴏғ Mᴀᴛᴛᴇʀ.—"Speaking of the eternal duration of matter, I said.—There is no such thing as immaterial matter. All spirit is matter, but is more fine or pure, and can only be discerned by purer eyes. We cannot see it; but when our bodies are purified, we shall see that it is all matter."

Tʜᴇ Pᴜɴɪsʜᴍᴇɴᴛ ᴏғ ᴛʜᴇ Dᴇᴠɪʟ.—*May* 21, 1843. "The spirits in the eternal world are like the spirits in this world. When those spirits have come into this world and received tabernacles, then died, and again have risen and received glorified bodies, they will have an ascendancy over the spirits who have no bodies, or kept not their first estate, like the Devil. The punishment of the Devil was, that he should not have a habitation like men. The Devil's retaliation is, he comes into this world, binds up men's bodies, and occupies them himself. When the authorities come along, they eject him from a stolen habitation."

Tʜᴇ Tʜʀᴇᴇ Kᴇʏs.—"We have no claim in our eternal compact, in relation to eternal things, unless our actions and contracts and all things tend to this end. But after all this, you have got to make your calling and election sure.

"If this injunction would lie largely on those to whom it was spoken, how much more those of the present generation. First key: Knowledge is the power of salvation. Second key: Make your calling and election sure. Third key: It is one thing to be on the mount and hear the excellent voice, &c., &c.; and another to hear the voice declare to you, you have a part and lot in that kingdom."

Jᴏʜɴ Tʜᴇ Bᴀᴘᴛɪsᴛ.—*May* 24, 1843. "After naming his text, the Prophet remarked that some one had asked him the meaning of the expression of Jesus—'Among those born of women, there has not arisen a greater than John;' and said he had promised to answer it in public and he would do it then.

"It could not have been on account of the miracles John performed, for he did no miracles; but it was—First, because he was trusted with a divine mission of preparing the way before the face of the Lord. Who was trusted with such a mission before or since? No man. Second, he was trusted and it was required at his hand to baptize the Son of Man. Whoever did that? Who ever had so great a privilege or glory? Who ever led the Son of God into the waters of baptism, beholding the *Holy Ghost* descend upon him in the sign of a dove? *No man.*

"Third, John at that time was the only legal administrator holding the keys of power there was on earth. The keys, the kingdom, the power, the glory had departed from the Jews; and John, the son of Zachariah, by the anointing and decree of heaven, held the keys of power at that time."

THE PRINCIPLE THAT CRUCIFIED JESUS CHRIST.—*June* 11, 1843. "Many men will say, 'I will never forsake you, but will stand by you at all times.' But the moment you teach them some of the mysteries of the kingdom of God that are retained in the heavens and are to be revealed to the children of men when they are prepared for them, they will be the first to stone you and put you to death. It was this same principle that crucified the Lord Jesus Christ, and will cause the people to kill the Prophets in this generation."

A FULNESS OF ORDINANCES NECESSARY.—"All men who become heirs of God and joint heirs of Jesus Christ will have to receive the fulness of the ordinances of his kingdom; and those who will not receive all the ordinances will come short of the fulness of that glory, if they do not lose the whole."

THE WORLD OF SPIRITS.—"Hades, the Greek, or Shaole, the Hebrew: these two significations mean a world of spirits. Hades, Shaole, paradise, spirits in prison, are all one: it is a world of spirits.

"The righteous and the wicked all go to the same world of spirits until the resurrection. * * The great misery of departed spirits in the world of spirits, where they go after death, is to know that they come short of the glory that others enjoy and that they might have enjoyed themselves, and they are their own accusers."

THREE PERSONS IN HEAVEN HOLDING THE KEYS OF POWER.—"Any person that has seen the heavens opened knows that there are three personages in the heavens who hold the keys of power, and one presides over all. * * * As the Father hath power in himself, so hath the Son power in himself, to lay down his life and take it again, so he has a body of his own. The Son doeth what he hath seen the Father do: then the Father hath some day laid down his life and taken it again; so he has a body of his own; each one will be in his own body."

FORGIVE ALL MEN.—*July* 9, 1843. "Joseph remarked that all was well between him and the heavens; that he had no enmity against anyone; and as the prayer of Jesus, or his pattern, so prayed Joseph—'Father, forgive me my trespasses as I forgive those who trespass against me,' for I freely forgive all men. If we would secure and cultivate the love of others, we must love others, even our enemies as well as friends."

NECESSITY OF BAPTISM.—The Gospel requires baptism by immersion for the remission of sins, which is the meaning of the word in the original language—namely, to bury or immerse. * * But I further believe in the gift of the Holy Ghost by the laying on of hands. * * Might as well baptize a bag of sand as a man, if not done in view of the remission of sins and getting of the Holy Ghost. Baptism by water is but half a baptism, and is good for nothing without the other half—that is, the baptism of the Holy Ghost.

SEALING OF THE SERVANTS OF GOD.—*August* 13, 1843. "Four destroying angels holding power over the four quarters of the earth until the servants of God are sealed in their foreheads, which signifies sealing the blessing upon their heads, meaning the everlasting covenant, thereby making their calling and election sure. When a seal is put upon the father and mother, it secures their posterity, so that they cannot be lost, but will be saved by virtue of the covenant of their father and mother."

THE KING OF SALEM.—*August* 18, 1843. "The King of Shiloam (Salem) had power and authority over that of Abraham, holding the key and the power of endless life."

"THE SACRIFICE REQUIRED OF ABRAHAM in the offering up of Isaac shows that if a man would attain to the keys of the kingdom of an endless life, he must sacrifice all things. When God offers a blessing or knowledge to a man, and he refuses to receive it, he will be damned."

THE FULNESS OF THE MELCHISEDEK PRIESTHOOD.—"Those holding the fulness of the Melchisedek Priesthood are kings and priests of the Most High God, holding the keys of power and blessings! In fact, that Priesthood is a perfect law of theocracy, and stands as God to give laws to the people, administering endless lives to the sons and daughters of Adam.

"Abram says to Melchisedek, I believe all that thou hast taught me concerning the Priesthood and the coming of the Son of Man; so Melchisedek ordained Abram, and sent him away. Abram rejoiced, saying, Now I have a Priesthood. * * Elijah shall reveal the covenants to seal the hearts of the fathers to the children, and the children to the fathers. The anointing and sealing is to be called, elected, and made sure."

SPIRITS OF THE JUST.—*October* 9, 1843. "Spirits can only be revealed in flaming fire or glory. Angels have advanced further, their light and glory being tabernacled; and hence they appear in bodily shape. The spirits of just men are made ministering servants to those who are sealed unto life eternal, and it is through them that the sealing power comes down. * *

"The spirits of the just are exalted to a greater and more glorious work; hence they are blessed in their departure to the world of spirits. Enveloped in flaming fire, they are not far from us, and know and understand our thoughts, feelings, and notions, and are often pained therewith.

"Flesh and blood cannot go there; but flesh and bones, quickened by the Spirit of God, can."

THE KINGDOM OF GOD.—*October* 15, 1843. "It is one thing to see the Kingdom of God, and another thing to enter into it. We must have a change of heart to see the Kingdom of God, and subscribe the articles of adoption to enter therein.

ADULTERY.—*November* 25, 1843. "If a man commit adultery, he cannot receive the celestial kingdom of God. Even if he is saved in any kingdom, it cannot be the celestial kingdom."

Saviors on Mount Zion.—*January* 20, 1844. "The Bible says, 'I will send you Elijah the Prophet before the coming of the great and dreadful day of the Lord; and he shall turn the hearts of the fathers to the children, and the hearts of the children to the fathers, lest I come and smite the earth with a curse.'

"Now, the word *turn* here should be translated *bind*, or seal. But what is the object of this important mission? or how is it to be fulfilled? The keys are to be delivered, the spirit of Elijah is to come, the Gospel to be established, the Saints of God gathered, Zion built up, and the Saints to come up as Saviors on Mount Zion.

"But how are they to become Saviors on Mount Zion? By building their temples, erecting their baptismal fonts, and going forth and receiving all the ordinances, baptisms, confirmations, washings, anointings, ordinations, and sealing powers upon their heads, in behalf of all their progenitors who are dead, and redeem them that they may come forth in the first resurrection and be exalted to thrones of glory with them; and herein is the chain that binds the hearts of the fathers to the children, and the children to the fathers, which fulfils the mission of Elijah. * *

"The Saints have not too much time to save and redeem their dead, and gather together their living relatives, that they may be saved also, before the earth will be smitten, and the consumption decreed falls upon the world."

The Spirit of Elias.—*March* 10, 1844. "The spirit of Elias is to prepare the way for a greater revelation of God, which is the Priesthood of Elias, or the Priesthood that Aaron was ordained unto. And when God sends a man into the world to prepare for a greater work, holding the keys of the power of Elias, it was called the doctrine of Elias, even from the early ages of the world. * * * This is the Elias spoken of in the last days, and here is the rock upon which many split, thinking the time was past in the days of John and Christ, and no more to be. But the spirit of Elias was revealed to me, and I know it is true; therefore I speak with boldness, for I know verily my doctrine is true."

The Spirit of Elijah.—"Now for Elijah. The spirit, power, and calling of Elijah is, that ye have power to hold the keys of the revelations, ordinances, oracles, powers, and endowments of the fulness of the Melchisedek Priesthood and of the kingdom of God on the earth; and to receive, obtain, and perform all the ordinances belonging to the kingdom of God, even unto the turning of the hearts of the fathers unto the children, and the hearts of the children unto the fathers, even those who are in heaven. * * Now comes the point. What is this office and work of Elijah? It is one of the greatest and most important subjects that God has revealed. He should send Elijah to seal the children to the fathers, and the fathers to the children. * * I wish you to understand this subject, for it is important; and if you will receive it, this is the spirit of Elijah, that we redeem our dead, and connect ourselves with our fathers which are in heaven, and seal up our dead to come forth in the first resurrection; and here we want the power of Elijah *to seal those who dwell on earth to those who dwell in heaven*. This is the power of Elijah and the keys of the kingdom of Jehovah. * * Then what you seal on earth, by the keys of Elijah, is sealed in heaven;

and this is the power of Elijah, and this is the difference between the spirit and power of Elias and Elijah; for while the spirit of Elias is a forerunner, the power of Elijah is sufficient to make our calling and election sure. * * We cannot be perfect without the fathers, etc. We must have revelations from them, and we can see that the doctrine of REVELATION as far transcends the doctrine of NO REVELATION as knowledge is above ignorance; for one truth revealed from heaven is worth all the sectarian notions in existence.

"This spirit of Elijah was manifest in the days of the apostles, in delivering certain ones to the buffetings of Satan, that they might be saved in the day of the Lord Jesus. They were sealed by the spirit of Elijah unto the damnation of hell until the day of the Lord, or revelation of Jesus Christ. * *

"According to the Scriptures, if men have received the good word of God, and tasted of the powers of the world to come, if they shall fall away, it is impossible to renew them again, seeing they have crucified the Son of God afresh, and put him to open shame; so there is a possibility of falling away: you could not be renewed again, and the power of Elijah cannot seal against this sin, for this is a reserve made in the seals and power of the Priesthood. * *

"A murderer, for instance, one that sheds innocent blood, cannot have forgiveness. David sought repentance at the hand of God carefully, with tears, for the murder of Uriah; but he could only get it through hell: he got a promise that his soul should not be left in hell. Although David was a king, he never did obtain the spirit and power of Elijah and the fulness of the Priesthood; and the Priesthood that he received, and the throne and kingdom of David is to be taken from him and given to another by the name of David in the last days, raised up out of his lineage.

"This is the case with murderers. They could not be baptized for the remission of sins, for they had shed innocent blood."

THE SPIRIT OF MESSIAH. — "The spirit of Elias is first, Elijah second, and Messiah last. Elias is a forerunner to prepare the way, and the spirit and power of Elijah is to come after, holding the keys of power, building the Temple to the cap stone, placing the seals of the Melchisedek Priesthood upon the house of Israel, and making all things ready; then *Messiah* comes to his Temple, which is last of all. Messiah is above the spirit and power of Elijah, for he made the world, and was that spiritual rock unto Moses in the wilderness. Elijah was to come and prepare the way and build up the kingdom before the coming of the great day of the Lord, although the spirit of Elias might begin it."

ETERNAL LIFE.—*April 7, 1844.* "Here, then, is eternal life—to know the only wise and true God; and you have got to learn how to be Gods yourselves, and to be kings and priests to God, the same as all Gods have done before you,—namely, by going from one small degree to another, and from a small capacity to a great one; from grace to grace, from exaltation to exaltation, until you attain to the resurrection of the dead, and are able to dwell in everlasting burnings, and to sit in glory, as do those who sit enthroned in everlasting power."

ALL REVELATIONS ARE SPIRITUAL. — "All things whatsoever God of his infinite wisdom has seen fit and proper to reveal to us, while we are dwelling in mortality, in regard to our mortal bodies, are revealed to us in the abstract and independent of affinity of this mortal tabernacle, but are revealed to our spirits precisely as though we had no bodies at all; and those revelations which will save our spirits will save our bodies. God reveals them to us in view of no eternal dissolution of the body, or tabernacle. Hence the responsibility, the awful responsibility, that rests upon us, in relation to our dead; for all the spirits who have not obeyed the Gospel in the flesh must either obey it in the spirit or be damned. * * * The greatest responsibility in this world that God has laid upon us is to seek after our dead. The Apostle says, 'They without us cannot be made perfect;' for it is necessary that the sealing power should be in our hands to seal our children and our dead for the fulness of the dispensation of times—a dispensation to meet the promises made by Jesus Christ before the foundation of the world for the salvation of man."

SIN AGAINST THE HOLY GHOST.—"All sins, and all blasphemies, and every transgression, except one, that man can be guilty of, may be forgiven; and there is a salvation for all men, either in this world or the world to come, who have not committed the unpardonable sin, there being a provision either in this world or the world of spirits. Hence God hath made a provision that every spirit in the eternal world can be ferreted out and saved, unless he has committed that unpardonable sin which cannot be remitted to him either in this world or the world of spirits. God has wrought out a salvation for all men, unless they have committed a certain sin; and every man who has a friend in the eternal world can save him, unless he has committed the unpardonable sin. And so you can see how you can be a savior."

THE CONTENTION IN HEAVEN.—"The contention in heaven was—Jesus said there would be certain souls that would not be saved; and the Devil said he could save them all, and laid his plans before the grand council, who gave their vote in favor of Jesus Christ. So the Devil rose up in rebellion against God, and was cast down, with all who put up their heads for him."

FOREORDINATION OF MAN.—*May* 12, 1844. "Every man who has a calling to minister to the inhabitants of the world was ordained to that very purpose in the Grand Council of heaven before this world was."

GOD DWELLS IN ETERNAL FIRE.—"God Almighty himself dwells in eternal fire: flesh and blood cannot go there, for all corruption is devoured by the fire. Our God is a consuming fire. When our flesh is quickened by the Spirit, there will be no blood in this tabernacle. Some dwell in higher glory than others."

THE RESURRECTION.—"All men who are immortal dwell in everlasting burnings. You cannot go anywhere but where God can find you out. All men are born to die, and all men must rise; all must enter eternity.

"In order for you to receive your children to yourself, you must have a promise—some ordinance, some blessing, in order to ascend above principalities, or else it may be an angel. They must rise just as they died: we can there hail our lovely infants with the same glory—the same loveliness in the celestial glory, where they all enjoy alike. They differ in stature, in size: the same glorious spirit gives them the likeness of glory and bloom; the old man with his silvery hairs will glory in bloom and beauty. No man can describe it to you—no man can write it."

Council of High Priests.—*February* 12, 1834. The Prophet Joseph said: "No man is capable of judging a matter, in Council, unless his own heart is pure; and that we frequently are so filled with prejudice, or have a beam in our own eye, that we are not capable of passing right decisions, etc.

"But to return to the subject of order: In ancient days, Councils were conducted with strict propriety, that no one was allowed to whisper, be weary, leave the room, or get uneasy in the least, until the voice of the Lord, by revelation, or the voice of the Council by the Spirit was obtained, which has not been observed in this Church to the present.

"It was understood in ancient days, that if one man could stay in Council, another could; and if the President could spend his time, the members could also; but in our Councils, generally, one will be uneasy, another asleep; one praying, another not; one's mind on the business of the Council, and another thinking on something else, etc.

"Our acts are rendered, and at a future day they will be laid before us, and if we should fail to judge right and injure our fellow beings, they may be there, perhaps, condemn us; there they are of great consequence, and to me the consequence appears to be of force, beyond anything which I am able to express, etc. Ask yourselves, brethren, how much you have exercised yourselves in prayer since you heard of this Council; and if you are now prepared to sit in Council upon the soul of your brother."

The High Council.—*July* 11, 1840. "The High Council met at my office, when I taught them principles relating to their duty as a Council, and that they might be guided by the same in future, I ordered it to be recorded as follows: 'That the Council should try no case without both parties being present, or having had an opportunity to be present, neither should they hear one party's complaint before his case is brought up for trial; neither should they suffer the character of any one to be exposed before the High Council without the person being present and ready to defend him or herself; that the minds of the Councilors be not prejudiced for or against any one whose case they may possibly have to act upon."

By the Prophet Joseph, *January* 5, 1841. "At the organization of a school of instruction. Description of Paul: He is about five feet high; very dark hair; dark complexion; dark skin; large Roman nose; sharp face; small black eyes, penetrating as eternity; round shoulders; a whining voice, except when elevated, and then it almost resembled the roaring of a lion. He was a good orator, active and diligent, always employing himself in doing good to his fellow man."

Different Degrees of the Priesthood of Melchisedek.—"Answer to the question, Was the Priesthood of Melchisedek taken away when Moses died? All Priesthood is Melchisedek, but there are different portions or degrees of it. That portion which brought Moses to speak with God face to face was taken away; but that which brought the ministry of angels remained. All the prophets had the Melchisedek Priesthood and were ordained by God himself.

The world and earth are not synonymous terms. The world is the human family.—This earth was organized or formed out of other planets which were broken up and remodeled and made into the one on which we live.

The elements are eternal. That which has a beginning will surely have an end; take a ring, it is without beginning or end—cut it for a beginning place and at the same time you have an ending place.

A key: Every principle proceeding from God is eternal and any principle which is not eternal is of the devil. The sun has no beginning or end; the rays which proceed from himself have no bounds, consequently are eternal.

So it is with God. If the soul of man had a beginning it will surely have an end. In the translation 'without form and void' it should read, empty and desolate. The word created should be formed, or organized.'"

OBSERVATION ON THE SECTARIAN GOD.—"That which is without body, parts and passions is nothing. There is no other God in heaven but that God who has flesh and bones. *John*, 5. 26, As the Father hath life in himself, even so hath he given to the Son to have life in himself. God the Father took life unto himself precisely as Jesus did.

"The first step in the salvation of man is the laws of eternal and self-existent principles. Spirits are eternal. At the first organization in heaven we were all present, and saw the Savior chosen and appointed and the plan of salvation made, and we sanctioned it.

We came to this earth that we might have a body and present it pure before God in the celestial kingdom. The great principle of happiness consists is having a body. The devil has no body, and herein is his punishment. He is pleased when he can obtain the tabernacle of man, and when cast out by the Savior he asked to go into the herd of swine, showing that he would prefer a swine's body to having none.

All beings who have bodies have power over those who have not. The devil has no power over us only as we permit him. The moment we revolt at anything which comes from God, the devil takes power. This earth will be rolled back into the presence of God, and crowned with celestial glory."

THREE INDEPENDENT PRINCIPLES.—*May* 16, 1841. "There are three independent principles; the Spirit of God, the spirit of man, and the spirit of the devil. All men have power to resist the devil.

"They who have tabernacles, have power over those who have not. The doctrine of eternal judgment; *Acts* 2. 41. Peter preached, Repent, and be baptized in the name of Jesus Christ, for the remission of sins, &c.; but in *Acts* 3. 19 he says, Repent and be converted, that your sins may be blotted out when the times of redemption shall come, and he shall send Jesus, &c.

"Remission of sins by baptism was not to be preached to murderers. All the priests of Christendom might pray for a murderer on the scaffold forever, but could not avail so much as a gnat towards their forgiveness. There is no forgiveness for murderers; they will have to wait until the times of redemption shall come, and that in hell. Peter had the keys of eternal judgment, and he saw David in hell, and knew for what reason, and that David would have to remain there until the resurrection at the coming of Christ. *Romans* 9. All election that can be found in the scriptures is according to the flesh, and pertaining to the Priesthood.

The Three Personages.—Everlasting covenant was made between three personages before the organization of this earth, and relates to their dispensation of things to men on the earth: these personages, according to Abraham's record, are called God the first, the Creator; God the second, the Redeemer; and God the third, the witness or Testator."

Lehi's Travels.—*Revelation to Joseph the Seer*. The course that Lehi and his company traveled from Jerusalem to the place of their destination:

They traveled nearly a south, southeast direction until they came to the nineteenth degree of north latitude; then, nearly east to the Sea of Arabia, then sailed in a southeast direction, and landed on the continent of South America, in Chili, thirty degrees south latitude.

BOOK OF MORMON CHRONOLOGY.

The events marked are those about which the record does not appear sufficiently explicit to make the year certain. It is occasionally difficult to decide whether the circumstance narrated took place near the close of one year, or in the commencement of the next.

The four dates marked thus ** are based upon the supposition that Zeniff re-occupied the land of Nephi, B. C. 200. This may not be the exact year, but it is approximate.

The three dates marked thus * are based upon the idea that the "young man," Alma, was twenty-five years old when the prophet Abinadi was martyred.

The Book of Mormon appears to furnish no clue to the date of Lehi's colony landing in South America. It is supposed to have been about twelve years after its departure from Jerusalem.

B. C. signifies before the birth of Christ; A. C. after Christ; N. A. signifies "Nephite Annals" or years after the departure of Lehi from Jerusalem; Y. J., years of the Judges, or of the Republic.

	B.C.	N.A.	Y.J.
Lehi and colony leave Jerusalem, and journey to the valley of Lemuel, by the Red sea.	600	1	
The sons of Lehi return to Jerusalem and obtain the sacred records kept by Laban.			
Lehi and colony reach the land Bountiful, where Nephi commences to build a ship.	592	9	
Mulek, son of King Zedekiah, with a colony leaves Jerusalem.			
Lehi and his colony reach South America.	590	11	
A temple built, Jacob and Joseph consecrated priests, &c. before.	571	30	
Wars and contentions, between Nephites and Lamanites, during ten years previous to.	561	40	
Nephi transfers the records to Jacob. The book of Jacob opens.	546	55	

Jacob, having committed the records into the hands of his son Enos, the latter transfers them to his son Jarom. Many wars between the Nephites and Lamanites during the days of Enos.	421	180
The Nephites have increased and scattered much over the land; they strictly observe the law of Moses and are prospered.		
The Lamanites, much more numerous than the Nephites, often invade the Nephite lands.	401	200
Jarom transfers the records to Omni. Many wars and contentions during Jarom's days.	362	239
Omni has frequent wars with the Lamanites.	324	277
Omni transfers the records to Ammaron.	318	283
The more wicked portion of the Nephites destroyed, The righteous preserved. Ammaron transfers the records to Chemish.	280	321
**About this date Zeniff leaves Zarahemla, with a colony, to re-occupy the land of Nephi. He makes a treaty with King Laman, and obtains the lands of Lehi-Nephi and Shemlon.	200	401
**The Lamanites make war with the people of Zeniff, but are repulsed with a loss of 3043 men.	183	418
Alma, the elder, born in the land of Nephi.	173	428
**King Laman having died, his son attacks the people of Zeniff, but is driven back.	161	440
**Zeniff confers the kingdom on his son Noah.	160	441
Mosiah I, born in the land of Zarahemla.	154	447
*The prophet Abinadi appears in the land of Nephi, and reproves Noah and his subjects for their iniquities.	150	451
*Abinadi again appears, prophesies, and is martyred.	148	453
*Alma establishes a Christian Church at the waters of Mormon, and afterwards, because of King Noah's persecutions, removes with his people to Helam.	147	454
First Christian Church established in Zarahemla, by King Benjamin, who, at the same time, consecrates his son Mosiah king.	125	476
A company sent by Limhi, son of Noah, to find Zarahemla, wander into the north country, and discover numerous relics of the Jaredites.	123	478

King Benjamin dies. A company of men, under Ammon, start from Zarahemla to find their brethren in the land of Nephi. They succeed, and help them to escape from the Lamanites, and bring them safely to Zarahemla.	122	479	
Moroni, commander in chief of the Nephite armies, born.	99	502	
Alma, the elder, dies, aged eighty-two. King Mosiah I, dies, aged sixty-three.			
Alma, the younger, elected Chief Judge of the Republic. The sons of Mosiah, with other Elders, start on a mission to the Lamanites in the land of Nephi.			
Priestcraft first introduced among the Nephites, by Nehor.			
Nehor slays the aged patriarch, Gideon, is tried, condemned and executed.			
?King Lamoni and his household converted by Ammon.	91	510	1
Priestcraft spreads among the Nephites; pride and contention develop in the church.			
?A church established by Ammon amongst the Lamanites, in the land of Ishmael.	90	511	2
Continued peace amongst the Nephites, notwithstanding persecutions and increased wickedness.	89	512	3
Amlici, a disciple of Nehor, desires to be king and to destroy the true church; his pretentions are rejected at a special election, by "the voice of the people:" he raises a rebellion, and is consecrated king by his followers.			
Amlici's forces are defeated by the Nephites under Alma at the hill Amnihu.			
The Lamanites invade Zarahemla, are joined by the Amlicites, and the united armies are defeated by Alma, on the west bank of the Sidon.			
Another invading Lamanite army is defeated on the east bank of the Sidon, and driven back to their own lands. Peace restored.			
Aaron, and other missionaries, imprisoned by the Lamanites in the land Middoni.	87	514	5
The Nephites, because of their late afflictions, are humble, and many are baptized.			
?Ammon and Lamoni proceed to Middoni, to release Aaron and his brethren. They meet Lamoni's father on the way: he attempts to slay Ammon.			
?Antiomno, King of Middoni, releases the captive missionaries.	86	515	6

3500 Nephites baptized into the church. Great peace and prosperity amongst them.

?Lamoni's father, king of all the Lamanites, baptized.

He issues a proclamation in favor of the Nephite missionaries.   85   516   7

Pride increasing in the Nephite church, causing envyings, malice, strife and persecutions.   84   517   8

Alma, on account of increasing iniquity, resigns the Chief-Judgeship, and nominates Nephihah as his successor, who is accepted by the voice of the people. Alma devotes himself entirely to the work of the ministry. He sets in order the churches in Zarahemla and Gideon.   83   518   9

Alma, as presiding High Priest, visits and ministers to the people in Melek and Ammonihah.

Amulek visited by an angel; he receives Alma into his house. They preach to the people of Ammonihah; are imprisoned and abused.

Zeezrom, the lawyer, converted, afterwards healed of a fever and baptized.

Those who accept the Gospel are cast out of Ammonihah, whilst others, men, women and children, are martyred by fire.

Alma and Amulek delivered, by the power of God, from prison. The prison is destroyed, and with it their persecutors.

Massacre of 1005 believing Lamanites.   82   519   10

The Lamanites, as foretold by Alma, destroy Ammonihah, with all its people, but are afterwards disastrously defeated by Zoram.   81   520   11

The church greatly increases during this and two following years.   80   521   12

?Second massacre of the people of Anti-Nephi-Lehi.   79   522   13

?The people of Anti-Nephi-Lehi arrive in the land of Zarahemla.   78   523   14

The people of Anti-Nephi-Lehi established in the land of Jershon.

The Lamanites pursue the Ammonites; are defeated by the Nephites with great slaughter.   77   524   15

Korihor, the Anti-Christ, struck dumb, and afterwards killed in a city of the Zoramites.

Amalickiah captures the Nephite cities of Moroni, Nephihah, Lehi, Gid, Morianton, Omner, Mulek, &c., on the Atlantic coast. He is defeated by Teancum. Teancum enters the Lamanite camp at night and slays Amalickiah. The Lamanites retreat into Mulek.   67   534   25

Ammoron, brother of Amalickiah, succeeds him as king of the Lamanites, and takes command of their armies on the Pacific coast.

Moroni pays a short visit to the Nephite forces in the southwest.

Teancum fortifies the Land Bountiful and the Isthmus of Panama.

The Ammonites desire to assist in the war, but because of their oath are not permitted; but 2000 of their sons, under Helaman, join the Nephite armies in the southwest, where they find that the Lamanites have captured the cities of Manti, Zeezrom, Cumeni and Antiparah.   66   535   26

Moroni gathers fresh troops and reinforces Teancum in Bountiful.

The Nephite forces in the southwest finish fortifying the city of Judea.

?Tremendous battle in the wilderness north of Judea; the Lamanites defeated, but Antipus, the Nephite commander, is slain.   65   536   27

Mulek re-captured by Moroni, Lehi and Teancum.

Jacob, the Lamanite General, killed. Lehi placed in command at Mulek.

The Lamanite prisoners compelled to dig a ditch around and fortify the city Bountiful.

The city of Antiparah vacated by the Lamanites and re-occupied by the Nephites.   64   537   28

Pachus revolts against the commonwealth, and endeavors to establish a monarchy.

Moroni re-captures Gid, and releases large numbers of Nephite prisoners.

Six thousand men, from Zarahemla, join the Nephite armies in the Southwest.

The Lamanites surrender Cumeni. The Nephites drive the Lamanites eastward to the land of Manti. They are afterwards driven out of that region by Helaman.

Pahoran dies. The Book of Alma closes.	53	518	39
The Book of Helaman commences. Tubaloth king of the Lamanites.			
Three of Pahoran's sons contend for the judgment seat. The people choose Pahoran, the younger. His brother, Paanchi, rebels, for which he is tried, condemned and executed. One of his adherents, Kishkumen, assassinates Pahoran. Pacumeni chosen Chief Judge.			
The Gadianton robber bands organized.	52	549	40
The Lamanites, under Coriantumr, invade Zarahemla, capture the city, slay Pacumeni, and advance northward. Afterwards the Nephite forces, under Moronihah and Lehi, destroy the invading army. Coriantumr slain.	51	550	41
Helaman elected Chief Judge; Kishkumen attempts to assassinate him, but is himself slain. Gadianton and his band retire into the wilderness.	50	551	42
Much contention among the Nephites. Many emigrate North, as far as the great lakes.	46	555	46
Great contentions. Helaman fills the judgment seat with justice and equity.	45	556	47
The contentions measurably cease; the church is greatly prospered: tens of thousands baptized.			
The Gadianton robbers secretly increase in the more thickly settled portions of the land.	43	558	49
Pride increases; the more humble members of the church persecuted.	41	560	51
Helaman dies; his son Nephi succeeds him as Chief Judge.	39	562	53
Contentions and bloodshed among the Nephites; the rebellious affiliate with the Lamanites.	38	563	54
More dissenters go over to the Lamanites, who are all the year preparing for war.	36	565	56
The Lamanites invade Zarahemla; the Nephites, owing to their dissensions and wickedness, are everywhere driven before them.	35	566	57
The Lamanites overrun all the Nephite possessions as far as the land Bountiful. The Nephites fortify the Isthmus.	34	567	58
The Lamanites obtain possession of all South America. Moronihah reconquers the most northern portions of South America.	32	569	60
The Nephites regain about half their possessions, Zarahemla remaining in the hands of the Lamanites.			

The internal wars, originating with the Gadianton robbers, still continue. To stay the bloodshed, Nephi prays for a famine: his prayer is answered.	19	582	73
The famine continues and spreads.	18	583	74
The whole land, both amongst the Nephites and Lamanites, smitten with the famine; thousands die of hunger and pestilence. The people, in their extremity, begin to repent; they exterminate the Gadianton bands.	17	584	75
The Lord sends rain, and the earth brings forth abundantly. Nephi is reverenced as a servant of God by all the people.	16	585	76
The people rapidly increase; the major part of both peoples belong to the church.	15	586	77
Slight contentions on doctrinal questions.	14	587	78
The controversies increase; Nephi and Lehi receive many revelations and put an end to the disputes.	13	588	79
Dissenters search out the ancient abominations, re- establish the Gadianton bands and commence war.	12	589	80
The robbers grow strong, defy the united armies of the Nephites and Lamanites, commit depredations and carry off many prisoners. Great loss of life on both sides.	11	590	81
The Nephites again begin to forget the Lord. The Lamanites remain faithful.	10	591	82
The people wax strong in iniquity.	9	592	83
The people do not mend their ways.	8	593	84
The people grow in wickedness and ripen for destruction.	7	594	85
Samuel, the Lamanite, prophesies on the walls of Zarahemla; some attempt to kill him, others believe. The latter seek Nephi and are baptized. Samuel escapes to his own land. Nephi performs many miracles.	6	595	86
The greater portion of the people remain in their pride and wickedness, the lesser portion walking more circumspectly before God.	5	596	87
The people grow more hardened.	3	598	89
The words of the prophets commence to be fulfilled, signs and wonders appear, betokening the near advent of the Savior; angels are seen by many: yet the people still harden their hearts. The Book of Helaman closes.	2	599	90
The Third Book of Nephi opens. Nephi departs out of the land, and is never again seen. Lachoneus Chief Judge and Governor.	1	600	91

	A.C.	N.A.	Y.J.
The promised signs of the Redeemer's birth appear, much to the joy of believers.			
The two days and nights of constant light; a new star appears.			
The majority of the people join the church.			
The Nephites reckon their time from the Messiah's advent.	1	601	92
The Gadianton robbers commit many murders; the people not strong enough to overpower them.	2	602	
Dissensions increase, owing to many joining the robber band, especially among the youth.	3	603	
Wickedness and unbelief greatly increase.	4	604	
Evil continues to gain strength to this time. Gadianton bands grow so numerous that both Nephites and Lamanites take up arms against them.	13	613	
The robbers driven into their secret fastnesses in the mountains and the wilderness.	14	614	
Owing to dissensions, the robbers gain many advantages.	15	615	
Giddianhi, the robber chief, writes an epistle to Lachoneus, calling upon the Nephites to surrender.			
Gidgiddoni chosen commander of the Nephite forces. Lachoneus decides to gather all the Nephites from both continents into the lands of Zarahemla and Bountiful, and fortify against the inroads of the robbers.	16	616	
The people, with all their movable substance and seven years' provisions, gather at the appointed place.	17	617	
In the latter part of the year the robbers sally out of their hiding places and occupy the lands deserted by the people.	18	618	
The robbers, under Giddianhi, attack the Nephites. The slaughter more terrible than in any previous battle amongst the children of Lehi; Giddianhi is slain, the robbers are defeated and pursued to the borders of the wilderness.	19	619	
The robbers do not venture to again attack the Nephites. Zemnarihah made chief of the robber bands.	20	620	
The robbers surround and ineffectually besiege the Nephites, who make many sorties and slay tens of thousands of them; the robbers attempt to concentrate on the northern continent, but are cut off, their armies destroyed, and many thousands taken prisoners, among whom is Zemnarihah, who is afterwards hanged.			

The Nephites greatly rejoice in their marvelous deliverance.	21	621
All the Nephites believe the words of the prophets; righteousness prevails. They preach to the robber prisoners; all who make a covenant to murder no more are set at liberty, those who refuse are punished according to the law.	22	622
The Nephites all return to their own lands on both continents.	26	626
The laws revised according to justice and equity; great order Throughout the land.	27	627
Many new cities built and old ones repaired; numerous other improvements made.	28	628
Disputings and contentions re-commence, pride and other evils increase.	29	629
Lachoneus, the younger, Governor. The church broken up, except among a few Lamanites. Many prophets testify and are persecuted, some are executed contrary to law. The officers committing these crimes, on being called to account, rebel and seek to establish a monarchy, with Jacob as king. The Chief Judge is assassinated, and the ancient iniquitous combinations re-introduced. The Nephite commonwealth is broken up, and the people divided into numerous tribes. Jacob leads his followers into the northernmost part of the land.	30	630
The various tribes more fully regulated. Nephi performs many miracles; among others, raises his brother Timothy from the dead. But few are converted to the Lord.	31	631
Nephi continues his preaching and ministry; a few accept his message.	32	632
Many join the church.	33	633
On the fourth day of the new year the signs of Christ's crucifixion commence. An unparalleled storm rages for three hours, convulsing the land and destroying many cities. It is followed by three days darkness. The voice of the Lord is heard proclaiming the destructions that had happened.		
Jesus appears to the people in the land Bountiful. He preaches his Gospel, performs many mighty works, and chooses twelve disciples.		
Nephi, the son of Nephi, takes the records.	34	634
All the people are converted, and the church becomes universal. The believers have all things common.	36	636
The disciples of Jesus work many wonderful miracles.	37	637

The people again becoming numerous. Zarahemla and other cities rebuilt.	59	659
All the original twelve disciples, except the three who were to tarry, have died by this date.	100	700
The first generation in Christ have passed away. Nephi, the recorder, dies, and his son Amos takes charge of the records.	110	710
All the second generation have passed away, except a few.	200	800
Pride appears in the church; its members have their goods no more in common, and sects arise.	201	801
Many churches established opposed to the true church of Christ.	210	810
The wicked increase; the disciples and saints persecuted. The three Nephites perform many miracles, from the last date to.	230	830
The people divided into Nephites and Lamanites.	231	831
The more wicked portion of the people have grown much stronger.	244	844
The wicked build up many expensive churches to their false faiths.	250	850
The members of the true church, or Nephites, begin to grow proud and sinful. The Gadianton iniquities are again developed.	260	860
Both Nephites and Lamanites have grown exceedingly wicked; none are righteous except the three disciples. The Gadianton robbers have spread over all the land.	300	900
Amos transfers the records to his brother Ammaron, and dies.	306	906
Mormon born.	311	911
Ammaron hides up the records in the hill Shim.	321	921
Mormon, the father of Mormon, brings his son to Zarahemla. War commences between the Nephites and Lamanites; a number of battles are fought, in which the Nephites are victorious. Commencement of Mormon's record.	322	922
The three Nephites cease to minister among the people, because of their iniquities. Things hidden in the earth become slippery. Mormon endeavors to preach, but his mouth is shut. War re-commences, and Mormon is chosen General of the Nephite armies.	326	926
The Nephites, under Mormon, retreat before the Lamanites to the north countries. The Lamanites capture the city of Angola.	327	927

?The Lamanites drive the Nephites out of the land of David into the land of Joshua.	328	928
?Revolution, blood and carnage throughout all the land. The Nephite warriors gathered for battle into one place.	329	929
The Lamanite king, Aaron, defeated by Mormon.	330	930
Great sorrow among the Nephites, because of their pitiable condition.	331	931
Mormon obtains the plates, as Ammaron directed.	335	935
Wars, with much slaughter, until.	344	944
The Lamanites drive the Nephites to the land Jashon, thence northward to the land of Shem. The Nephites fortify the city of Shem.	345	945
Mormon, with 30,000 Nephites, defeats 50,000 Lamanites in the land of Shem; he pursues and again defeats the enemy.	346	946
The Nephites regain the lands of their inheritance by the year.	349	949
The Nephites as one party, and the Lamanites and Gadiantons as the other, make a treaty, by which the Nephites possess the country north of the Isthmus, and the Lamanites the south of it. Ten years' peace follows.	350	950
By the command of the Lord, Mormon preaches repentance, but the Nephites harden their hearts, during the ten years ending.	360	960
The Lamanite king declares war; the Nephites gather at the land Desolation.	360	960
The Lamanites march to Desolation, are defeated and return home.	361	961
The Lamanites make another invasion and are defeated. Mormon refuses to lead the wicked Nephites any longer.	362	962
The Nephites invade South America, and are driven back to Desolation. The Lamanites capture the city of Desolation.	363	963
The Lamanites besiege Teancum, are repulsed, and the Nephites re-capture Desolation.	364	964
The Lamanites re-commence war; they capture the cities of Desolation and Teancum, but are afterwards driven entirely out of the lands of the Nephites.	367	967
The Lamanites again commence war. An exceedingly fierce battle is fought in the land of Desolation. The Lamanites capture Desolation, Boaz and other cities. Mormon takes up all the records from the hill Shim.	375	975

TEMPLES AND SACRED PLACES.

When the Lord brought Israel out of Egypt, determined to make that people a nation to himself, as soon as they had arrived at a safe distance from surrounding peoples, he required them to build a Tabernacle, which is sometimes called the Temple, wherein he could institute certain ordinances and regulations for their guidance and worship.

This, at the commencement of their pilgrimage in the wilderness, was made portable, and of the costliest and best material within their reach, and one of the tribes was set apart to have charge of it and its appurtenances. Such has ever been the purpose of the Lord. This served them through their journey and in the promised Canaan, until suitable wealth enabled Solomon to erect a magnificent Temple on Mount Moriah, since called "The Hill of Zion," to which all Israel came annually to worship or attend Conference.

The Lord has informed us *Doc. & Cov., Sec.* 124, *v.* 39, that his people are always commanded to build Temples, or holy houses, unto his holy name. This accounts for our reading in the Book of Mormon of so many Temples having been erected on this continent. It also explains why the Prophet Joseph so early taught the commencement of a Temple in every important location of the Saints.

Not less than eight Temples have been designated, and their sites consecrated, of which there have been dedicated and ordinances administered therein—one at Kirtland, Ohio; Nauvoo, Illinois; St. George, and Logan, Utah. Those at Salt Lake City and Manti are progressing satisfactorily, the latter nearing completion. The places appointed in Independence and Far West are in the hands of our persecutors, who have driven the Saints from their homes, and from the State.

The site for a Temple at Independence was dedicated Aug. 3, 1831. Those present were Joseph Smith, Jr., Sidney Rigdon, Edward Partridge, Wm. W. Phelps, Oliver Cowdery, Martin Harris, Joseph Coe and Newel Knight. Description of Temple and city plot in History of Joseph Smith, under date of June 23 and 24, 1883. This was the first ground dedicated for a Temple in this dispensation.

The Temple at Kirtland was 55x65 feet; the corner stones were laid July 23, 1833. Reynolds Cahoon and Jared Carter were building committee. This was accomplished by donation and voluntary contribution; was completed and dedicated March 27, 1836.

The corner stone for a Temple at Far West was laid July 4, 1838, with appropriate ceremony. Dimensions of building to be 110 feet long and 80 feet wide. Particulars given in the History of Joseph Smith under this date. Work was re-commenced on this foundation April 26, 1839, and abandoned for the time on account of exterminating order of Governor Boggs, expelling the Saints from the State. Apostles Wilford Woodruff and George A. Smith were ordained on the corner stone of this building, and took leave of the Saints for a foreign mission, with the other Apostles who were present, at that time.

The Temple at Nauvoo, Illinois, was about 128 feet long by 88 feet wide. The corner stones were laid in the presence of the Nauvoo Legion, by the various authorities of the Priesthood, on the 6th day of April, 1841. The history of this date gives details of the proceedings. The building was erected by the tithing and free-will offerings of the people, and was so rapidly advanced that on the 8th of November of the same year the Baptismal Font was dedicated, and baptisms for the dead were administered. The cap stone was laid May 24, 1845. The upper rooms were dedicated Sunday, December 7, 1845, and sacrament was administered. Endowments were commenced on the 10th inst. The lower part of the building was dedicated with public services on Saturday and Sunday, the 2d and 3d of May, 1846.

The Salt Lake City site was consecrated and the ground broken for the foundation Feb. 14, 1853. The corner stones were laid April 6, 1853. It is 186 ½ feet by 99 feet in length and width, and is constructed of hard granite rock, brought from the mouth of Little Cottonwood Canyon, a distance of about twenty miles. With ordinary prosperity, its walls will be up to the square by the Autumn of 1883. We will not undertake a description of the harmony of its parts, the beauty or grandeur of its appearance, but refer our readers to the Deseret News of Aug. 17, 1854, and the Millennial Star, Vol. 16, page 753, for a full description given by its architect, Truman O. Angell.

The Temple at St. George, the site of which was dedicated by prayer by President George A. Smith, and ground broken November 9, 1871, is 141 feet 8 inches by 93 feet 4 inches; 84 feet from ground to top of parapet. The basement is of volcanic rock, the upper part of red sandstone, and contains about 1900 cords of rock, and 1,000,000 feet of lumber, and cost about $800,000.

The first foundation rock was laid March 10, 1873. On the first of April following, a deposit of records was made by President Brigham Young. On the first day of January, 1877, the Font, lower story and first main floor were dedicated by President Wilford Woodruff, and April 6, following, a general Conference of all the authorities of the Church consummated its consecration, at which Counselor Daniel H. Wells offered the dedication prayer.

The Manti Temple site was dedicated and the ground broken by President Brigham Young April 25, 1877. The corner stones were laid April 14, 1879. Its size is 172x95 feet, and 82 feet to square. Its Eastern Tower is to be 179 feet high; the Western Tower 169 feet high. This edifice stand on a hill, which required 2400 cords of rock terrace to provide for its location.

The site of the Logan Temple is situated on an elevation of table land in the eastern part of the city bearing that name. It was dedicated with prayer offered by Apostle Orson Pratt, May 18, 1877, and the ground was broken the same day.

Instructions were given by Presidents Brigham Young and John Taylor. The corner stones were laid September 17, 1877. The building, including tower and buttresses, is 171 feet long by 95 in width, with a tower 28 feet square at each end, the Eastern tower is 156 feet, and the Western tower 151 feet in height, and 87 feet from the surface to top of battlements. It was dedicated May 17, 1884, President John Taylor offering the dedicatory prayer.

The location of the Temple sites at Independence, Kirtland, Far West and Nauvoo were determined and consecrated by or under direction of the Prophet Joseph Smith, who also directed the designs and construction of the Kirtland and Nauvoo Temples.

The locations of the Temples at Salt Lake City, at St. George, at Manti and at Logan were determined and dedicated by President Brigham Young, or by his direction. He also directed the designs of the Salt Lake City and St. George Temples, and presided at the dedication services of the latter house.

Bible.

Exo. Chapters 25, 26, 27, 28 give a description of the Tabernacle constructed in the wilderness, with its appointments. This Tabernacle is frequently called a Temple in the Old Testament; as in 1 *Sam.* 1. 9.

1 *Kings, Chapters* 6, 7, and 8. Temple of Solomon is described, with the dedication ceremonies.

Ezra, Chap. 6. The rebuilding of Solomon's Temple by Cyrus is given. The decree is found in *verse* 3.

The final demolition of this Temple was foretold by Christ in *Matt.* 24. 2. This terrible prophecy was fulfilled by the Romans under Titus about the year seventy of our Lord.

Book of Mormon.

2. *Nephi* 5. 16 and I, Nephi, did build a Temple after the manner of the Temple of Solomon, etc.

Jacob 1. 17 wherefore I, Jacob, gave unto them these words, as I taught them in the Temple, etc.

2. 2 I come up unto the Temple this day, that I might declare unto you the word of God.

2. 11 get thee up into the Temple on the morrow, etc.

Mos. 1. 18 might gather themselves together to go up to the Temple, to hear the words which his father should speak unto them.

2. 6, 7 pitched their tents around the Temple, with their doors toward the Temple.

Alma 16. 13 and Alma and Amulek went forth preaching repentance to the people in their Temples, and in their sanctuaries, and in their synagogues, which were built after the manner of the Jews.

23. 2 but that they should have free access to their houses, and also their Temples and their sanctuaries.

26. 29 we have taught them in their houses, in their streets, upon their hills, and we have also entered into their Temples, and their synagogues, and taught them.

Hel. 3. 9 have timber to build houses, cities, Temples, synagogues, sanctuaries and all manner of buildings.

3. 14 an hundreth part of their building of ships, of Temples, synagogues and sanctuaries cannot be contained in this work.

10. 8 if ye shall say unto this Temple, it shall be rent in twain, it shall be done.

Doctrine & Covenants.

Sec. 84. 3 which city (New Jerusalem) shall be built, beginning at the Temple lot, which shall be appointed by the finger of the Lord.

4 even the place of the Temple, which Temple shall be reared in this generation.

5 this generation shall not all pass away, until an house shall be built unto the Lord, and a cloud shall rest upon it, etc.

31 which House shall be built unto the Lord in this generation, upon the consecrated spot as I have appointed.

97. 10 it is my will that an house should be built unto me in the land of Zion, like unto the pattern which I have given you.

124. 29, 30 that they, my Saints, may be baptized for those who are dead; for this ordinance belongeth to my House.

31 but I command you, all ye, my Saints, to build a House unto me.

39 for the beginning of the revelations and foundation of Zion, and for the glory, honor and endowment of all her municipals, are ordained by the ordinance of my Holy House, which my people are always commanded to build unto my Holy Name.

55 and again, verily I say unto you, I command you again to build a House to my name, even in this place.

127. 9 let all the records be had in order, that they may be put in the archives of my Holy Temple, to be held in remembrance from generation to generation, saith the Lord of Hosts.

See Sermon by B. Young, J. of D., Vol. I, page 277.

See Sermon by B. Young, J. of D., Vol. I, page 131.

See Sermon by B. Young, J. of D., Vol. 2, page 29.

See Sermon by B. Young, J. of D., Vol. 9, page 239.

See Sermon by O. Pratt, J. of D., Vol. 14, page 271.

See Sermon by O. Pratt, J. of D., Vol. 16, page 251.

See Sermon by G. A. Smith, J. of D., Vol. 17, page 160.

An Article entitled, The Order of Laying Temple Corner Stones, Deseret Weekly News, Vol. 27, page 214.

History of Joseph Smith, date of Aug. 3, 1831, and July 4, 1838.

History of Joseph Smith, date of May 6, June 6, and July 23, 1833, and March 27, 1836.

GEMS FROM THE HISTORY OF JOSEPH SMITH.

How the book of Mormon was Obtained.—*May* 8, 1838. Joseph Smith's answer to the question, "How and where did you obtain the Book of Mormon?" "Moroni, who deposited the plates (from whence the Book of Mormon was translated,) in a hill in Manchester, Ontario County, New York, being dead and raised again therefrom, appeared unto me, and told me where they were, and gave me directions how to obtain them. I obtained them, and the Urim and Thummim with them, by the means of which I translated the plates; and thus came the Book of Mormon."

Plurality of Wives.—*October* 5, 1843. "Gave instructions to try those persons who were preaching, teaching, or practising the doctrine of plurality of wives; for, according to the law, I hold the keys of this power in the last days; for there is never but one on earth at a time on whom the power and its keys are conferred; and I have constantly said no man shall have but one wife at a time, unless the Lord directs otherwise."

October 8, 1843. The Organization of the Spiritual and Heavenly Worlds, and of spiritual and heavenly beings, was agreeable to the most perfect order and harmony; their limits and bounds were fixed irrevocably, and voluntarily subscribed to in their heavenly estate by themselves, and were by our first parents subscribed to upon the earth. Hence the importance of embracing and subscribing to principles of eternal truth by all men upon the earth that expect eternal life.

CHURCH CHRONOLOGY.

This Compendium being designed for the elucidation of theological rather than of historical subjects, we have only given the dates of a few important events in the development of the great latter-day work.

1805.—Joseph Smith, Jun., was born on the 23d of December, in Sharon, Windsor Co., Vermont.

1820.—Early in the Spring, Joseph Smith, Jun., had his first vision.

1823.—*September* 21; Joseph Smith, Jun., had his second vision, in which the existence of the Plates of the Book of Mormon was revealed to him. The following day he opened the place where the Plates were deposited, and saw them.

1827.—*September* 22. Joseph Smith, Jun., obtained the Plates of the Book of Mormon, the Urim and Thummim, and Breastplate.

1828.—*February*; Martin Harris showed some of the characters transcribed from the Plates, and the translation of them to Professor Anthon and Dr. Mitchell, of New York.

1829.—*May* 15; Joseph Smith, Jun., and O. Cowdery were ordained to the Aaronic Priesthood, by John the Baptist, and were baptized by each other.

1830.—*April* 6. The Church of Jesus Christ of Latter-day Saints was organized, Elders were ordained, the Sacrament was administered, and, for the first time in the Church, hands were laid on for the reception of the Holy Ghost.

June 1. The Church held its first Conference, in Fayette, Seneca County, New York. In October the first missionaries to the Lamanites were appointed.

1831.—*January*. Joseph Smith, Jun., moved to Kirtland, Ohio where he arrived about the first of February.

August 2. The land of Zion was consecrated and dedicated by prayer for the gathering of the Saints.

August 4. The first Conference of the Church in the land of Zion was held.

1832.—*April* 26. Joseph Smith, Jun., was acknowledged President of the High Priesthood, at a General Council of the Church.

May 1. At a Council held at Independence, it was decided to publish the Book of Doctrine and Covenants.

June. The first periodical, "The Evening and Morning Star," was published by the Church in Independence.

1833.—*February* 2. Joseph Smith, Jun., completed the translation of the New Testament.

March 18. The Quorum of High Priests was first organized in Kirtland.

July 2. Joseph Smith, Jun., finished the translation of the Bible.

July 23. The corner stones of the Lord's house in Kirtland were laid.

September 11. It was decided to publish a paper in Kirtland, entitled "The Latter-day Saints' Messenger and Advocate." Bishop Edward Partridge was acknowledged head of the Church in Zion.

December 18. Joseph Smith, Sen., was ordained Patriarch.

1834.—*February* 17. A First Presidency of three and a High Council of twelve were first organized.

May 3. At a Conference of Elders in Kirtland, the Church was first named "The Church of Jesus Christ of Latter-day Saints."

May 5. Zion's Camp left Kirtland for Missouri.

1835.—*February* 28. The organization of the Quorums of Seventies commenced.

May 3. The Twelve left Kirtland on their first mission.

July. In the early part of this month the rolls of Egyptian papyrus, which contained the writings of Abraham and Joseph in Egypt, were obtained.

August 17. At a general assembly at Kirtland, the Book of Doctrine and Covenants was accepted as a rule of faith and practice.

1836.—*January* 21. The authorities of the Church attended to the ordinances of anointing and blessing each other in the Kirtland Temple.

March 27. The House of the Lord in Kirtland was dedicated.

April 3. In the House of the Lord in Kirtland, the Savior, Moses, Elias and Elijah appeared to Joseph Smith, Jun., and Oliver Cowdery.

1837.—*June*. In this month Heber C. Kimball, O. Hyde and W. Richards were set apart for a mission to England. This was the first foreign mission of the Church.

July 1. The mission for England sailed from New York on the ship *Garrick*.

July 20. The English mission landed in Liverpool, England.

July 30. The first baptism in England, by divine authority took place in the River Ribble.

August 4. The first confirmation of members in the Church took place in England, in Walkerfold, Chaidgley.

September 27. Joseph Smith, Jun., left Kirtland to visit the Saints in Missouri and establish gathering places. He arrived in Far West about the last of October, or first of November.

December 10. About this time Joseph Smith, Jun., arrived in Kirtland from Missouri.

December 25. The first Conference of the Latter-day Saints in England was held in the Cock Pit, Preston. During this month a somewhat extensive apostacy took place in Kirtland.

1838.—*March* 14. Joseph Smith, Jun., and family arrived at Far West.

July 6. 515 Saints left Kirtland for Missouri.

October 27. Governor Boggs' exterminating order was issued.

October 30. The massacre at Haun's Mill took place.

October 31. Joseph Smith, Jun., and others were betrayed by G. M. Hinckle.

November 1. Joseph Smith, Jun., and others condemned to be shot. Far West plundered.

1839.—*February* 14. Brigham Young fled from Far West to Illinois.

April 15. Joseph Smith, Jun., and his companions in bonds, left Davies for Broome County, and on their way made their escape from the guard.

April 26. The Saints commenced evacuating Far West.

April 22. Joseph Smith, Jun., arrived in Quincy, Illinois.

June 11. The first house was put up by the Saints in Commerce, afterward named Nauvoo.

September 18. Elder Brigham Young, accompanied by H. C. Kimball, left Nauvoo on his first mission to England.

October 29. Joseph Smith, Jun., and others left Nauvoo for Washington, D.C., as delegates from the Church to the general government.

November 28. Joseph Smith, Jun., arrived in Washington.

1840—*March* 4. Joseph Smith, Jun., arrived in Nauvoo from Washington.

1840.—*April* 15. Elder O. Hyde left Commerce, on his mission to Jerusalem.

May 27. The first number of "The Latter-day Saints' Millennial Star" was published at Manchester, England.

June 6. The first company of emigrating Saints, from Europe, sailed from Liverpool for New York.

July 20. The company of Saints who left Liverpool in June arrived in New York.

About the first of this month, the first English edition of the Latter-day Saints' Hymn Book was published.

September 14. Joseph Smith, Sen., died in Nauvoo.

December 16. The charter of the city of Nauvoo became a law.

1841.—*January*. During this month the first English edition of the Book of Mormon was published.

November 8. The Baptismal Font in the Nauvoo Temple was dedicated.

1842.—*December* 7. Elder O. Hyde returned from his mission to Jerusalem.

1844.—*June* 27. Joseph and Hyrum Smith were assassinated in Carthage jail.

1845.—*September* 24. The authorities of the Church made a treaty with the mob, to evacuate Nauvoo the following spring.

1846.—*February*. In the beginning of this month, the exodus of the Saints from Nauvoo commenced.

May 16. The Pioneer camp of the Saints arrived at Mount Pisgah, Iowa Territory.

June. A call was made, by the general government, for the Mormon Battalion.

September 10, 11, 12. Battles took place between the citizens of Nauvoo and the mob.

September 16. The Trustees of the Church, in Nauvoo, made a treaty with the mob for the surrender of the city, and its immediate evacuation by the remnant of the Saints.

1847.—*April* 14. The Pioneers left Winter Quarters for the Rocky Mountains.

July 24. The Pioneers entered Great Salt Lake Valley.

December 23. The Twelve sent forth an epistle to the Saints to recommence the gathering.

1848.—*May*. Presidents B. Young and Heber C. Kimball left Winter Quarters, the second time, for Great Salt Lake Valley.

September 20. Presidents B. Young and H. C. Kimball arrived, the second time, in Great Salt Lake Valley.

November 19. The Nauvoo Temple was burned.

1849.—*October* 6. The organization of the P. E. Fund Company was commenced.

1850.—*June* 14. The first missionaries to Scandinavia landed in Copenhagen, Denmark.

June 15. The first number of the "Deseret News" was published.

August 12. The first baptisms in Denmark, by legal authority, in this dispensation, took place.

September 9. The "Act" for organizing the Territory of Utah became a law.

October 13. The first company of P. E. Fund emigrants arrived in Salt Lake City, from the United States.

December 7. The first branch of the Church, in France, was organized at Paris.

1851.—*January* 9. Salt Lake City was incorporated.

January 13. The first settlers of Iron County, U.T., arrived on Centre Creek, near where the city of Parowan now stands.

1852.—*August* 29. The revelation on the law of Celestial Marriage was first made public.

September 3. The first company of P. E. Fund emigrants from Europe arrived in Utah.

December 13. The Legislative Assembly of Utah Territory met, for the first time.

1853.—*January* 25. Elders O. Spencer and J. Houtz, missionaries, arrived in Berlin, Prussia, and were banished from there on the second of February following.

February 14. The Temple Block in Salt Lake City was consecrated.

March 7. The first missionaries to Gibraltar arrived there.

November 1. The first number of the "Journal of Discourses" was published in England.

1854.—*May* 23. Patriarch John Smith died.

June 28. John Smith, son of Hyrum Smith, was appointed Patriarch over the Church.

1855.—*May* 5. The Endowment House in Salt Lake City was dedicated.

October. A branch of the Church was organized in Dresden, Germany.

During this year grasshoppers and drouth caused a great failure of crops in Utah.

October 29. The First Presidency of the Church, in their General Epistle, proposed, for the Saints who should emigrate by the P. E. Fund, to cross the plains with handcarts.

1856.—During this year the practice of paying tithing was generally introduced among the Saints in Europe. During the winter and spring there was a great scarcity of food in Utah, and many domestic animals perished.

September 26. The first company of Saints, who crossed the plains with handcarts, arrived.

1857.—*April* 23. A company of about seventy missionary elders left Salt Lake City to cross the plains with handcarts.

July 11. A. Cumming, of Georgia, was appointed governor of Utah.

July 23. Messrs. J. Stoddard and A. O. Smoot arrived from Independence without the mails, the postmaster there having received orders not to forward them. They brought the news that General Harney, with over 2000 men, was ordered to Utah.

Near the close of the year, the U. S. army, under General Johnson, took possession of Fort Bridger.

1858.—*March* 21. The citizens of Utah, living north of Utah County, agreed to abandon their homes and move south. This was deemed advisable as a defensive measure.

In the meantime Col. Thos. L. Kane had arrived in Salt Lake City, via California, for the purpose of bringing about a peaceful solution of the difficulties between the U. S. and Utah.

April 19. Gov. Cumming and Col. Kane visited the Utah library, where they were shown the records and seal of the U.S. court, which was said to have been destroyed.

June 7. Messrs. Powell and McCullough, sent out as peace commissioners, by the general government, arrived in Salt Lake City.

June 26. The "Army of Utah," under Col. Johnson, passed through Salt Lake City and camped on the west side of the river Jordan.

June 30. The people who had moved south began to return to their homes.

October 28. Jacob Hamblin, with eleven men, left Southern Utah to open intercourse with the Indians on the east side of the river Colorado.

1861.—*April* 23. Two hundred wagons, with four yoke of cattle each, carrying 15,000 pounds of flour, started for the Missouri river, to bring the poor of the Saints to Utah.

October 18. President B. Young sent the first message over the overland wire to the U.S.

October 24. The first telegram was sent to San Francisco. In the autumn of this year a large colony of Saints was sent to southern Utah.

1862.—*October* 24. Camp Douglas, near Salt Lake City, was located by Col. P. E. Connor.

1863.—Col. P. E. Connor defeated a band of the Shoshone Indians near Bear river.

March 3. Great mass meeting held in the Tabernacle, Salt Lake City, to protest against the infamous course of U.S. officials.

1864.—*April* 10. Moves were made for building a telegraph line in Utah.

1866.—*January* 1. The first number of the "Juvenile Instructor" was issued in Salt Lake City.

1867.—The Deseret Telegraph Company was organized.

1868.—*June* 19.—Ground was broken in Weber Canyon, on the U. P. Railroad.

October 16. Co-operative Mercantile Institution was organized. B. Young, president.

March 8.—U.S. Land Office opened in Salt Lake City.

March 15. A company was partially organized for building a railroad between Ogden and Salt Lake City.

May 9. The last rail was laid connecting the U. P. and C. P. railroads, thus completing the first railroad across the continent.

May 17. The first ground was broken for the Utah Central Railroad.

June 25. The first company of Latter-day Saint emigrants reached Ogden, per U. P. R. R.

December 24. In the evening street lamps were first used in Salt Lake City.

1870.—*January* 10. The last rail of the Utah Central Railroad was laid.

January 13. General mass meeting of the ladies of Salt Lake City, to protest against the passage of the Cullom bill.

February 12. "An act conferring the elective franchise upon women," became a law of Utah Territory.

April 27, An abandoned child was left at the door of Mrs. The first circumstance of the kind known in Salt Lake City.

August 12. A discussion commenced, in Salt Lake City, between Professor O. Pratt and Dr. J. P. Newman, chaplain of the U.S. Senate. Question, "Does the Bible sanction polygamy?"

September 15. Gov. J. W. Shafer issued a proclamation, forbidding the assembly of the militia of Utah Territory for any purpose except by his orders.

1871.—*May* 1. Ground was first broken for the Utah Southern Railroad.

June 30. Acting-Governor of Utah, George A. Black, issued a proclamation forbidding any of the militia of the Territory to assemble for the purpose of celebrating the ninety-fifth anniversary of American Independence.

October 10. President B. Young was arrested by U.S. Marshal on an indictment founded on a charge of "lascivious cohabitation."

1872.—*June* 1. The first number of the "Woman's Exponent was issued in Salt Lake City.

September 3 Ground was dedicated and broken for the Salt Lake City water works.

October 14. President G. A. Smith and others left Salt Lake City on their Palestine tour.

1873.—*February* 24. President Smith and party arrived in Jerusalem.

June 18. President Smith arrived in Salt Lake City.

LATTER-DAY SAINTS' EMIGRATION.

The publications of the church show that, commencing with the year 1840 and ending with the year 1883, there have been emigrated from the European countries to the United States, by the church emigration agencies, 78,219 souls, who have crossed the sea in 243 sail vessels and steamships.

These have come in companies of varied numbers, from a dozen or two at a time to as many as eight hundred or more, which latter number has embarked several times on double decked ships.

We regret our inability to give a tabulated statement of the number of persons from each country of their nativity. The greater proportions have been from Great Britain and Scandinavia, while Switzerland, Germany, Italy, Iceland, Finland, East India, South Africa and other countries have contributed to make up the number.

A very remarkable feature in this work of gathering Israel is that of all these vessels that have gone to sea, no one with a Latter-day Saint on it has ever gone down. Some have been driven back to Port before they could get out of the Irish channel, one was dismasted before reaching New Orleans, but all have yielded up their precious souls and freight to the ports of their destination.

The organization, cleanliness and consequent health, peace and safety, have rendered the Saints' emigration notorious and proverbial among European shippers and ship captains, many of whom have been heard to say that a company of Mormon emigrants on their ship they considered better insurance than the underwriters at Lloyd's could give.

THE BOOK OF MORMON.

The Book of Mormon is the name of a record which was engraved upon plates of gold, about 400 years after the crucifixion of our Lord and Savior Jesus Christ, by a celebrated prophet named Mormon. These plates were deposited by his son, Moroni, in a stone box, in a hill in the western part of the State of New York, called by the Nephites, Cumorah. The language in which this record was made was said by Mormon to be Reformed Egyptian. On the 22d of September, 1823, Moroni discovered the stone box which contained these plates, the Urim and Thummim, a sword and breastplate, to the young Prophet, Joseph Smith, Jr., and he, by the aid of the Urim and Thummim, translated the record from the plates into the English language. This is the most ancient, the most accurate and reliable history of America, its ancient inhabitants and its antiquities, that is now extant; and has since been translated from the English into the French, German, Italian, Danish, Swedish, Welsh, Kanaka, Hindostanee, Dutch and Spanish. It has also been printed and published in all those languages except Spanish, Hindostanee and Dutch, and will soon be published in the Spanish also.

Lector House believes that a society develops through a two-fold approach of continuous learning and adaptation, which is derived from the study of classic literary works spread across the historic timeline of literature records. Therefore, we aim at reviving, repairing and redeveloping all those inaccessible or damaged but historically as well as culturally important literature across subjects so that the future generations may have an opportunity to study and learn from past works to embark upon a journey of creating a better future.

This book is a result of an effort made by Lector House towards making a contribution to the preservation and repair of original ancient works which might hold historical significance to the approach of continuous learning across subjects.

HAPPY READING & LEARNING!

LECTOR HOUSE
LECTOR HOUSE LLP
E-MAIL: lectorpublishing@gmail.com

9 789356 141124